COME
THE SUN

C000182014

COMPANION
TO THE
SUNDAY MISSAL

NOTES ON ALL THE PASSAGES
OF SCRIPTURE FOR

SUNDAY MASSES
FOR THE THREE YEAR CYCLE
THE FEASTS OF THE LORD
SOLEMNITIES

William Coleborne

COLLINS

Collins Liturgical Publications
8 Grafton Street, London W1X 3LA

Distributed in USA by
Harper & Row, Publishers, Inc., San Francisco
Icehouse One — 401
151 Union Street, San Francisco, CA 94111-1299

Distributed in Canada by
Novalis, Box 9700, Terminal,
375 Rideau Street, Ottawa, Ontario K1G 4B4

Distributed in Ireland by
Educational Company of Ireland
21 Talbot Street, Dublin 1

Collins Liturgical Australia
PO Box 316, Blackburn, Victoria 3130

Collins Liturgical New Zealand
PO Box 1, Auckland

First published by William Coleborne, 1984
First published this edition, 1987

ISBN 0 00 599072 6

Imprimatur + William Murray, Bishop of Wollongong

Made and printed by William Collins Sons & Co, Glasgow

IN MEMORY OF MY WIFE
KATHLEEN

CONTENTS

BISHOP'S HOUSE
WOLLONGONG

TELEPHONE 042 28 6511

P.O. BOX 1254
WOLLONGONG 2500

COMPANION TO THE SUNDAY MISSAL

Dr. W. Coleborne.

Dr. Coleborne's Companion to the Sunday Missal is quite delightful. The readings and the Psalms for the Sundays in the year and the major feast days are illuminated in the light of their Social Conditions, Customs and History. Where it is of interest, the subtle meanings of the original languages are brought out.

Dr. Coleborne has managed to combine the precious talents of good Biblical Scholarship with easy Communication.

For the homilist - but more especially for the Layperson wishing to reflect upon the readings - the Companion to the Sunday Missal will prove to be a 'Spring of Living-water'.

+ William E. Murray

+ WILLIAM E. MURRAY, D.D., D.Sc.Soc.,
Bishop of Wollongong.

INTRODUCTION

The diversity of opinions expressed down through the ages in matters of Biblical interpretation attests the difficulties and problems presented by the literature of the *Bible*. The situation is not made easier when readers, and more often listeners, are presented with Scripture taken out of its context.

The *Companion to the Sunday Missal* had its origin in a Parish Priest's appreciation of this problem and in his request for the type of material contained in the book, much of which appeared in his parish bulletins. It was the author's privilege to read each paragraph of notes at the Vigil Mass in Holy Family Church Ulladulla before the lector presented the passage of Scripture.

The aim of the *Companion* is not homiletic, but rather to place each passage in its context with such additional remarks as will help to bring it to life. It is felt that there is a great need to educate our people at all levels, in their understanding of the circumstances that produced the various parts of the *Bible* and so it is hoped that the *Companion* will appeal to lectors, readers of the parish bulletin and to study groups, especially in schools and that it will provide an aid in preparation for attendance at Mass. To any who may decry the writer's failure to come to grips with some problem, the exigencies of space and the needs of a congregation are offered as excuses.

Many passages of Scripture are used more than once in the Missal; the notes have likewise been repeated in part or whole, a fact which illustrates their contextual rather than their homiletic content.

In the course of reading and lecturing over a long period of time, so much passes into the compost of the mind that sources are no longer remembered. In any case, a heavily annotated *Companion* is the last thing that is wanted.

The book has been adjusted to the latest edition of the *Sunday Missal*.

It is hoped that the Index of Passages may attract friends from outside the Catholic Church. In this connexion the problem of the numeration of the *Psalms* must be mentioned. The *Companion* has followed the numbering in the Missal which observes the Grail system and so, in general, is one behind the numeration in any translation that follows the Hebrew.

All profits from the sale of this book will be donated to the missionary work of the Columban Fathers.

There are debts of gratitude that I am happy to acknowledge: to the Most Reverend Dr W. E. Murray, Bishop of Wollongong, for his commendation of the book; to *Australasian Catholic Record* for permission to draw on material I contributed to Homilies for the Sundays of January and February 1983 (Vol. LIX No. 4); to the Reverend P. M. Kenna, P. P. Kiama who during his ministry at Star of the Sea Milton, Holy Family Ulladulla and St Patrick's Sussex Inlet, saw the need for these notes and has given the author constant help and encouragement; to Mrs Cynthia Sajko and Mrs Gaye Fogarty whose labours and skill as typists have been an offering to the Church; last and by no means least, to my wife who as critic, proof reader and unfailing helper gave that assistance without which the book could not have been completed.

Introduction to Second Edition
The first edition which was a private publication was well received by clergy and laity throughout Australia and beyond. The author is grateful to Collins Liturgical Publications for their willingness to present *Companion to the Sunday Missal* as a second edition. The opportunity has been taken to correct a few errors in the first edition. Royalties from the second edition will be an offering of gratitude towards the building of a new Catholic church in Ulladulla. This edition is dedicated to the memory of my wife Kathleen who died peacefully on 2 July 1986.

Ulladulla, NSW, Australia   William Coleborne
22 February 1987
Feast of the Chair of St Peter Apostle

SUNDAY MASSES
Year A

SEASON OF ADVENT
FIRST SUNDAY OF ADVENT
YEAR A

First Reading: *Isaiah 2. 1—5*
During Advent, First Readings will be taken from the early
chapters of *Isaiah*. Written mainly in verse, a frequent medium
of prophecy, they belong to the period 750—700 B.C. and are
set against an uneasy background. The prophet looks beyond the
fears created by powerful Assyrian armies to a future in which
Jerusalem is a world centre, weapons of war are no more and
nations walk in the ways of peace.

Responsorial Psalm: *Psalm 121. 1—2, 4—5, 6—9*
In this Gradual Psalm there is an expression of a pilgrim's joy
when he joins others who have invited him to go up to Jerusalem.
Travel in groups was a necessary protection against brigands. Then
comes the delight of being in the city of cities. The second stanza
stresses the unity of which Jerusalem is the symbol; this is
followed by remembrance from long ago of their city as the seat
of kings. The psalm concludes with a call for prayer for the peace
of Jerusalem, for her well-being in every way.

Second Reading: *Romans 13. 11—14*
Like some of Paul's other letters, *Romans* concludes with
exhortations arising out of the doctrinal content of Chapters 1-11.
The portion to be read expresses an intense belief in the
imminence of the Lord's Return. The night of spiritual darkness
is nearly over; in the new era when righteousness shall rule, old
habits and ways will change, for love must prevail.

Gospel: *Matthew 24. 37—44*
Matthew's Gospel will be much before our attention this year.
Written probably between 70 and 80 A.D. it absorbs most of
Mark, has material found elsewhere only in *Luke* and contains
information not recorded in any other writer. Matthew wrote for
Jewish Christians. The portion to be read contains a positive
message for Advent, a warning to be ready for the Lord's Return.
In the days of the Flood there was laxity; it was so when the
Gospel was proclaimed; its message is even more pertinent today.
Stay awake, is the challenge, and wait for the Lord's Coming.

First Reading: *Isaiah 11. 1—10*
Against gathering clouds and a dismal picture of current society,
Isaiah projects the well known picture of the Messianic rule. The
Messiah of David's stock will reveal new qualities of spirit,
especially such justice as the poor have never known. A new
relationship between man and the order of nature will be like
Paradise revisited. The scattered of God's people, far flung in
many wars, will rally to the Messiah. This ancient Messianic vision
prepares us for the Christmas season.

Responsorial Psalm: *Psalm 71. 1—2, 7—8, 12—13, 17*
The psalmist celebrates a king's accession and prays for the
quality of his reign, that he may understand God's justice and
pass it on in his judgments. It will be an era of peace; his role
will extend far and wide; the poor and needy will benefit. Though
the psalm is not quoted in the *New Testament,* its note is
universal and helps us fix our minds on the Advent message, the
coming of the righteous King.

Second Reading: *Romans 15. 4—9*
The great epistle is drawing to a close with some moral exhortations on matters possibly affecting the church in Rome. Paul has
been dealing with respect for the scruples of others and proves by
an appeal to Scriptures, i.e, the *Old Testament,* that Christ did
not seek to please himself. At this point the reading begins. Love
is the only solution of human differences and problems, as Christ
himself showed in his dealings with his own people.

Gospel: *Matthew 3. 1—12*
John the Baptist, so like Elijah even in dress and food *(II Kings
1.8),* breaks suddenly into Matthew's narrative. His role was to be
the Lord's forerunner proclaiming the nearness of the Kingdom
of Heaven, God's rule on earth so fervently awaited by the Jews.
He drew enormous crowds, preaching repentance and baptising in
the river Jordan. He lashed out fearlessly at religious hypocrisy,
warning that God's Kingdom was not limited to the Jews, but
that his own baptising with water would be followed by Christ
baptising with the Holy Spirit.

First Reading: *Isaiah 35, 1—6, 10*
We are to hear some of the loveliest words in Scripture. Isaiah, setting aside the gloom and fear of the current political situation, looks to a Golden Age when God's salvation will transform everything. The deprived places of nature will blossom; the weak, the frail and the handicapped will be strong; Jerusalem shall be a new centre of creation. Lovers of Handel's *Messiah* will hear in stanza five the contralto recitative set in the words of the King James' *Bible*.

Responsorial Psalm:*Psalm 145. 6—10*
This is the first of the Alleluia Psalms, so called because they begin and end with Alleluia. The thought in the psalm before us echoes the First Reading. Five times the psalmist puts 'The Lord' at the beginning of a sentence. In Hebrew this is more emphatic than in English. The Lord, judge and deliverer, unlike kings on earth, is eternal.

Second Reading: *James 5. 7—10*
Descriptions of this letter range from "a string of pearls" to "a bundle of straw". The reading stresses the need for patience in awaiting the Lord's Return. There are good reasons for thinking the letter was late in composition. If so, it could well have been written to those undergoing persecution. The idea of harvest as a consummation is found in *Matthew 13. 30*.

Gospel: *Matthew 11. 2—11*
John the Baptist could not reconcile what he has heard in prison *(Luke 3. 19—20)* with what he expected of the Messiah and so sent messengers to inquire. Jesus gives a resume of his activity. Listen for words like "lame", used already in the readings of this Mass. To the departing messengers he speaks appreciatively of John and quotes loosely from *Malachi 3.1* to show that John is God's messenger and by inference that Jesus is himself the Messiah. The reading contains two words of interest: the reeds in the wind are the long cane-like grass growing on Jordan's banks; it was the symbol stamped on Herod's coins. The words "does not lose faith in me" are a weak translation built around the verb "to have the bait stick of a bird trap sprung on someone", with the idea of ensnaring or tripping up.

First Reading: *Isaiah 7. 10—14*
There is special need to see this prophecy against its historical
background. Israel, the northern kingdom of the Jews, was court-
ing Damascus against the rising power of Assyria. An attempt to
draw Ahaz, king of Judah, the southern kingdom, into the alliance
failed. Israel then invaded Judah which turned to Assyria for help.
Isaiah pleads against this action and gives as a sign, the prophecy
that a young woman would soon bear a son in the royal line,
and through him God would deal with present problems. The
prophecy is a powerful symbol of Our Lord's Coming.

Responsorial Psalm: *Psalm 23. 1—6*
The psalm was used at one of the great festivals. The first stanza
affirms the divine creation and the Lord's possession of his own.
Then a priest in the pilgrims' midst asks who may climb Zion's
hill; the question is answered by another priest and in stanza
three the rewards of those fit to ascend are set out.

Second Reading: *Romans 1. 1—7*
The opening of Paul's letter follows the format of hundreds of
letters surviving from the ancient world, written on papyrus, from
people in all walks of life. Paul's letter was to precede his visit.
As there were no text books on Christian doctrine, Paul prepares
what has been called a handbook of the faith. In the reading, it
is the humanity and the divinity of Our Lord that stand out.

Gospel: *Matthew 1. 18—24*
Two points will bring more understanding to this lovely incident:
betrothal created a bond so close that if the man died the girl
became a widow. In Mary's condition, Joseph could not simply
walk away from her. The scandal of a public divorce or a writ and
payment of a fine were the options. Joseph, intending to take the
latter course, was stopped by an angel. Secondly, Matthew's
quotation from the First Reading is preceded by: "to fulfil the
words spoken by the Lord ..." Those who find this deterministic
interpretation of the *Old Testament* difficult — it is frequent in
Matthew — will welcome an alternate and equally sound translation: "with the result that the words were fulfilled".

SEASON OF CHRISTMAS
25th December
NATIVITY OF OUR LORD
VIGIL MASS
YEARS A, B, C

First Reading: *Isaiah 62. 1—5*
The book we call *Isaiah* is really two books, the work of two
different hands. The second part starts at Ch. 40 and belongs to
the time after the exile. The first part was written when Assyria
was threatening the Jews. Babylon absorbed Assyria, took the
Jews into captivity and was in turn overrun by the Persian Cyrus,
who allowed the Jews to return to their shattered city. The
second part of *Isaiah* belongs to this period and in the First Reading, using the imagery of marriage, creates a beautiful description
of the restored city; her new names are Hephzibah (my delight is
in her) and Beulah (married).

Responsorial Psalm: *Psalm 88. 4—5, 16—17, 27,29*
The portion of the psalm before us is part of a composite psalm.
The first stanza tells of God's covenant with David which will last
for ever. In the second the blessings of God's people are set forth
and finally the psalmist returns to the Covenant with David. In
II Samuel (7.14) we read of God promising a father-son relation-
ship with Solomon. In the psalm it is applied to David. In the
Gospel for the Mass, we will be reminded that Our Lord was of
David's line; the promise holds.

Second Reading: *Acts 13. 16—17, 22—25*
Coming to Antioch — there were several cities so named — in the
Roman province of Galatia in the south of Asia Minor, Paul
as often, made for the Synagogue to preach to the Jews. In a thumb-
nail sketch of Jewish history, he showed how Jesus was of David's
line and therefore the Messiah of Jews everywhere.

Gospel: *Matthew 1. 1—25*
The second part of this reading was covered in the notes for
Advent IV. Possibly the first part may not be read, though it is
none the less important. Jews generally set great store on their
genealogies. Matthew here traces Our Lord's lineage through
Joseph back to Abraham, the father of the Jewish race. There are
some unexpected names in the list, "not moral saints, but
forgiven sinners".

First Reading: *Isaiah 9. 1—7*
This prophecy has for its background the situation described in the First Reading, Advent IV, Israel's invasion of Judah and Judah's alliance with Assyria. Looking over the embattled scene the prophet sees first the lifting of the darkness that war always casts over people, then the destruction of the gear of war and finally the birth of the Messiah who will inaugurate a new era. The latter is a beautiful foreshadowing of Our Lord. Again the music of Handel's *Messiah* runs through our minds.

Responsorial Psalm: *Psalm 95. 1—3, 11—13*
This is one of a group of psalms that celebrate the Kingship of God, possibly in association with the festival of the New Year. These are the Enthronement Psalms. What is before us falls into three parts, a call to all the world to praise God, an invocation to the whole of nature to join the praise and finally a brief statement of God's justice and truth. "He comes to rule the earth" are words most appropriate in this Mass.

Second Reading: *Titus 2. 11—14*
Paul, having given Titus some advice on various matters, offers in the passage before us the doctrinal basis of his teaching, namely what God did for us in sending his Son into the world and what obligations it imposes on us. Two points may be made: the words "giving up everything that does not lead to God" look like a definite renunciation such as was made at Baptism in the early Church and is made now at Confirmation. Then comes the "appearing of the glory of the great God". "Appearing" is "epiphaneia", epiphany. We will be celebrating Epiphany on January 6.

Gospel: *Luke 2.1—14*
The imperfect state of our historical knowledge enables us neither to confirm nor deny the census to which Luke refers. If one were to write a fictitious account of God's entry into this world, would its main elements be a dubious conception, an unattended birth in a stable under near impossible conditions and angels singing to some rough shepherds out on the hills in freezing cold late at night? God's truth often cuts gloriously across our ideas of credibility.

NATIVITY OF OUR LORD
MASS AT DAWN
YEAR A,B,C

First Reading: *Isaiah 62.11—12*

The prophet is speaking to his people who have returned from exile to a shattered city.[1] The Temple had been rebuilt in 520 B.C., but the way was hard. Isaiah's message is a prophecy of hope. Jerusalem will be a New Jerusalem; its present inhabitants are to open their gates and prepare for the coming of their Saviour. The new names by which they will be called indicate their new status.

Responsorial Psalm: *Psalm 96.1,6,11—12*

This is another psalm in the short series of Enthronement Psalms that celebrate the Kingship of God. The writer looks to a future when God's Reign will be over all the earth. Light, the symbol of well-being and happiness, and joy, the expression of God's blessing, describe this time. The universal note in the first stanza and the blessedness of the second are fitting thoughts for the Mass.

Second Reading: *Titus 3.4—7*

Paul is giving further advice to Titus, this time on a Christian's responsibility to the world about him. Then follows in the reading another summary of the Gospel which expresses the reason for a Christian acting as Paul indicates. It was God's kindness that lay behind his saving of us.

Gospel: *Luke 2.15—20*

Two thoughts emerge from this exquisite narrative: when Luke wrote that the shepherds said to one another "Let us go to Bethlehem" he expressed his thought in a way that suggests a lot of talk before the action. We can see them standing out in the hillside in the frosty night excitedly working out their plan to go to Bethlehem. Then we observe that "all were astonished", but that blessed Mary "pondered". Again the tenses are revealing. For the shepherds it was a single action; for Mary it was a habit that was part of her life.

---

[1] See Notes on the First Reading, Christmas Vigil Mass.

First Reading: *Isaiah 52. 7–10*
Deliverance from exile in Babylon[1] is imminent. A messenger comes running over the hills to tell the people to return to Jerusalem with God going on before. The call then goes out to the remnant in Jerusalem (or is it to the very ruins themselves?) to break into joy, for God is to show his strength for the whole world to see. Even so come, Lord Jesus.

Responsorial Psalm: *Psalm 97. 1–6*
This is a new psalm in the Enthronement series that celebrates the Kingship of God. There is a call to praise him for his salvation of his people, beyond and within Israel. This salvation is God's righteousness which he has revealed to the nations. His covenant with Israel has been kept. All the earth is called to rejoice in what God has done for his people. Finally instruments of various kinds will be used in the joyful noise of praise.

Second Reading: *Hebrews 1. 1–6*
Centuries of speculation have failed to come up with a convincing solution to the authorship of *Hebrews*. We cannot be certain where, to whom or when the letter was written. The passage before us is as lovely a picture of God's Son as one could find anywhere in Scripture. He is so presented in order to establish later in the letter his absolute superiority. The words a "perfect copy" are a translation of the Greek word "kharakter" (English, "character") meaning first an engraving tool, and then the engraved object.

Gospel: *John 1. 1–18*
The reading is John's Prologue to his Gospel, one of the noblest passages in the *Bible*. Christ is represented as the Word, a concept which is a mixture of two streams of thought, one from the Wisdom literature of the *Old Testament*, the other from Greek philosophy. During the year passages from the Wisdom writings will be used in First Readings. Wisdom is almost a person, a "pure flowing forth from the Almighty." In the passage to be read details about the Word alternate with facts about John the Baptist.

---

[1] See Notes, First Reading Christmas Vigil Mass

SUNDAY IN THE OCTAVE OF CHRISTMAS
THE HOLY FAMILY
OF JESUS,MARY AND JOSEPH
YEAR A

First Reading: *Ecclesiasticus 3.2-6, 12-14*
Ecclesiasticus has been described as the "gem of the Apocrypha"
(books of the *Old Testament* not considered genuine by the
Jews). It was a late composition, best known in a Greek
translation and regarded as a kind of handbook covering a wide
range of life's circumstances which are treated in relation to
Wisdom. The reading deals with honouring our parents.

Responsorial Psalm: *Psalm 127. 1-5*
This is one of the Songs of Ascent or Gradual Psalms (120-134),
sung by pilgrims ascending Zion's hill as they returned for one of
the great festivals. It sings the blessedness of the God-fearing man
in his family life; he will have enough to provide for his own; his
wife will bear him children and they shall be like shoots of the
spreading, ever green olive (Jeremiah 11.16). A benediction brings
the psalm to its conclusion.

Second Reading: *Colossians 3. 12-21*
Paul wrote to the Colossians to correct serious errors in their
faith. Having done this, he asserts that "they have been brought
back to true life with Christ" (Ch.3.1), and this involves a
reorganisation of their lives. So Paul gives rules for the regulation
of conduct; before us is what he has to say about family
relationships. Paul's vocabulary is always vivid. We note the
familiar idea of the putting on and off of garments to express a
change in life style. Last to go on is love, the fairest of all the
garments of redemption.

Gospel: *Matthew 2. 13-15, 19-23*
King Herod, whose throne had been secured by brutality,
misinterpreted the significance of the adoration of the Magi and
planned a rampage of slaughter to eliminate Jesus, the alleged
threat to his throne. The Holy Family fled to Egypt and stayed
possibly seven years. Though recorded only by Matthew the
account has the full ring of truth. The career of Moses began
amid the slaughter of children (*Exodus 1.22ff*). He fled before his
work of redemption began. So it was with one greater than Moses.
This is what Matthew is trying to say in his quote from *Hosea
(11.1)* "I am calling my son out of Egypt".

First Reading: *Numbers 6.22-27*
In the brevity of these verses lies the ancient recognition that
Israel owed everything to God who was the shield of his people
and the source of all that served their true interests. Here is the
invocation with which the priest from earliest times blessed the
people. In it there is a progression from the material to the
spiritual. In *Ecclesiasticus (50.20ff.)* we are told that the blessing
was pronounced each morning at the hour of sacrifice. The
shining of God's face is an expression of his delight in his people.

Responsorial Psalm: *Psalm 66.2-3,5,6,8*
This psalm which was used as harvest thanksgiving gathers up the
precious grain of the Aaronic blessing. In the first stanza the
gathered grain causes the psalmist to realise how dependent on
God the people are. The thought then passes to God's beneficent
rule of the nations. The psalm closes on a universal note that the
very ends of the earth may come to know God. *Deus misereatur.*

Second Reading: *Galatians 4.4-7*
Paul speaks bluntly to the Galatians who had been led astray
from the faith that he had taught them. They had been enticed
into a legalistic form of Christianity. Paul asserts that Jesus, Son
of Mary, had in reality freed them (as slaves were freed) from the
Law and given them the status of adopted sons. Note the use of
Abba. The word is Aramaic for "Father " and Aramaic was the
language Our Lord spoke. Tender and intimate, it fell from his
lips in prayer, especially in Gethsemane.

Gospel: *Luke 2. 16-21*
The liturgy of the Church invites us to let our minds range over
the whole octave of Christmas and in so doing we turn from Child
to Mother. The reaction of the shepherds was like an explosion of
wonder; Mary pondered the events in long and silent reflection.
In the first two chapters Luke is using a document written in
Aramaic as his source. If the writer of the document got his facts
from Blessed Mary, as has been suggested, what we read today is
largely her gift to us.

First Reading: *Ecclesiasticus 24.1-2,8-12*
Ecclesiasticus is part of the Wisdom literature which includes
Proverbs, Job etc. These writings cover a wide range of topics
such as the problem of suffering *(Job)*, advice on a great range
of life situations and the nature of Wisdom. She is conceived as
a person, "a clear flowing forth from the Almighty". These
writings are a product of the time after the exile. The writer of
Ecclesiasticus deals with the nature of Wisdom, Wisdom in
creation, and in our reading tells of Wisdom's special association
with God's people.

Responsorial Psalm: *Psalm 147.12-15,19-20*
This psalm is one of the Alleluia psalms, so called because they
begin and end with Alleluia. God is praised in this psalm for
having rebuilt Jerusalem, then for his sustaining nature, and in
the part before us as the God of Zion. He has strengthened her
defences, given peace and revealed himself to his own as to no
others.

Second Reading: *Ephesians 1.3-6,15-18*
Ephesians was a circular letter written to the churches of Asia
Minor and is considered by some to be Paul's greatest
composition. Its purpose, unlike some of his other epistles, is not
corrective, but is the flowering of Paul's spiritual genius to be
shared with his Christian converts. Its theme is the Church as the
Body of Christ. We read first, part of a magnificent doxology that
sweeps the range of God's plan for mankind and second, a prayer
for his readers' enlightenment in spiritual matters.

Gospel: *John 1.1-18*
This reading which was used also on Christmas Day is John's
prologue to his Gospel; it is one of the noblest passages in the
Bible. Christ is represented as the Word, a concept which is a
mixture of two streams of thought, one from the Wisdom
literature of the *Old Testament,* the other from Greek philosophy.
The presentation of Wisdom in the first reading is particularly
apt. In the passage to be read, details about the Word alternate
with facts concerning John the Baptist.

6 January or
Sunday between 2 January and 8 January
EPIPHANY OF THE LORD
YEARS A,B,C

First Reading: *Isaiah 60.1-6*

In this extract from the second part of *Isaiah* the prophet, living in the period after the exile and aware of the moral anarchy that gripped the Jews, saw a new Jerusalem bathed in light, while everything below lay in gross darkness. From East and West, wealth and people with a new heart were streaming into the city. So the passage prefigures the men who with their precious gifts came to Bethlehem for the first Epiphany. Notice the last two lines: "Bringing gold and incense and singing the praise of the Lord". In the first Epiphany there was the adoration of the East; in the hope of Epiphany is the worship of the whole world.

Responsorial Psalm: *Psalm 71.1-2,7-8,10-13*

This is part of a royal psalm intended for the accession of a king in Jerusalem. The prayer that the king may have the noblest attitudes of royalty passes into a vision of these qualities in operation; then comes a petition for world-wide dominion; the places mentioned are on the outer fringes of the world; the psalm ends with another vision of the blessedness of the era. The psalm is never quoted in the *New Testament* and is not Messianic, yet it points unerringly to the time when the spirit of the Epiphany is realised in the universal worship of Christ the King.

Second Reading: *Ephesians 3.2-3,5-6*

Set in the great discourse on the Church, this little gem deals with God's secret (not "mystery") hidden from time immemorial and revealed to holy men of the writer's generation. This secret, now open to the belief of all, is that salvation is not for the Jews only, but for all people everywhere. The homage of the world which is the hope of Epiphany is brought one stage nearer by the revelation of God's plan for all his sons and daughters.

Gospel: *Mattew 2.1-12*

We are indebted to Matthew alone for the account of the Wise Men and their coming to adore the infant Jesus. They were Persian astrologers who shared, in one of many forms, the contemporary longing for a Saviour. Their coming unleashed the fury of Herod and the slaughter of the Holy Innocents followed, for the *de facto* fears the genuine and seeks to eliminate it. In the custom of the day the Magi brought gifts which some think symbolised royalty, divinity and mortality. The word "epiphany" is a technical term to describe the manifestation of a deity; the word is used now to denote Christ's appearing to the nations.

Sunday after Epiphany
THE BAPTISM OF THE LORD
(First Sunday in Ordinary Time)
YEAR A

First Reading: *Isaiah 42.1-4,6-7*
This passage is part of the first Song of the Suffering Servant of which there are four in *Isaiah*. Speaking of the Servant, the writer describes his mission and later in direct address to the Servant, God the Creator speaks more specifically of what he has to do. Holding the work of creation and redemption in balance through the Spirit of God, the Church has identified Christ with the Suffering Servant.

Responsorial Psalm: *Psalm 28.1-4,9-10*
This psalm is one of the oldest in the Psalter and in its full form reflects the awesome description of Mount Sinai. God, full of power and full of splendour, is Lord of the storm. He is greater than that phenomenon that can wreak havoc and also bring relief to man's parched crops. His power is also a call to worship. The peace which is invoked in the response is not only freedom from war, but the full range of God-given blessings both material and spiritual.

Second Reading: *Acts 10.34-38*
Peter dominates the first part of *Acts*; among his great moments was the conversion of Cornelius, an officer in the Roman army who, like many Romans of his day, found no reality in their national religion. Now in Cornelius' house, Peter gives a quick sketch of the life of Jesus. He refers to Jesus as anointed with the Holy Spirit. Peter, remembering how great men of old were anointed with oil for special tasks, represents Our Lord's baptism as a divine anointing, not with oil, but with the Holy Spirit.

Gospel: *Matthew 3.13-17*
John's feeling of unworthiness in the presence of the Lord is understandable, yet when Jesus consented to be baptised, he who knew no sin was making a symbolic cleansing for the sin of the world, in the same way that he became sin on the Cross. Also, in his Baptism he was confirmed in the future role for which everything so far had shaped him. The dove has many meanings; the primitive church adopted it as a symbol of the Holy Spirit. The final seal of approval was the voice from heaven, the voice that was heard again at the Transfiguration.

First Reading: *Joel 2.12-18*

Joel prophesied in the years of spiritual depression following the return from exile. The land had been devastated by locusts; the Day of the Lord was at hand, as Joel saw it. And so the prophet called for national repentance, but it had to be with a sincere heart for the formality of torn garments was not enough. There was yet time, for God is compassionate. Then the prophet issues a call for a fast; all must come, elders and children, even the bride and her bridegroom in the first flush of their union and all must plead with God in humiliation and penitence.

Responsorial Psalm: *Psalm 50.3-6,12-14,17*

It has been said of this psalm that "it is the greatest of all penitential prayers, biblical and extrabiblical". Traditionally, though very dubiously, the psalm has been associated with David's sin in the company of Bathsheba. Through the centuries, men and women distressed by their sin have found the psalm a way to God's grace. The thoughts of the psalmist turn on a plea for mercy, confession, a desire for a fresh beginning and the joy of restored fellowship with God. The last stanza is like a light at the end of the tunnel, for it shows what the sinner has lost and what he hopes to regain.

Second Reading: *II Corinthians 5.20-6.2*

II Corinthians has no plan, only contents. It is a very difficult letter because what we have is probably bits and pieces of three letters. A great row between Paul and the Corinthians had been resolved and in part of *II Corinthians* we have a letter which reviews the conflict. No wonder it concludes with profound thoughts on reconciliation, some of which are before us. We are urged to be reconciled, not to avoid the anger of God, but — and the thought is stupendous — that we may through Christ become the goodness of God. The reading concludes with a quotation from *Isaiah (49.8)* in which the Lord speaks to the Suffering Servant of salvation (i.e. victory). Paul changes the sense of salvation and applies it to Christ's followers.

Gospel: *Matthew 6.1-6,16-18*

In this portion of the Sermon on the Mount the disciples are required to persevere in the observances of giving, praying and fasting, but to examine the motive behind these spiritual exercises, for these disciplines have as much inherent power for mischief as for good. It deserves to be noted that "hypocrite" comes from the Greek word for an actor, one who speaks from under a mask.

First Reading: *Genesis 2. 7—9, 3. 1—7*
From one of the earliest strands in *Genesis* comes this account of
        Mans First Disobedience , and the Fruit
        Of that Forbidden Tree,
and with it centuries of argument about original sin. The narrative
is rich in psychological detail. It has the form of a lovely story,
naive, but penetrating; in it we see how long ago it was realised
that God created man for his companionship and that it was man
who broke the bond.

Responsorial Psalm: *Psalm 50. 3—6, 12—14, 17*
In this, the greatest of the penitential psalms, it is of no significance who the penitent was. What is supremely important is that
we have the ideal form of penitential approach to God. In the
first stanza there is an appeal for mercy; then comes confession;
in the third stanza there is a longing for a clean heart that will
save the penitent from future error. The psalm closes with desire
for restored communion with God.

Second Reading: *Romans 5. 12—19*
The Second Reading perfectly complements the first. Into Paul's
discourse on righteousness by faith comes Christ, the second
Adam, to restore what was lost in man's Fall and to bring him
again into communion with his God. Paul is at pains to point out
that what Christ conferred was greater than what was lost in the
Fall. In place of condemnation for sin came acquittal through the
grace of Christ freely given to everyone who will accept it.

Gospel: *Matthew 4. 1—11*
The temptations of Our Lord follow immediately after the
baptism. As he was alone in this experience he must have talked
to the disciples about it and so passed the details into circulation.
Matthew and Luke who record the temptations do not follow the
same order. It is observed that the temptations came to Our Lord,
as they often do to us, when physical resources were at a low ebb;
that in each instance the tempter was rebuffed by appeals to
Deuteronomy, and that the temptations in each case were a
caricature of what the Messianic age stood for, full and plenty,
powers greater than the forces of nature and world-wide dominion. The Lord's victory was a triumph for the forces of the Spirit.

First Reading: *Genesis 12. 1–4*
Genesis has been compiled from five main sources; at Chapter 12
the narrative emerges as history. Here the record of the patriarchs
begins with the call of Abram. He had already left his home near
the head of the Persian Gulf and travelled to Haran in
Mesopotamia where God again confronted him and gave him and
his wife, a childless couple, the commission to travel south and
become the great nation of God's people.

Responsorial Psalm: *Psalm 32. 4–5, 18–20, 22*
One of the distinctive features of the Hebrew religion was its
moral quality. The first stanza of this psalm shows God as the
source of that morality. The writer then records God's care for
those who hope in his love. Finally there is the expectancy of
those who trust in him.

Second Reading: *II Timothy 1.8–10*
Paul appeals to Timothy, his son in Christ, to witness with
courage to Christ's saving work. In a brief, but powerful statement
Paul reviews God's salvation of mankind through the redeeming
Christ. It is also stressed that redemption was part of God's
eternal purpose and that nearer to Paul's own time the Incarnate
Christ has bestowed eternal life on those who receive him.

Gospel: *Matthew 17. 1–9*
When Paul wrote to the Philippians (2.6) and referred to Christ
as "being in the form of God" he used a word which is embedded
in the Greek verb "to be transfigured." Our Lord was changed
into a form that revealed the Godhead. The presence of Moses
and Elijah on the Mount of Transfiguration symbolised the Law
and the Prophets, the old order summed up in two persons.
Peter the impetuous wanted to hold the moment for all time, not
realising that as the voice at the Lord's baptism set the seal on his
ministry, so now it confirmed the way to the Cross.

First reading: *Exodus 17. 3—7*
God's people in the wilderness were not immune to physical
needs, but they did have a God willing and able to meet them,
and on this occasion it was by releasing water from a rock. The
name Massah has captured the mood of the Israelites in requiring
proof that God was still with them; Meribah records their finding
fault with Moses and ultimately with God.

Responsorial Psalm: *Psalm 94. 1—2, 6—9*
This psalm was sung on the way to the Temple. S. Benedict in the
sixth century required the monks of his order to say it daily on
waking. In the psalm God is approached with a joyful noise in
characteristic Oriental manner. In the second stanza one feels the
hush of awe. References to the rock, Meribah and Massah, show
how the desert experience stands as a perpetual warning to God's
people.

Second Reading: *Romans 5. 1—2, 5—8*
In previous chapters of *Romans*, Paul lays the foundation for the
new life. The reading begins at the point where the erection of
the structure based on it begins. The Christian in the new status
given by his faith has blessings to look forward to and they are
not illusions. God's love has been poured out as the emptying of a
vessel upon us, and all this because, in spite of our unworthiness,
Christ died for us to reconcile us to God.

Gospel: *John 4. 5—42*
All Our Lord's dealings with the Samaritans were compassionate
as this reading shows. His teaching often centres on the simplest
things, bread, wine and here water, living water, a term found
in the *Old Testament (Jeremiah 2. 13)*. His thoughts may have
been drawn in part from the content of the First Reading. He
offered not the water that required daily toil to draw, but such as
would quench the needs of the spirit continuously. There were
defects, as the Jews saw them, in the faith of the Samaritans.
They worshipped only on Mount Gerizim near the well. Jesus
insists that it is the quality and not the place of worship that
matters.

First Reading: *I Samuel 16. 1, 6—7, 10—13*
For his disobedience Saul was rejected as king and Samuel was
told to find and anoint a successor. The reading records the
search and the process of rejection until David, of whom God
approved, was found. Three points are worth observing: God's
choice is not made by human standards; by anointing, the
recipient was given a special gift of God's Spirit, and from the
verb "to anoint" comes the word Messiah, in Greek "Christos".
Samuel anointed David and David became Christ's ancestor.

Responsorial Psalm: *Psalm 22*
The Shepherd psalm is unique in the Psalter and probably the
best known. Into his image of the good shepherd, the writer,
traditionally said to be David, projects all the qualities of the
keeper of sheep on the hill side. What more could he do for his
charges than is set out in the first two stanzas? Then the picture
changes to a banquet where God is the host. The psalm ends with
a feeling of security prompted by the divine Shepherd. All we
like sheep have gone astray, and we find in this psalm the Great
Shepherd who gently leads the lost back to the fold.

Second Reading: *Ephesians 5. 8—14*
Ephesians is a circular letter addressed to the churches of Asia
Minor, not written to correct errors of faith, but to share the
full flower of a spiritual development with God's people. The
theme of the letter is the Church as the Body of Christ. After the
doctrine comes the practical application; in the reading we are
urged to discover what God wants of us as children of light.
The quotation at the end is otherwise unknown, possibly a
fragment of a hymn.

Gospel: *John 9. 1—41*
The passage to be read begins with the miracle of sight restored
to the blind man and of his turning to the true Light. The
Pharisees make of the occasion a battle of words with the man
and lose badly. From the first part it is observed that Our Lord,
contrary to some ideas in the *Old Testament* discounts any
necessary connexion between sin and suffering; from the second
part comes the condemnation of those who have the gift of
spiritual sight and do not use it. It is they who are blind.

First Reading: *Ezekiel 37. 12—14*
Ezekiel is a difficult book with complex problems and so the
passage before us must be handled carefully. The Jews were in
exile in Babylon and it is to them that Ezekiel speaks. The
opening of graves refers to the bringing of exiles from their
bondage. Then comes the promise of restoration as a living
nation with the Spirit of God upon them.

Responsorial Psalm: *Psalm 129*
This is one of the Gradual Psalms or songs sung by pilgrims
ascending Mount Zion; it is also, and more pertinently, a
penitential psalm. The deep emotion of the penitent is reflected
in the irregularity of the Hebrew verse. First there is a long cry
of distress in which, as we say in English, the psalmist is in deep
water. The second half reveals a mood of expectancy as he
waits for deliverance and forgiveness.

Second Reading: *Romans 8.8—11*
Paul's theme in this well known passage is the new life in the
Spirit, a word used nearly thirty times in this chapter. As a result
of our being declared righteous there is a transformation brought
about by the Holy Spirit. This indwelling Spirit raises us from our
former life just as God raised Jesus from the dead.

Gospel: *John 11. 1—45*
So much has been said about the raising of Lazarus that two
comments must suffice: the events reveal the human and the
divine natures in Our Lord. He did not hurry to Lazarus' bedside
because he knew that he would restore him to life, yet he burst
into tears (a word unique in the *New Testament*) when he saw the
dead man. Then too John uses a very powerful word with the
primary sense of the snorting of horses to express Our Lord's
emotional reaction to the same sight. The whole occasion was the
vehicle of the Lord's fifth utterance "I am", in this case "I am the
Resurrection and the Life". These form a distinctive feature of
this Gospel.

PASSION SUNDAY
(Palm Sunday)
YEARS A,B,C
FIRST FORM: THE PROCESSION

YEAR A *Matthew 21. 1—11*
The secret his disciples had been forbidden to reveal was now proclaimed as Jesus made his triumphal entry into Jerusalem. All four Gospels record the event; Matthew's is stamped with its own individuality in the composite quotation chiefly from *Zechariah (9.9)*. Here the unknown writer sees a cessation of the war with which his people are beset; the paraphernalia of battle will no longer be needed; peace will be widespread; the king will enter "riding on a donkey, on a colt the foal of a donkey", not on a horse, the animal of war. All this is applied to Jesus as he makes his Messianic entry into Jerusalem.

YEAR B *Mark 11. 1—10*
Jesus is now approaching Jerusalem the holy city into which a Messiah will have to enter as the climax of his progress. Careful preparation has been made as the release of the colt indicates. A touch of realism is given by the mention of Bethany and Bethpage, about three km from the city, and seen as the party travelled up the steep road to Jerusalem. Mark is predominantly interested in the colt. Usually triumphal entries were made on horses, beasts of war, but this rider comes in peace; his warfare was spiritual.

ALTERNATE GOSPEL: *John 12. 12—16*
John's account of the triumphal entry differs from those of the Synoptics; there is less detail and more interpretation as is typical of John. In this account Jesus is hailed as King (and also in *Luke*); only John refers to the strewn branches of date palms (Mark calls them "leafy branches," a very rare word). These date palms were an ancient symbol of victory *(II Maccabees 10.7)*. Furthermore John prefaces the very brief reference to Zechariah's prophecy with "Do not be afraid", because the Roman authorities were sensitive to anything that suggested a political challenge. The Evangelist records a very human note at the end of the reading, an awareness only after the event of the full significance of what was happening.

YEAR C *Luke 19. 28—40*

Luke's narrative of the triumphal entry catches the exuberance of the crowd. There are, as one would expect, details not given elsewhere; only Luke records the complaint of the Pharisees and the Lord's reply. Luke, grounded in Greek, disliked Hebrew words and omitted the Hosanna ("save us") of the other Evangelists and substituted "glory in the highest heavens" for Gentile ears. Missing, too, is the reference to *Zechariah*, with its overtones in the original setting of the progress of a political king. In its place are liturgical fragments from the psalms.

First Reading: *Isaiah 50. 4—7*
From Ch. 40 onwards the *Book of Isaiah* is commonly called
Deutero— or Second Isaiah, the work of another hand. In the
portion to be read, the Jews were in exile in Babylon where their
captors, the Chaldeans, had taken them in 587 B.C. The prophet
never ceased to encourage the people to have hope in the future.
Between Chs. 42 and 53 there are four Songs of the Suffering
Servant. Here we have the third and in it the Servant discloses the
source of his power which is trust and obedience. Though
persecuted, the Servant does not doubt God's vindication. The
Church has naturally seen Christ as the Suffering Servant.

Responsorial Psalm: *Psalm 21. 8—9, 17—20, 23—24*
There are other psalms in which the writer laments his lot, but
none like this one. There is no reference to sin as the cause of his
trouble, nor is there any cry for vengeance on his enemies. Often
called the "Passion Psalm", it is quoted in all four Gospels.
Nothing so exalts it as Our Lord's first word on the Cross: "My
God, My God, why have you forsaken me?", words taken from
the first line of the psalm. Our Lord thus applies the psalm to
himself.

Second Reading: *Philippians 2.6—11*
Paul writing to the Philippians from prison, is speaking about the
Christian life and in Ch. 2, in response to a local situation, makes
a plea for unity. Into this setting he places what is generally
agreed was a Christian hymn, and it is this that constitutes the
reading. This is not the only hymn that has found its way into the
New Testament. Their identification is not easy as there was no
literary code regarding quotations. The hymn to Christ falls into
two parts, his Humiliation and his subsequent Glorification.

YEAR A

Gospel: *Matthew 26.14–27. 66*
In mediaeval times the Gospel on this day was sung in assigned
parts and during the singing it was customary to hold palm
branches in the hand. The long reading covers events from Judas'
agreement with the chief Pharisees, to the Lord's death and burial
and includes the institution of the Lord's Supper, the betrayal,
Jesus on trial, the crucifixion and one account of Judas' death.
Matthew follows the Marcan account with additions.

YEAR B

Gospel: *Mark 14. 1–15.47*
In a narrative that is both the end and the beginning, the
deepening crisis in Our Lord's life moves to its conclusion. Tightly
woven into the chain of events presented in this, the oldest
known account of Our Lord's last two days, are the anointing at
Bethany, the treachery of Judas, the Last Supper, the arrest,
trial and crucifixion. The secret hidden from the beginning of
time will soon be revealed.

YEAR C

Gospel: *Luke 22. 14–23. 56*
We begin the Lucan account of the Passion with the institution
of the Lord's Supper and this is followed by Peter's denial, the
trial and crucifixion. Luke appears to follow sources not
available to Matthew and Mark and this results in greater detail,
especially in regard to the Institution of the Supper. Probably
from the same source also come words from the Cross otherwise
unrecorded, the first, second and last: "Father forgive ....,"
"Today you will be with me in Paradise", and "Father, into your
hands ....".

First Reading: *Isaiah 61. 1—3,6,8—9*
The writer of the second part of *Isaiah* is speaking to his people
who have returned from exile in Babylon to a shattered city. The
way of restoration was long, slow and hard. In the reading the
prophet, anointed with the Spirit of the Lord, speaks words of
comfort to the people. Their new function in the world will be a
priestly one; they will be seen as a race under God's blessing.
Listen for the first part of this reading in the gospel.

Responsorial Psalm: *Psalm 88. 21—22,25,27*
The full version is a long psalm, perhaps three psalms of different
times and circumstances. The few lines before us tell of God's
covenant with David and of God's promises to him.In this Chrism
Mass we recall that in the blessing of the holy oil, God gives his
power and his Spirit for a specific purpose as of old.

Second Reading: *Apocalypse 1.5—8*
The *Apocalypse* is addressed to the Seven Churches of Asia, but
the mystic number suggests that in reality there are no
geographical boundaries to its reception. Our reading begins with
an elaborate salutation which covers Our Lord's redemptive work
and ends with a kind of "Thus saith the Lord", expressed symbolically through the first and last letters of the Greek alphabet.
There is an echo from the First Reading in "priests of the Lord":
in fact the echo comes from as far away as *Exodus (19.6)* and
reaches to this Mass with its renewal of priestly vows.

Gospel: *Luke 4.16—21*
Jesus returns from the wilderness experience to visit his home
town of Nazara where he participates in the Synagogue service by
reading. The passage as quoted in *Luke* is from the First Reading
with some minor differences. Our Lord applies the prophecy in
Isaiah to himself and in so doing gives a glimpse of the line his
ministry will follow. For the intention of this Mass the opening
lines of the quoted passage are specially important with their
reminder how prophets and priests of old were anointed with oil
for their calling.

EASTER TRIDUUM
HOLY THURSDAY
Evening Mass of the Lord's Supper
YEARS A,B,C

First Reading: *Exodus 12.1–8,11–14*
Nine plagues had failed to move Pharaoh. Before carrying out the tenth, God gives instructions for the institution of the Passover, details of which are set out in the reading. There are three elements in this ancient rite, the sacrifice of a victim, a celebration at night and protection afforded by shed blood. The Passover became an annual event in the religious life of the Jews.

Responsorial Psalm: *Psalm 115. 12–13,15–18*
This is one of the great Hallel (Hebrew:praise) or Egyptian Hallel Psalms (113–118[1]) traditionally sung while the Passover lambs were being slain and possibly sung by Our Lord and the disciples after the Last Supper. In the portion before us, the psalmist thanks God for some great deliverance. The cup of salvation suggests the pouring of a drink offering. Vows made during distress will be paid in the sight of all.

Second Reading: *I Corinthians 11.23–26*
As none of the Gospels existed when Paul wrote his letters, this account of the Institution of the Lord's Supper is the first ever set down. Later Matthew, Mark and Luke recorded their versions. Paul tells the Corinthians in the context of public worship that this account was given by direct inspiration and was not drawn from documentary sources. He writes because there were disorders in the Corinthian church due to party spirit and originating also from failure to appreciate the solemn nature of the occasion, by misuse of the "agape" or love feast.

Gospel: *John 13.1–15*
From this point in the narrative Our Lord's teaching is directed to his disciples. The present occasion shows how much, even at this late hour, they were in need of instruction. Common courtesy required a servant to wash the feet of guests who had come off the dusty ways of the village. None of the disciples was willing to undertake this menial task and so Our Lord, to teach them a lesson in humility and service, performs the task himself.

---

[1] In the numeration of the *Jerusalem Bible*

First Reading: *Isaiah 52.13—53.12*
The *Book of Isaiah* from Chapter 40 onwards is later than what precedes it and is from another hand. In this second part there are four Songs of the Suffering Servant and before us now is the last of these. Set against the times of exile in Babylon, the Servant appears as one humiliated and suffering, only to be revealed at the end in triumph. Who was the Suffering Servant in the contemporary scene? An individual? Israel? The faithful remnant? The Church has found the full expression of the Servant in Christ.

Responsorial Psalm: *Psalm 30.2,6,12—13,15—17,25*
The psalmist's great distress alternates with his trust in God. Stanzas two and three suggest that he has been ostracised by his fellows. Yet his faith rises above his trials and finds beautiful expression in the last two stanzas. The response is actually an omitted line and is one of the treasures of the Christian faith, for it is Our Lord's last word on the Cross recorded only in *Luke (23. 46)* "Into your hands I commend my spirit".

Second Reading: *Hebrews 4.14—16,5.7—9*
The unknown writer of the *Letter to the Hebrews* has dealt with the superiority of Jesus to all that the Old Covenant implied and now explains his heavenly high priesthood. Tempted, but without sin, he can be approached by us in our need. Though a high priest, he learned obedience through suffering. From sharing our nature came his sympathy with us and his gift of salvation.

Gospel: *John 18.1—19.42*
John's account of the glorification of Jesus in his passion and death presents the Lord as always being in control of the situation. John gives details not recorded elsewhere, notably in respect of Pontius Pilate. In particular it is observed that the third, fifth and sixth words from the Cross are found only in *John*, "Behold your mother," "I thirst" and "It is finished".

First Reading: *Genesis 1.1-2.2*
When *Genesis* took its final form, the strand to which this reading
belongs was late in composition though a precise date is
impossible to give. This account is distinct from the second
version which is recorded in Ch.2. It is marked by a great dignity
in its presentation and unlike other contemporary accounts of
creation, in *Genesis* the existence of God is assumed. In the
opening words, the mind naturally turns to the beginning of
John's Gospel.

Responsorial Psalm: *Psalms 103.1-2,5-6,10,12-14,24,35*
This lovely creation psalm — there are others in the Psalter — praises
the Creator for the various aspects of creation and ideally follows
the First Reading. The psalmist also glorifies the beneficence of
the Creator as in the fourth stanza. The reference to light in the
first stanza not only recalls the account of creation in *Genesis* but
indicates, as do other omitted parts of the psalm, the influence of
an alien culture.

Alternate Psalm: *Psalm 32.4-7,12-13,20,22*
The goodness and moral beauty of God are evident in creation.
The psalmist sees the love of God for his people and sings of his
people's rest in that love; they wait for him and recognise him as
their defence.

Second Reading: *Genesis 22.1-18*
God's provision for a race more numerous than the stars or the
sand on the shore seemed to have come to an intolerable
contradiction. The sacrifice of Isaac was the supreme test of
Abraham's faith. Had he come so far to face family extinction?
Paul summed up the whole crisis which is ours in many forms:
"with any trial he will give you a way out of it" *(1 Corinthians
10.13).*

Responsorial Psalm *Psalm 15.5,8-11*
The psalmist lives near to his God and finds joy in his oneness
with him. First he states what amounts to his creed, then comes
confidence that he will be spared untimely death, for
contemporary ideas of the hereafter were undeveloped and
offered little consolation. Finally the psalmist sees himself
enjoying a life guided by the hand of God.

Third Reading: *Exodus 14.15-15.1*
Israel in flight from Egypt crossed the sea to safety. But where ?
The Hebrew means "The Reed Sea"; the Greek version has "Red
Sea". The argument continues interminably without solution.
What matters most is that the Israelites did cross over and God's
deliverance for his people was accomplished. Deliverance is the
keynote to the Easter season.

Responsorial Psalm: *Exodus 15.1-6,17-18*
Not all the songs of the *Old Testament* are in the Psalter (e.g. the
Song of Hannah, 1 *Samuel* 2). This abridged version of Moses'
song follows immediately after the Third Reading. The occasion
was momentous, an escape by the hand of God, an enemy no
more, a nation born, indeed reborn, and ahead lay the terrifying
experience of years in wandering. This period in time was a
watershed and Moses sings. Three stanzas of the song exalt the
warrior God; in the last there is an assurance of arrival in the
Promised Land.

Fourth Reading: *Isaiah 54.5-14*
The author of the second part of *Isaiah* is writing words of
encouragement to his people who are still in exile in Babylon.
Themes from marriage convey the prophet's message: God will
reclaim his people as a husband takes back a forsaken wife; never
again will God's love be withheld from them. The new city which
is promised to them will have a splendour that has not been seen
before, and righteousness will be its foundation.

Responsorial Psalm: *Psalm 29.2,4-6,11-13*
The psalmist is full of joy because God has brought him through a
time of serious illness. How near he was to death is evident from
the first stanza. In the second he praises God whose favour is
only briefly withdrawn. Joy breaks through the last stanza. The
psalm as a whole reflects the main thought in the Fourth Reading.

Fifth Reading: *Isaiah 55.1-11*
The scene is unchanged; God's people are still in exile. The
prophet issues a great invitation to the Messiah's banquet,
admission free. Through the basics of water, grain, wine and milk
the needs of the spirit will be satisfied. There is a promise of a
new covenant and with it a command to return to God. The
conclusion affirms that God's word is never frustrated; it is as
sure as the seasons.

40

Responsorial Psalm: *Isaiah 12.2-6*
The reading has been described as two small psalms sung by those
who have been redeemed. It is considerably later than the part of
Isaiah in which it has become embedded and should be read in
connexion with the end of the previous chapter which speaks of
times of deliverance. While not being specifically Messianic, it has
a Messianic quality. The reading overflows with the joy of God's
salvation which is like the inexhaustible springs of water from a
well.

Sixth Reading: *Baruch 3.9-15,32-4.4*
Baruch is one of the books of the *Apocrypha* (the books in the
Old Testament not recognised by the Jews); it is very late in
composition, possibly belonging to the early Christian era.
Traditionally a disciple of Jeremiah, Baruch is supposed to have
written part of the book in Babylon and to have read it to the
exiles. The reading deals with Wisdom [1] as the privileged
possession of Israel.

Responsorial Psalm: *Psalm 18.8-11*
This psalm begins with praise of the God of the universe and ends
with the praise of God's Law; it is in fact two psalms joined
together, so much so that even the metre of the two parts is
different. The portion of the psalm before us praises the Law of
God, the Law before the Pharisees converted it with their burdens
into a yoke, the Law as God gave it to Moses.

Seventh Reading: *Ezekiel 36.16-28*
This section of *Ezekiel* (Chs 33-39) contains prophecies that deal
with the redemption of God's people who are in exile in Babylon,
awaiting the rebuilding of their national hopes. The prophet
explains why God who controls the course of nations exiled his
people and how in their exile they continue to shame him. God
will vindicate himself in the eyes of the nations and then cleanse
his people before gathering them in again from exile.

---

[1] See Notes, First Reading, Second Sunday after Christmas.

Responsorial Psalm: *Psalm 41.3,5,42.3-4*
Though difficult to date, these two psalms reflect the mind of
one absent, for whatever reason, from his home and its religious
life. They aptly express the thoughts of anyone who had heard
Ezekiel's message. In the full text we learn that the psalmist is ill
also. He longs for God and sees himself leading crowds to worship
This becomes a prayer that it may happen. The psalm ends in
confidence that it will.

If a baptism takes place

Responsorial Psalm[1]: *Psalm 50.12-15,18,19*
This psalm has been called "the greatest of all penitential prayers,
biblical and extrabiblical". It is dubious whether the penitent was
David, but penitents through the ages have made it their longing
for a restored relationship with God. First there is a cry for God's
forgiveness, then an expression of a desire to help others to avoid
the way he has trodden and finally a recognition that penitence is
the only propitiatory offering God will receive.

---

[1] See the rubric in the Missal. See also Notes for Ash Wednesday.

EASTER VIGIL
MASS OF EASTER NIGHT
YEARS A. B. C

First Reading: *Romans 6.3-11*
The *Letter to the Romans* was not occasioned by any known
situation in the church, but was written by Paul as a means of
introducing himself before his proposed visit. It is the first text
book on systematic theology. The reading expresses the closeness
of the bond between Christ and the believer in baptism, death,
resurrection and the new life. Four vital Greek words in the
passage are compounds involving "with", an expression of the
intimacy of the bond.

Responsorial Psalm: *Psalm 117,1-2,16-17,22-23*
This psalm is the last of the Hallel psalms [1] and was used at the
Feast of Tabernacles, a festival celebrating the ingathering of
harvest. There is a call for general thanksgiving. In the second
stanza a deliverance from peril is brought to mind. The third
contains a reference to the rejected stone and this is most apt at
Easter. The corner stone was a huge block put in the ground to
tie two walls together. The stone symbolises the Jewish nation
rejected by the pagan world, but restored by God to a place of
honour. In the *New Testament* Our Lord is seen as the corner
stone.

Gospel: YEAR A *Matthew 28.1-10*
The women who had been faithful to the end came "at the
outgoing of the sabbath" to minister to Jesus' dead body and for
their devotion were rewarded with the first Resurrection
appearance, preceded by earthquake, the moved stone, the flight
of the guards and the presence of angels. The reading will now
present what is the corner stone in our faith, the Lord's
Resurrection.

Gospel: YEAR B *Mark 16.1-7*
Mark's account of the empty tomb is characterised by an
economy of words. What he describes "with dignity and restraint"
does not contain the details found in the other Evangelists,
but the argument from silence means little. The writer aims to
present the events as the very crux of the Christian faith, that
Christ rose from the tomb.

---

[1] See Notes, Holy Thursday's Responsorial Psalm.

Gospel: YEAR C *Luke 24.1-12*
None of the synoptic accounts agree in the details of the empty
tomb. Luke, for instance, records two angels, as also does John.
These apparent discrepancies rather tend to be proofs of
historicity. A dishonest writer would have synchronised his
version with other existing accounts. Furthermore the
information provided by those who were present, the source
material of the Evangelists, was bound to vary for they had
witnessed the most stupendous event in human history, the event
without which the Christian faith would have no meaning.

SEASON OF EASTER
EASTER SUNDAY
Mass of the Day
YEARS A B C

First Reading: *Acts 10.34,37-43*
Peter dominates the first part of *Acts*. It was he who first
addressed the Jews, and here in the household of the Roman
Cornelius whose conversion was one of the great events in the
early Church, Peter delivers the first address to the pagans. It
represents in the main the *kerygma* or line of preaching adopted
in the primitive Church, a survey and a very good one, of the
main events in the life of Jesus Christ.

Responsorial Psalm: *Psalm 117.1-2,16-17,22-23*
This psalm is the last of the Hallel psalms [1] and was used at the
Feast of Tabernacles, a festival celebrating the ingathering of the
harvest. There is a call for general thanksgiving. In the second
stanza a deliverance from peril is brought to mind. The third
contains a reference to the rejected stone and this is most apt at
Easter. The corner stone was a huge block put in the ground to
tie two walls together. In the *New Testament* Our Lord is seen as
the corner stone. The stone symbolises the Jewish nation,
rejected by the pagan world, but restored by God to a place of
honour.

Second Reading: *Colossians 3.1-4*
In his *Letter to the Colossians* Paul deals with the errors in their
faith and brings them face to face with the risen Christ. In the
reading they are urged to turn from the things of earth to
heavenly things. In four short verses the Greek for "with"occurs
three times, thus defining the new relationship in Christ.

Alternate Second Reading: *I Corinthians 5.6-8*
A basic law of morality had been breached and Paul bluntly tells
the Corinthian Church to expel the offender. Yeast, because of
its fermenting, was usually used to denote something evil. So the
Corinthians must get rid of every trace of this corrupting
influence, just as the Jews cleansed the house of every particle
of yeast before the Passover at which only bread without yeast
was used.

Gospel: *John 20.1-9*
John's narrative of the Resurrection passes over much detail
found in the other Gospels. In fact the same may be said of the
Gospel as a whole. The reason is that he selected aspects of Our
Lord's life to make them vehicles of the teaching he wished to
impart. So here John gives enough to serve his purpose, the final
Glorification of Christ.

---

[1] See Notes, the Responsorial Psalm on Holy Thursday.

First Reading: *Acts 2.42–47*

We are at the beginning of the history of the Church and will be reading from the *Acts of the Apostles* for several weeks to come. After Pentecost, Peter preached to a large gathering of Jews and about three thousand were converted and baptised. Our reading describes the new life style of these people. They shared everything and to faithful attendance in a body at the Temple, they added the Eucharist in house meetings. In their religious observances we note the grafting of the new onto the old.

Responsorial Psalm: *Psalm 117.2–4,13–15,22–24*

This is the last of the praise or Hallel psalms which were sung at the important festivals. The full version suggests that a deliverance was the reason for the composition of the psalm. In the first stanza God's love is acknowledged by all; in the second the reasons for praise are stated and they include a victory in war. Finally there is the thought so dear to Christians, the final acceptance of the rejected stone.

Second Reading: *I Peter 1.3–9*

Letters make up a considerable portion of the *New Testament* and in the main, but with variations, they follow the format of a pagan letter. The reading consists of a doxology instead of the more usual thanksgiving. Then comes an assurance of salvation and of God's protection in time of trial. "The paradox of joy in suffering" has caught the attention of more than one commentator.

Gospel: *John 20.19–31*

The Resurrection appearance recorded in the reading serves a theological purpose as the narrative does elsewhere in John's Gospel. Coming through closed doors, Jesus gave his disciples his peace, a peace which covered the whole range of spiritual well-being. The Risen Lord breathed on the disciples as his Father breathed on the world at its creation. They received their commission with priestly authority to forgive and to retain sins. The passage contains the only reference in the Gospels to the nails of the Cross.

First Reading: *Acts 2.14,22–23*

Following the amazing events of Pentecost, Peter spoke to the crowd with a courage that even now makes the reader gasp. It was in fact the first Christian sermon ever delivered and it was a Jewish audience to which he spoke. Having rebutted the charge that they were drunk, he who once denied any knowledge of Jesus, fearlessly accused the Jews of murdering him. Because he was addressing Jews he quotes from *Psalm 16*,[1] altering the original meaning to prove Christ's Resurrection from the tomb.

Responsorial Psalm: *Psalm 15.1–2,5,7–11*

The psalmist walks closely with his God and finds many sources of strength in him. God directs his way and watches over him at night. In the third stanza the psalmist expresses confidence that Sheol, or the place of the dead will not make an untimely claim on him. The quotation in the First Reading is from this psalm. "For you will not leave my soul among the dead" does not amount to a plea for immortality nor is it a prophecy of the Resurrection; it is only a prayer for life of normal length.

Second Reading: *I Peter 1.17–21*

The letter is addressed to Christians in Asia Minor who were undergoing a time of trial. As the letter cannot be dated with certainty, it is hard to say to which of the known persecutions the writer is referring. Living in a world of slavery, Peter is on familiar ground when he speaks of ransom and applies this idea to his readers' release from the bondage of sin. The price paid for their ransom is stressed. References to the Resurrection and Glorification of Christ make the reading very appropriate to the time of the year. The words "as long as you are living away from home" involve a word that means "residence in a foreign country without citizenship".

Gospel: *Luke 24.13–35*

The appearance of the risen Lord to the disciples on the way to Emmaus is one of the best loved of the Resurrection stories and is found only in *Luke*. Three points come to mind: the courtesy of the travellers in pressing the stranger to dine with them; the significance of the breaking of bread and the searching of the Scriptures. There is evidence that the Gospels may have developed by stages. If so then one of these was the collection of *Old Testament* material paralleled by incidents in Our Lord's life. This was exactly what happened on the way to Emmaus.

---

[1] i.e. in the *Jerusalem Bible*, 15 in the *Grail* translation, used in the Responsorial Psalms in the Missal.

First Reading: *Acts 2.14,36—41*

The events recorded in this reading follow the speech to the Jews which was read last Sunday. In an electrified atmosphere the audience was stung with remorse over what had been perpetrated at the Crucifixion, and after another speech from Peter which is not recorded, they sought baptism and the gift of the Holy Spirit.

Responsorial Psalm: *Psalm 22.1—6*

The Shepherd psalm is unique in the psalter and probably the best known. Into his image of the good shepherd, the writer, traditionally said to be David, projects all the qualities of the keeper of the sheep on the hill side. What more could he do for his charges than is set out in the first two stanzas? Then the picture changes to a banquet where God is host. The psalm ends with a feeling of security prompted by the divine Shepherd. All we like sheep have gone astray and we find in this psalm the Great Shepherd who gently leads the lost back to the fold.

Second Reading: *I Peter 2.20—25*

Accepting the fact of slavery, as Paul did, Peter urges members of a household to endure the master's severity . Christ's followers must endure, because Christ also endured, not as a wrongdoer, as slaves often were, but one who was cruelly treated for our sakes. The Greek text is full of interesting words, like the word behind "example," defined as a "model to be copied in writing or drawing".

Gospel: *John 10.1—10*

Drawing as usual from the common scenes of life, John wants us to picture a farmstead and courtyard where shepherds take their flocks for nightly protection. The only door is guarded against those who would steal by force or cunning. The sheep recognise only their own shepherd's voice. It is not difficult to work out the application. The passage ends with the third of the "I am" statements, "I am the Gate of the sheepfold". These are peculiar to *John.*

First Reading: *Acts 6.1—7*
As the Church grew, so also did the number of widows requiring
assistance. It was therefore decided by the Twelve — Matthias
replaced Judas — that the disciples should appoint seven
spiritually minded men from their own number to attend to the
day by day administration of the Church. We note that hands were
laid on them by the apostles for their work. Thus the apostles were
left free to evangelise. The fact that all seven bore Greek names
shows that the Church was recognising the universal nature of its
calling.

Responsorial Psalm: *Psalm 32.1—2,4—5,18—19*
Only a ringing cry of joy with musical instruments will suffice to
praise the moral qualities of God. The full version of the psalm
makes it clear that some deliverance prompted the writer. The
third stanza suggests that the ever recurring spectre of famine
has no terror for those who trust in God. The same trust will also
take away the fear of untimely death.

Second Reading: *I Peter 2.4—9*
Continuing his letter to Christians in Asia Minor, Peter, with
possible thoughts of his own denial of Christ, takes up the theme
of the rejected stone which as *Isaiah*[1] declares, God will restore
to its position of honour. Peter transfers this idea of rejection and
glorification to Jesus Christ and bids his readers and us become
living stones with Christ and enjoy the privileges thus bestowed.

Gospel: *John 14.1—12*
Our Lord continues to prepare his disciples for his impending
departure and encourages them to face what lies ahead by trusting in him as they do in God. The phrase "rooms in my Father's
house" has provoked much discussion; the best view is along the
line that the many rooms in a palace are meant. The reading is
notable also for the sixth use of "I am" in the form "I am the
Way", the way to follow for the goal of true life. The passage
closes with the assurance that belief in Christ will give disciples
power to do the same work as he does.

---

[1] *Isaiah 28.16* rather than *Psalm 117.*

First Reading: *Acts 8.5-8,14-17*

After the martydom of Stephen and the persecution in Jerusalem, the Church scattered; Philip went to Samaria where there had been an expectation of the Messiah though the Jews had no dealings with the Samaritans. This move towards a people to whom the Lord had shown great compassion indicates an early recognition of the Church's universal message. Philip's mission resulted in healing and the gift of the Holy Spirit to Samaritan believers.

Responsorial Psalm: *Psalm 65.1-7,16,20*

The Jews were very conscious of God's goodness to their nation in the past. The third stanza makes this clear. The psalm rings with the praise of God for his deliverance and all the earth is invited to see. Because the psalm ends on a note of personal deliverance, there is a strong body of opinion that we have here two psalms joined into one. The last stanza shows that God's concern for the individual is as real as his concern for the world.

Second Reading: *I Peter 3.15-18*

The Christians of Asia Minor to whom the letter was addressed were suffering for their faith, though in what way, is not clear. Peter continues his encouragement. Reverence for the Lord will be the source of prompt and courteous replies to those who want to question others about their faith. They are to remember that Christ is the supreme example of being persecuted for righteousness' sake. Peter's vocabulary is always colourful; the word for "answer" is "apologia", a speech of defence made in court.

Gospel: *John 14.15-21*

It is four days to Ascension and most fitting that we should read part of the Lord's farewell discourse to his disciples. The passage before us contains reference to the "Advocate", a word almost impossible to translate, but with the basic meaning of "one called to be beside". However translated, the word refers to the Holy Spirit who will guide believers in the way of truth. The passage concludes with a reference to the possible intimacy of the bond between Christ and the believer.

First Reading: *Acts 1.1-11*
The reading begins with a reference to "my earlier work" which is
Luke's Gospel, and to "Theophilus"who is anybody's guess. The
writer then mentions in general terms Our Lord's Resurrection
appearances. The promise of the gift of the Holy Spirit— *Acts* has
been called the *Book of the Holy Spirit* — is repeated; questions
about the political future of Jerusalem are not answered and with
that, the earthly ministry of Our Lord ends in his Ascension.

Responsorial Psalm: *Psalm 46.2-3,6-9*
This is one of the Enthronement Psalms used to celebrate the
Kingship of God, possibly in association with the festival of the
New Year. While there may be reference to some great
deliverance, more probably the writer in this psalm looks towards
God's future universal rule. It has a traditional association with
Ascension Day.

Second Reading: *Ephesians 1.17-23*
Paul's *Letter to the Ephesians,* written from prison, was a circular
letter written to the churches of Asia Minor; it represents his
spiritual genius in full flower. The theme is the Church as the
Body of Christ, embracing Jews and pagans without distinction.
The reading deals with Christ's supremacy and sets out what he
who has triumphed over angelic and demonic hosts will confer on
believers.

Gospel: *Matthew 28.16-20*
These closing words of Matthew's Gospel record Our Lord's last
charge to his disciples in the threefold instruction to engage in
missionary work, to baptise the converts and to give instruction
in the faith. We observe too, the emergence of the Trinitarian
formula "in the name of the Father and of the Son and of the
Holy Spirit". His very last word was an assurance of his abiding
presence.

First Reading: *Acts 1.12-14*
This is the occasion of the first service after the Ascension. The
disciples had walked from the Mount of Olives, about 1 km-the
maximum allowed on the Sabbath – and were gathered in the
upper room. Was it the upper room? The company consisted of
all eleven apostles, the faithful women and blessed Mary who is
mentioned here in Scripture for the last time. The Lord's cousins
who are loosely called "brothers" are also in the company.

Responsorial Psalm: *Psalm 26.1,4,7-8*
The portion in the Missal suggests a man whose joy in the Lord
comes from a life without a care. The full version which is in fact
two psalms joined together, shows him battered and bruised by
the calumnies of men, a fact that makes his joy all the more
attractive. The second stanza expresses a beautiful thought, the
peace that comes from being in the house of the Lord. He knew
the presence that is so real in holy places.

Second Reading: *I Peter 4.13-16*
The theme of suffering is continued and must reflect some acute
situation; whether it was persecution in a physical sense or being
made the butt of harassment, we do not know. Peter's argument
is that submission is sharing in Christ's suffering. In early usage
"Christian" was a term of reproach; "informer" is apparently
a word coined by the writer, literally "an overseer of other
people's affairs", possibly with some sinister overtone.

Gospel: *John 17.1-11*
Perhaps best described as a prayer of consecration, Our Lord's
consecration of himself before Calvary, the reading consists of
two parts, a prayer for himself and a prayer for his disciples.
Possibly the most sacred point in the passage is his asking God to
allow him to resume his pre-existent Glory. The passage must be
read and read again.

First Reading: *Genesis 11.1-9*
From one of the oldest strands in *Genesis* comes a piece of folk
lore, the story, how for their arrogance in trying to reach heaven
with a colossal building, God scattered the people over the earth
and willed them to speak different languages. The story has no
foundation in science, but like other early chapters in Genesis, is
rich in theological truth, in this instance that impiety is punished.
For the present occasion the relevance lies in the **fact** of diverse
languages. It ties in with the First Reading of tomorrow's Mass.

                   2

              Exodus 19.3-8,16-20
Compounded in the main from two very old sources, this account
of the Law-giving on Sinai contains the Covenant of agreement
between God and his people. Of greatest interest for this Vigil
Mass of Pentecost is the graphic description of the smoke and the
fire and the sound of the trumpet, all forming a superb backdrop
for the tongues of fire described in *Acts Ch. 2.*

                   3

              Ezekiel 37.1-14
The Valley of Dry Bones is one of the most brilliantly executed
prophecies in the *Old Testament*. The *Book of Ezekiel* presents
acute problems, but it may be said with confidence that Ch.37
belongs to a portion of the book written in Babylon, where
Ezekiel was with his countrymen after the fall of Jerusalem in
586 B.C. The prophecy is not about the resurrection of
individuals, but about the resurrection of the nation and its
restoration to its own land. Of special significance in the Mass are
the words, "breath" and "wind", all reminders of the Pentecostal
mighty rushing wind. In Hebrew and in Greek the same words
signify wind and breath.

4

Joel 3.1-5

Joel lived many years after the Jews had returned from exile. Amid outward signs of prosperity all was not well. Morality was at a low ebb; worship was formal and sterile. Locusts and famine enabled Joel to see signs of the Day of the Lord and the beginning of a new order. We see two of these signs in the First Reading, an outpouring of the Spirit and violent disturbances in nature. This spiritual activity will embrace **all** sections of the people. Amid the warning of doom there is hope, for all who "call on the name of the Lord will be saved". The reading is particularly apt for this Mass of Pentecost.

Responsorial Psalm: *Psalm 103.1-2,24,27-30,35*

In a long psalm consisting of 35 stanzas, the writer, in beautiful Hebrew poetry, glorifies God for his work of creation. This comes through in the first three stanzas in the Missal. In the last stanza we see how the whole creation depends for its life on the Spirit of God. Because the Hebrew for "spirit" and "breath" are one and the same word, it is not easy to see which applies. Truth is better served, perhaps, by fusing the two meanings into a powerful pointer to Pentecost.

Second Reading: *Romans 8.22-27*

Chapter 8 begins with a description of life in the Spirit and then, in the passage to be read, speaks of the glory that will be. The second paragraph is wonderful news: the Holy Spirit intercedes for us before the eternal throne and puts into words what we cannot express.

Gospel: *John 7.37-39*

The Spirit has been a prominent thought in all readings so far. We will be pulled up with a round turn in the Gospel with the words: "There was no Spirit as yet". We know that some of the wisest of the early Fathers of the Church had before them a Greek text which read: "For the Spirit was not yet GIVEN". The Holy Spirit **was** active before Pentecost, but he was not given as a source of Christ's life until after the Resurrection, to continue, as it were, Christ's life on earth.

PENTECOST SUNDAY
YEAR A
MASS DURING THE DAY

First Reading: *Acts 2.1-11*
Pentecost, originally a festival of the crops, became one of the greatest occasions in history when God, the Holy Spirit, burst into human affairs. In all great religious experiences words become inadequate. In spite of his mastery of language, all Luke can say is that the coming of the Holy Spirit was **like** a powerful wind and **like** tongues of fire. There were in Jerusalem, Jews long resident in many foreign places, but staying in the city for Pentecost. These were caught up in the outpouring of the Spirit . The apostles were reported as speaking in foreign tongues. This may have been so; it could also be a case of mass glossolalia, the ecstatic speech of intense religious experience, in this instance mistaken for foreign tongues.

Responsorial Psalm: *Psalm 103.1,24,29-31*
Gathering thoughts from various accounts of creation that circulated in other lands, the psalmist has put together a magnificent hymn of praise to God, the Maker of all things. The Missal quotes only a fragment of the whole which, seen in its full form, shows how poetry can be used in praise.

Second Reading: *I Corinthians 12.3-7,12-13*
This letter deals with situations in the Corinthian Church needing Paul's advice. The question of spiritual gifts is here discussed, though it is not clear why. In this brief reading four points emerge: all have these gifts in some form, for just to say "Jesus is Lord" is evidence of such a gift; the activity of the Holy Spirit manifests itself in many ways; there is however only one Holy Spirit; our baptism by the Holy Spirit ought to have produced unity among us.

Gospel: *John 20.19-23*
The risen Lord greets his disciples with the customary "Peace be with you", a greeting that had the additional effect of stilling their fears occasioned by recent events. He gave them their commission and with it the gift of the Holy Spirit for their work, and in particular their priestly function of forgiving the sins of penitents. The whole scene was a foretaste of the Pentecostal effusion of the Spirit.

First Reading: *Exodus 34.4-6,8-9.*

Three months after the Israelites had left Egypt, God made a
Covenant with them through Moses on Sinai and gave them laws
to regulate their life and worship, but because Moses was a long
time coming down from the mountain, the people made a golden
calf and worshipped it. Moses in frustration and anger broke the
tablets, but was recalled to the mountain with two more. In the
reading God declares his compassion for his erring people.

Responsorial Psalm: *Daniel 3.52-56*

Portions of *Daniel* are known only in the Greek translation; the
passage before us is one of these. The book was written in the
second century B.C. during a time when the Jews were being
fiercely persecuted by Antiochus Epiphanes[1]. The aim of the
book in its first six chapters was to encourage the Jews with
details of the resistance of Daniel and his friends at the court of
the Babylonian king Nebuchadnezzar. For refusing to worship a
golden statue of the king three men were thrown into a fiery
furnace. Before us is part of a song of praise to God from the
furnace.

Second Reading: *I I Corinthians 13.11-13*

The so-called *Second Letter to the Corinthians* is very difficult.
Enough is said if the reading is regarded as part of a benediction
following a painful disagreement between Paul and the
Corinthians. Of prime importance in this Mass is the fact that
here we have the first association in the *New Testament* of the
three persons of the Trinity, though it took centuries of heresy
and bitterness to work out the inter-relationship of the three
Persons.

Gospel: *John 3.16-18*

The reading records the latter part of the incident in which
Nicodemus came to Jesus under cover of darkness. It explains
God's great love for man and his desire that man should be a
spiritual being. The passage, with its references to God and the
Son, is set in the context of the Spirit and so gathers up the
Trinitarian implications of the Mass.

---

[1] See Notes, Thirty-second Sunday in Ordinary Time, Year C.

First Reading: *Deuteronomy 8.2-3,14-16*
The *Book of Deuteronomy* contains three discourses by Moses, a
code of laws for life in the Promised Land and an account of
Moses' death. The First Reading belongs to the second discourse
in which Moses reminds the people of God's provision of food in
the form of manna, in the wilderness. This is described in *Exodus
Ch. 16* as a white substance which fell with the dew. It may have
been a sweet deposit left on tamarisk bushes by sucking insects.
If so, God provided for his people from the natural circumstances
of the desert. God works like that.

Responsorial Psalm: *Psalm 147.12-15,19-20*
The Psalter concludes with a bracket of five Alleluia psalms, so
called because they begin and end with Alleluia (Hebrew for
"Praise the Lord"). The psalm before us commences with praise
to God for rebuilding Jerusalem after the exile. The reference to
his feeding "with finest wheat" is appropriate to this Mass.

Second Reading: *I Corinthians 10.16-17*
It is not in the Gospels that the first reference to the Lord's
Supper is preserved, but in the *Letter to the Corinthians.* Having
recalled God's provision for his people in the wilderness and their
pursuit of idolatry, Paul urges his Corinthians to avoid the use of
foods offered to pagan idols. Between the practices of idolatry
and the rites of the Church there can be no compromise. The
Eucharist bonds believers into a single body, for they have made
their communion with Christ in his Body and Blood.

Gospel: *John 6.51-58*
There are seven "I am" discourses in John's Gospel and the first
of these will be read in a moment. This discourse was delivered in
the general context of the miraculous Feeding of the Five
Thousand. It contains a reference to the manna in the wilderness
and goes on to deal with the life-giving quality of the Body and
Blood in the Eucharist.

First Reading: *Deuteronomy 7.6—11*
The *Book of Deuteronomy* contains in the main three discourses
by Moses, a code of laws for life in the Promised Land and an
account of Moses' death. The First Reading belongs to Moses'
second discourse and in it Israel is described as a people on whom
God had set a seal of difference. They are the special objects of
divine love and favour. For this they are required to observe what
God requires.

Responsorial Psalm: *Psalm 102.1—4,6—8,10*
The psalm is dominated by thoughts of God's infinite goodness
and love. Into the second stanza the psalmist has crowded four
qualities of God. his forgiveness, healing, redemption and his love.
The last two stanzas suggest that God is concerned with all the
world. Unlike man, God knows no spite; he does not retaliate.

Second Reading: *I John 4.7—16*
John who wrote the Gospel also wrote this letter. In the discourse
on love which forms the basis of the reading, one quickly senses
the Johannine spirit. What emerges very strongly is that in loving
one another, we are giving back what God has given us. Our
loving others is of the very essence of the spiritual life. This
passage must be read and read again.

Gospel: *Matthew 11. 25—30*
The passage has two distinct sections: the first part which has
been called both "Matthew's pearl of great price" and the
"ecstasy of Jesus". has almost a Johannine character as Our Lord
gives a self-revelation that indicates a oneness with the Father;
then like Isaiah with his call to come to the waters and drink, Our
Lord issues a gracious invitation that has been accepted through
the centuries by those who have sought relief from the burdens
of life. The yoke to which Our Lord refers is primarily the burden
of the Pharisaic law. His yoke, like those he made in his workshop, fits lightly and does not chafe.

First Sunday in Ordinary Time
BAPTISM OF THE LORD
YEAR A

See above page 24

First Reading: *Isaiah 49.3,5—6*
The *Book of Isaiah* is the work of two different hands. Chapters
1—39 belong to the period before the fall of Jerusalem in 586B.C.
while Chapters 40—66 relate to events after that date. Set in the
second part are four Songs of the Suffering Servant, and the
second of these is in the First Reading. Speaking in exile, the
Servant sees the restoration of his country as a God-given task.
But greater still, the Servant is to be the means whereby salvation
reaches the ends of the world.

Responsorial Psalm: *Psalm 39.2,4,7—10*
In the portion before us there is an expression of gratitude for
recovery from illness. The psalmist had been ill for a long time,
but God heard his cry. In the second stanza the futility of
sacrifice is recognised; only the willing heart prevails with God.
The reference to the "scroll of the book" is not clear. Ready to
do the will of God, the psalmist feels he must speak out to others
of the justice of God.

Second Reading: *I Corinthians 1.1—13*
In this and the next six Second Readings the first four chapters
of *I Corinthians* will be read. Paul wrote because he had heard
that all was not well in the Corinthian church. Subsequent readings will reveal aspects of one of these problems. "Holy people"
and "saints" are difficult words to translate. Their basic meaning
is not superlative spiritual excellence; they simply denote the fact
of being set apart by virtue of Christian faith.

Gospel: *John 1.29—34*
When John the Baptist was asked if he were the Christ he replied
in the negative and explaining his own mission as the forerunner
of the Messiah, pointed to Christ and hailed him as the Lamb of God,
a term with many *Old Testament* overtones, perhaps most
notably the Suffering Servant in *Isaiah (53.7).*   The Baptist had
seen the Spirit descending on Jesus at his baptism and so was able
to assert that he was the Messiah, the Chosen One of God.

First Reading: *Isaiah 8.23—9.3*
The prophecy in this reading must be seen against its political background. Israel, the northern kingdom of the Jews, made an alliance with Syria to hold Assyria in check and tried to force Judah, the southern kingdom, to join the alliance. The situation was bleak. Yet with enormous faith in God, Isaiah could see light in place of darkness and the coming rule of a Messiah King under whom burdens would fall away. Zebulun and Naphtali were provinces of the northern kingdom previously lost to Assyria.

Responsorial Psalm: *Psalm 26. 1,4,13—14*
Two psalms have been joined to give us the full version of which only part is used in the Missal. In the complete text one sees the real quality of the psalmist's faith, for he has been through a great deal. His faith is unshakable; he knows the mystic presence of God in his holy places; his confidence in the future is unbounded.

Second Reading: *I Corinthians 1.10—13,17*
Losing no time, Paul addresses himself to the problems in the Corinthian church. The congregation was divided, polarising around leading personalities, probably not in serious opposition to one another, but split nevertheless in true Greek fashion. These divisions were intolerable and Paul pleads for a closing of the ranks, for Christ was not divided.

Gospel: *Matthew 4.12—23*
Matthew is much concerned to give his own interpretation of Old Testament prophecy. Using the passage from *Isaiah* of the First Reading he applies it to Our Lord. This consistent direction of the *Old Testament* prophecies away from what the prophets envisaged is one of the special features of *Matthew*. Isaiah saw hope for Zebulun and Naphtali, the provinces lost from Israel to Assyria. Matthew sees Jesus as this hope. The rest of the reading records the call of the first disciples.

First Reading: *Zephaniah 2.3,3.12—13*
Zephaniah is later than *Isaiah* Chapters 1—39 and the political
background has changed. In place of Assyria, Egypt and the
nomadic Scythians posed a new threat. The East was like a
seething cauldron. During the time of Assyrian ascendency many
elements false to Jewish religion had been adopted. Zephaniah
attacked these abuses with threats of divine judgment. Central
to the reading is the concept of a righteous remnant which will
escape God's wrath. This remnant will consist not of the oppressive
rich, but of the poor, the humble and lowly.

Responsorial Psalm: *Psalm 145.7—10*
The alternate response is apt, for this is one of the Alleluia psalms.
After decrying the value of trusting in people, in the portion to
be read, the psalmist praises God who makes the socially deprived
his special care and concern. Kings on earth reign only for a time,
but God's rule is for ever.

Second Reading: *I Corinthians 1.26—31*
Paul has condemned party spirit in Corinth and after speaking of
the "foolishness" of the Cross, deals in the reading with God's
way of using weak things of the world to achieve his ends. The
spread of Christianity among the lower classes both in Corinth
and elsewhere proves Paul's point. Not philosophical argument,
but the simple preaching of a carpenter on the gallows was Paul's
way of winning souls for Christ. The passage concludes with
reference to the true wisdom, knowledge of God in Christ.

Gospel: *Matthew 5.1—12*
The Beatitudes, ten in number and forming a new decalogue
reverse all the world's values regarding what constitutes happiness.
They were delivered on a mountain, as was the original decalogue.
Mountains play a big part in Matthew's Gospel as places of
importance in the life of Jesus. The phrase "poor in spirit" (Luke
omits "in spirit") means having an awareness of spiritual need,
absence of intellectual pride.

First Reading: *Isaiah 58.7-10*
The Jews had returned from exile; the Temple was rebuilt by 516
B.C., but the nation was not being restored. After the first flush
of excitement, the life went out of religious observance and
worship became more and more formal. The prophet draws
attention to the improper motive in the people's fasting and then
in the First Reading sets out what they will do if fasting is sincere.
As a result, their light will shine through the darkness and their
own wounds will be healed.

Responsorial Psalm: *Psalm 111.4-9*
The psalm is one of the Alleluia group and is also acrostic, i.e.
each verse begins with successive letters of the Hebrew alphabet.
Two aspects of the noble character here depicted are his excellent
qualities and his willingness to assist others in financial difficulty;
this help was more real than apparent, for the Law required a Jew
to lend to his fellows without interest.

Second Reading: *I Corinthians 2.1-5*
The Corinthians were Greeks and as such were a people with a
distinguished contribution to philosophy. It was in their blood to
argue and to talk. But Paul declares that he did not preach to
them in philosophic terms; in fact he avoided human wisdom and
presented Christ crucified to them, not with self-confidence, but
with fear and trembling.

Gospel: *Matthew 5.13-16*
Matthew alone makes salt and light the symbols of the disciples'
life. The preservative qualities of salt were well known in ancient
times. Our Lord was referring at least partly to the role of the
disciples as a force against the corrupting processes of the world.
Salt could be adulterated and so lose its savour. A disciple who
loses his is useless. Light was a word of varied application in the
Old Testament. The oil lamp in a dimly lit house was a precious
thing. It was only natural that Our Lord should apply this idea to
his disciples whose light must shine in the world.

First Reading: *Ecclesiasticus 15. 15-20*[1]
The *Book of Ecclesiasticus* was written about 200 B.C. and is part of what is known as the Wisdom Literature which includes *Proverbs. Job etc.* Wisdom is represented as a flowing forth from God, almost a person. Much space is devoted in *Ecclesiasticus* to the treatment of Wisdom, first its nature and then its application to life. Speaking of individual responsibility in Ch. 15, the writer talks of the happy lot of him who seeks Wisdom which only the godly can find. Then in the First Reading the question of freedom of choice is discussed.

Responsorial Psalm: *Psalm 118. 1-2,4-5,17-18,33-34*
This is the longest psalm in the Psalter, twenty-one stanzas of eight lines, all eight lines of each stanza beginning with the same letter of the Hebrew alphabet and each stanza using a successive letter of the same alphabet. The psalm is an acrostic on a huge and unique scale. The subject is the Law of God and, in the portion before us, the blessedness of the man who follows it.

Second Reading: *I Corinthians 2.6-10*
Continuing his theme of wisdom, Paul declares that he does have a wisdom to offer, but not in the sense the world understands the term, but a secret, God's hidden wisdom, kept since time began. Paul is referring to the revealing of this secret in the crucified Christ, a wisdom made known through the Holy Spirit.

Gospel: *Matthew 5.17-37*
In this long reading, Our Lord's attitude to the Law of Moses is revealed. He regards himself as its fulfilment. Reformers often create chaos with their break from the past. Our Lord's teaching, on the other hand, was firmly rooted in the Law. So far from deviating from it, his interpretation of adultery shows a more refined insight. Only two comments are possible: in the phrase "not one dot, one little stroke", "dot" refers to the smallest letter of the Hebrew alphabet; "one little stroke" is probably a sign of abbreviation. "Fool" is not an offensive word in English, but *raca* in Hebrew was grossly libellous and could involve a law-suit.

[1] See Notes, Holy Family, Year A and Second Sunday after Christmas.

First Reading: *Leviticus 19.1-2,17-18*
Leviticus contains mostly laws to regulate religious and ethical aspects of life. Chs. 17-26 are a separate set of laws and are older than the rest of the book. These chapters are known as the Holiness Code in which the holiness of God is presented as the motive for striving after holiness. In the reading which is from this code the holiness of God's people is revealed in their treatment of others.

Responsorial Psalm: *Psalm 102,1-4,8,10,12-13*
Thoughts of God's infinite goodness and love are prominent in this psalm. The second and third stanzas are a compact statement of God's qualities of forgiveness, healing, redemption, love and mercy. The last stanza is a beautiful expression of God's forgiveness.

Second Reading: *I Corinthians 3.16-23*
Thoughts of buildings, of foundations and of him who is **the** foundation, lead Paul to think of the building that is above all buildings, the Temple, and in particular of its inmost shrine. We are God's temple and must preserve it inviolate. Then he returns to his theme of wisdom. The wisdom of the world is nothing; Paul, Apollos and Cephas around whom the parties in Corinth had polarised, are nothing; Christ is everything.

Gospel: *Matthew 5.38-48*
Our Lord's remarks regarding retaliation turn upside down what is found in the Holiness Code in *Leviticus* on the subject and cut across what is basic in human nature. The *lex talionis* or law of retaliation in kind was common to several ancient codes outside Israel. The reference to tunic and cloak are to an inner and an outer garment. A creditor was forbidden to hold a garment over night *(Exodus 22.26)*. The verb "to order" in the expression "if any one orders you to go a mile", is of Persian origin and refers to the right of couriers in the Persian mail system to press anyone into service in an emergency.

First Reading: *Isaiah 49.14-15*
This portion of *Isaiah* is set in Babylon where the Jewish exiles had been deported after the capture of Jerusalem in 586 B.C. Hopes of return to their own country must have risen and fallen during their enforced stay. The reading sees the captives at a low ebb. They feel that God has forsaken them. To refute this comes an assurance of his care. Their release is near.

Responsorial Psalm: *Psalm 61.2-3,6-9*
The text and the background of the psalm present difficulties. Be that as it may, the psalmist has emerged from some deep crisis to find God as his rock and stronghold against his adversaries who set upon him. In the last stanza he invites others - whether in the congregation or beyond, is not clear — to put their trust also in God.

Second Reading: *I Corinthians 4. 1-5*
This is the beginning of Paul's last word on the subject of the divisions in Corinth. He stresses that he and other teachers are stewards in the Church, but that God alone is entitled to pass judgement on them. With this Paul calls for an end to criticism. This is the final reading from *I Corinthians* in the present series.

Gospel: *Matthew 6.24-34*
Matthew begins with Our Lord's warning on the peril of divided loyalty. This is brought out with two words that stand in stark opposition to each other: "to serve" means "to be a slave" and slaves were the total possession of their masters, while "masters" were those who had absolute ownership of slaves. Mammon, an Aramaic word, represents riches, a force that makes slaves of men and ultimately destroys them. Matthew then goes on to deal with Our Lord's teaching on the subject of the human tendency to worry. Nature has no such cares; anxiety is as futile as trying to increase one's life span (or to add to one's height). The panacea for worry is to seek the Kingdom of God and to trust him for what we cannot control.

First Reading: *Deuteronomy 11.18,26-28,32*
The *Book of Deuteronomy* contains in the main three discourses
by Moses, a code of laws for life in the Promised Land and an
account of Moses' death. The First Reading belongs to Moses'
second discourse and having previously reviewed all that God had
done and promised, Moses warns against seeking other gods, the
worship of which was and would be all about them. The reading
puts it all succinctly and bluntly: blessing will follow obedience; a
curse will fall on disobedience.

Responsorial Psalm: *Psalm 30.2-4,17,25*
This psalm was offered in more detail than here on Good Friday
and on that occasion it can be seen how the writer's great distress
alternates with trust in God. Clearly he had been ostracised by his
fellows. Yet God is his refuge, rock of defence, the one who will
free him from his troubles. In the last stanza the psalmist invites
all - and the invitation reaches to us − to share his trust in God.

Second Reading: *Romans 3.21-25,28*
This is the first of sixteen readings taken from *Romans*, which is
regarded by most (but not all) as Paul's greatest work. He was
planning to visit Rome and sent the letter in advance to prepare
the way. It is a kind of handbook of the faith. In the reading Paul
asserts that the justice of God, which may be a quality or an
activity, has been revealed apart from the Law, through Christ, to
all who believe. Reconciliation through faith alone is the new way
to oneness with God.

Gospel: *Matthew 7.21-27*
Jesus continues to instruct his disciples in preparation for sending
them out as Evangelists. The reading deals first with practice and
profession and then with the two builders. To say and to do the
appropriate things which are not supported by faith is simply
self-deception and to build on the wrong foundations whether
one is making a house to live in or the house of life is sheer folly.
Rock is a frequent metaphor in the *Psalms*, as in the Responsorial
Psalm.

First Reading: *Hosea 6.3-6*
Hosea is one of the tragic figures of history. A prophet of God, he was married to an unfaithful wife, a prostitute either before or after marriage. He belonged to the northern kingdom which he calls Ephraim. Morality was at a low ebb and idolatry was rife. In one of the most damaged pieces of text in the *Old Testament*, the message appears to be that God is coming to judge both kingdoms; there is no substance in the people's religion; God wants their love rather than their sacrifices.

Responsorial Psalm: *Psalm 49.1,8,12-15*
The true nature of the psalm is seen in the full version; it represents the inhabitants of the world before the bar of divine judgment in the matter of worship. God does not complain of their sacrifices, but rejects the primitive idea that he is nourished by them. Spiritual sacrifice is what God requires; then may he be called upon in the day of trouble.

Second Reading: *Romans 4.18-25*
Last Sunday Paul's concept of the new righteousness that is acquired through faith in Christ was explained. Now, as an example of what faith can accomplish, we read of Abraham and Sarah, old and childless, yet destined to be parents of a nation, and how faith in God's word won through. The verb "to consider" occurs three times in the reading and many times in the letter as a whole. It is a word from the world of business and means "to put on someone's account".

Gospel: *Matthew 9.9-13*
In the account of Matthew's call to discipleship, there is a subtlety in the Greek tense of the imperative that is lost in English. The form of "follow me" emphasises that the action was to be continuous and ongoing. Taxes were collected for the Roman government by "tax farming" syndicates which employed local people to do the actual collecting. Their greed, coupled with the fact that they were of the native population, made them particular objects of hatred. Matthew was one of these. Our Lord's association with him was yet another outrage to public opinion.

First Reading: *Exodus 19.2-6*
The events in the reading take place three months after the departure from Egypt when the Israelites have reached Sinai. Before making the Covenant with his people God promises that in return for their obedience he will make them his very own. This is expressed in Hebrew by one word meaning "a king's private treasure of gold and silver".

Responsorial Psalm: *Psalm 99.2-3,5*
This is the psalm widely known as "Old Hundredth"[1]. It was sung in procession to the Temple when the thank offering was to be made. A call to sing with gladness to the Lord is followed by the people's acknowledgement of their allegiance to God. The psalm ends on the note of God's eternal goodness.

Second Reading: *Romans 5.6-11*
Continuing the theme of righteousness through faith, Paul deals with the efficacy of Christ's sacrifice which was made not for godly men, but for sinners. Thus reconciled to God, we are assured of salvation in the consummation of all things, to which we look forward now, not in fear, but in "joyful hope".

Gospel: *Matthew 9.36-10.8*
The disciples have been instructed; moved by compassion for his own, Our Lord sends them out to minister. The urgency of the situation is emphasised by the crowds who lack guidance. As a harvest cannot wait, so the need of the masses was equally urgent. The twelve apostles ("sent out ones") are named and commissioned with power to do as they had seen their Lord do. They are to exercise their ministry at this stage only among the lost sheep of Israel.

---

[1] *Psalm* 100 in most translations of the Bible including the *Jerusalem Bible*

First Reading: *Jeremiah 20.10-13*
Jeremiah was not by nature a prophet of woe; one of the noblest characters in the *Old Testament*, he was required over a long period to deliver strong and painful denunciations to his people. He is the prophet of a personal relationship with God. When the might of Assyria was declining, the Jews courted Egypt against Babylon. For advising submission to Babylon, Jeremiah was immensely unpopular. Having endured a painful and humiliating punishment in the public stocks, he speaks out in the First Reading. He tells of the loss of old friends, and his own trust in God. The date is about 600 B.C.

Responsorial Psalm: *Psalm 68.8-10,14,17,33-35*
The psalmist is in the deepest distress; his trust in God is all that he has left; even his own family has turned against him. Who he was or what his plight was, we do not know. Some older scholars have said he was Jeremiah. In the first stanza he pours out his soul; in the second he states his confidence in God; finally the psalmist declares that when God turns to him, some will rejoice.

Second Reading: *Romans 5.12-15*
We may not accept the historical situation implied in the references to Adam and the Fall of man. But no age has more reason than the present to believe in the bondage of sin whatever its origin. Into this hopeless situation came the second Adam, Christ, conferring in his grace more than was lost in the Fall.

Gospel: *Matthew 10.26-33*
The Twelve have received their apostolic commission. With no mincing of words they are warned of treatment they can except. The reading then gives advice and above all encouragement: there must be open profession of their message; God will take care of them as he does of all his creatures. Our Lord likewise assures his champions that he will uphold their cause before the Father. The resources of English are not equal to the Greek behind "Do not be afraid" and "fear". The former suggests that the fear has not begun, but probably will; the latter implies continuous and habitual fear.

First Reading: *I I Kings 4.8-11,14-16*
The *Books of Kings* cover the history of Israel and Judah from
the accession of Solomon (978 B.C.) to the fall of Jerusalem in
586 B.C. Before the prophets who gave their names to several
books of the *Old Testament,* there were bands of men who called
themselves "sons of the prophets". One of these was Elisha,
successor to the greater Elijah and it is of Elisha that the reading
speaks. His holiness so impresses a Shunammite woman that she
and her husband offered him shelter and in gratitude he assured
them that they would have the son they so longed for.

Responsorial Psalm: *Psalm 88.2-3,16-19*
The full version is a long psalm, perhaps three psalms of
different times and circumstances. The first stanza tells of God's
everlasting love and of the psalmist's desire ever to proclaim it.
In the second and third stanzas the writer refers to the spiritual
blessings this love confers; they are mediated through the earthly
king who is ruling at the time.

Second Reading: *Romans 6.3-4,8-11*
The mystic union between Christ and the believer is brought
about in the first place by baptism, which has more significance
when it is recalled that baptism was total immersion and for
adults. It admits us into a re-enactment, as it were, of Christ's
death and Resurrection. He died to meet and cancel sin; he
lives for ever. If we are part of him, we too are dead to sin with
the prospect of eternal life.

Gospel: *Matthew 10.37-42*
Speaking further on the cost of discipleship, Our Lord emphasises
that it is total involvement even to the exclusion of the normal
place given in life to family. The common sight of a condemned
criminal carrying the beam of his cross to the place of execution
prompted the remark about taking up one's cross. The chapter
concludes with some thoughts on the reception given to
missionaries and with that there is a return to the thought of the
First Reading.

First Reading: *Zechariah 9.9-10*
Like the *Book of Isaiah, Zechariah* is the work of two different hands, centuries apart. Chs. 9-14 belong to a period much later than the period of return from exile. Near at hand, neighbouring nations are restless. The prophet sees the Messianic King entering Jerusalem on an animal of peace and in humility. War will be no more; universal peace will be established. The reading brings back thoughts of Passion (Palm) Sunday.

Responsorial Psalm: *Psalm 144.1-2,8-11,13-14*
This hymn of praise, described as "one of the most inspiring in the Psalter" could have been composed only by one who had had a profound experience of God. It is the last of the alphabetical or acrostic psalms in which each verse begins with the succeeding letter of the Hebrew alphabet. First the greatness of God, then his compassion are praised. In the third stanza the psalmist strikes a universal note and concludes with praise for God's faithfulness and love.

Second Reading: *Romans 8.9,11-13*
Baptism with Christ creates a new life for the believer, a life directed by the indwelling Spirit, a word used nearly thirty times in this chapter alone. There is the familiar reminder of what disobedience to the Spirit means, but by the same token, victorious living results from this same power in us. "Body" is not an easy word to define in Pauline usage. Here it means our lower self prone to sin.

Gospel: *Matthew 11.25-30*
Following the pronouncement of doom on the unrepentant cities, comes this passage with its two distinct sections, first, what has been called "Matthew's pearl of great price", and then the "ecstasy of Jesus" which is almost Johannine in character as Our Lord gives a self revelation that indicates a oneness with the Father. Then like Isaiah with his call to come to the waters and drink, Our Lord issues a gracious invitation that has been accepted through the centuries by those who have sought relief from the burdens of life. The yoke to which Our Lord refers is primarily the burden of the Pharisaic law. His yoke, like those he made in his workshop, fits lightly and does not chafe.

First Reading: *Isaiah 55,10-11*
These beautiful words can be seen apart from a political
background. They assert the effectiveness of God's word which is
as sure in its working as the seasons are in promoting the
sustaining powers of life. The passage forms a backdrop against
which the Gospel for the day may be read with even more telling
effect.

Responsorial Psalm: *Psalm 64.10-14*
The portion of the psalm before us is possibly the second of two
psalms joined together. The writer has no doubt to whom thanks
are due for a bountiful season with good autumn rains. In the
fourth stanza even the hills and valleys react with human
expressions of joy. We are moving from the First Reading through
the Responsorial Psalm to the Gospel for a spiritual application
of the processes of growth in nature.

Second Reading: *Romans 8.18-23*
For Paul the best is yet to be for man and nature. Both have
shared in the decadence created by the Fall; both have a better
hope. The reference to suffering is probably to the trials of life
and in Paul's case to what he has suffered for Christ *(II
Corinthians 11.24-27)*. Creation is going through a labour
comparable to child-birth, though what form the redemption of
creation will take is not revealed. We too await our liberation
from the lower self. The expression "creation is eagerly waiting"
is built around a Greek word found only in Christian literature
and derived from the athletics track, the word that means
"straining forward, head back and eyes off the spectators".

Gospel: *Matthew 13.1-23*
Seven parables make up this long chapter. A parable has been
defined as "an earthly story with a heavenly meaning." The
details should not be minutely pressed; an explanation is required;
parables vary in kind and are a vivid form of teaching in which
Our Lord was without equal. In the reading the Parable of the
Sower is presented, but before the application is given, interest
is heightened by Our Lord's explanation why he uses this form of
teaching. It is a vehicle by which secrets are made known to the
disciples. The quotation is from *Isaiah 6.9-10* and represents God
speaking after the call of Isaiah to a people who are set against
his salvation.

First Reading: *Wisdom 12.13,16-19*
The *Book of Wisdom* was written about 100 B.C. and is divided
into three sections: Wisdom and the destiny of man, the character
of Wisdom and Wisdom in history. Wisdom is more than the
quality of being wise; in fact she is almost a person, a flowing
forth from the Almighty. The First Reading is from the last
section of the book in which it is explained how God with
forbearance prepared Canaan for "a colony of God's children"
and in the reading the forbearance and leniency are further
explained.

Responsorial Psalm: *Psalm 85.5-6,9-10,15-16*
The psalm is a cry of distress and has been called a mosaic of
quotations from different parts of the *Old Testament.* Outside
our portion, the writer says he is poor and needy and that he
invokes God all day long. In the first stanza his reference to God
as forgiving, suggests his own need of absolution. A return to this
theme in the third stanza brings the reader to the heart of his
problem.

Second Reading: *Romans 8.26-27*
These two verses are like a flash of light; they tell us so much
about the Holy Spirit whose activity lies in prayer. It is all part of
what Our Lord said when he promised to send the Holy Spirit,
the Advocate. "Our weakness" is our inability to pray.
The translation "in a way that could never be put into words"
does not do justice to the Greek which means "with groans that
are unspoken (or cannot be expressed)". The focal word
"unspoken" is unique in Greek literature. "Unspoken" is
preferable with its implication that in the final analysis, prayer
passes beyond the need of words.

Gospel: *Matthew 13.24-43*

The reading gives three more parables from the treasure house of
Ch.13. The Darnel and the Wheat signify the intermixture of
good and evil in the Church until the consummation of all things.
Darnel, one of the four main weeds in Palestine is a kind of rye,
similar to wheat, with possible narcotic properties. The Mustard
Seed suggests the final extent of the Kingdom from a tiny
beginning, while the Yeast, here used in a good sense[1] reinforces the
second parable. The term "Kingdom of Heaven" is Matthew's
equivalent of the "Kingdom of God", used by the other
Evangelists.

---

[1] See Alternative Second Reading, Easter Day for a different
meaning.

First Reading: *I Kings 3.5,7-12*
The *Books of Kings* trace the history of the Jews in their two kingdoms from the accession of Solomon to the fall of Jerusalem. The name Solomon (978-938 B.C.) was a by-word for wisdom and insight. The reading which tells the origin of Solomon's special gift belongs to the beginning of the king's reign. A famous story illustrating Solomon's wisdom follows in verses 16-27.

Responsorial Psalm: *Psalm 118. 57,72,76—77,127—130*
This is the second reading from the long acrostic poem[1] in which the Law is extolled for its divine qualities. It is not the Pharisaic law, but God's revealed truth. In every verse but one of the full psalm the writer refers to the law by some other name such as decrees, precepts, statutes etc. To find these different ways of presenting the Law in the Responsorial Psalm makes a useful meditation.

Second Reading: *Romans 8.28—30*
The spiritual union which has been developed in successive Second Readings now offers us the certainty that our lives will be ordered according to a divine purpose. Yet the passage presents two acute difficulties: there will always be those who would translate the first sentence by "all things work for good for those who love God"; some of the bitterest controversies in the long history of the Church have stemmed from what is known as predestination. Are we puppets in the divine purpose? Can we be sure there is no predestination to damnation? Belief in the love of God overrules strict logic.

Gospel: *Matthew 13.44-52*
The chapter of parables concludes with four more, three of which are peculiar to *Matthew*. The Treasure in the Field illustrates the joy of finding the Kingdom and its immense wealth; the Pearl Merchant also indicates the worth of the Kingdom and the sacrifice made to attain it. The Net stresses selection and rejection within the Kingdom. Finally the phrase "new and old" suggests what Our Lord is offering and the treasures of Jewish teaching.

---

[1] See Notes, Sixth Sunday in Ordinary Time, Year A.

First Reading: *Isaiah 55.1-3*
The author of the second part of *Isaiah (Chs 49-66)* is writing
words of encouragement to his people who are still in exile in
Babylon. The prophet issues a great invitation to the Messiah's
banquet, admission free. Through the basics of water, grain, wine
and milk the needs of the spirit will be satisfied. There is also a
promise of a renewed covenant.

Responsorial Psalm: *Psalm 144.8-9,15-18*
This psalm was probably rendered as a solo before the
congregation, a hymn of praise to God. There are six themes in
the full version; two of them are in the portion before us, God's
compassionate nature and his provision for his people. Listen in
the second stanza for the words "You give them their food in due
time". This is the last of the alphabetical psalms.

Second Reading: *Romans 8.35,37-39*
Paul has explained how we are united with Christ. He now
expresses the absolute conviction (literally: "I have been
persuaded and am in this state of certainty") that nothing can
separate us from Christ's love for us. His confidence covers the
disasters of life, troubles from within and troubles from without.
He is clearly thinking too of the hostile spirit world which was
part of Paul's belief and over which Christ triumphed.

Gospel: *Matthew 14.13-21*
Jesus needed solitude, but this was not to be. A vast crowd
followed him and eventually required feeding. What happened is
the only miracle recorded in all four Gospels. It reveals Our Lord's
concern for people's basic needs. Of old, the Israelites had been
fed in the wilderness; Elisha gave sustenance to a hundred men
(11 Kings 4.43). With next to nothing Jesus fed this large crowd
and provided a foretaste of every Eucharist the Church celebrates.

First Reading / *Kings 19.9,11-13*
The great prophet Elijah had gained the triumph of his life in the victory of God over the followers of Baal in the contest on Mount Carmel. It is a fact of life that great heights often create deep valleys. It was so for Elijah. Fearing for his life because of Jezebel, Ahab's wicked queen, he fled far to the south. In the reading, God speaks to Elijah and gives him a new commission, but the divine revelation is not made in the terrifying phenomena of nature as at Sinai, but in a still small voice, the sound of a gentle breeze.

Responsorial Psalm: *Psalm 84.9-14*
The psalmist is listening for God's voice and what he hears suggests the coming of a golden age. His glory will dwell in the land. The noblest virtues will flourish and material blessings will come from the earth. Peace, or the general well-being of all, will result from God's footsteps, his movement among his people.

Second Reading: *Romans 9.1-5*
With argument spread over almost eight chapters, Paul has concluded his treatment of righteousness by faith and turns, in the Second Reading, to a matter over which as a Jew he has anguished, the rejection of Christ by his own people. He declares with conviction that he is speaking the truth, his conscience in unison with the Holy Spirit, when he records all the privileges that the Israelites have enjoyed from God. These are all stated in the concluding part of the reading which ends with a statement that the Messiah is of the lineage of the Patriarchs.

Gospel: *Matthew 14.22-33*
Jesus was alone in the hills, in prayer. Below, the disciples who a while before had plans to manage a huge crowd, could not control a boat in one of those storms that arise so suddenly on the lake. Leaving them until about three o'clock in the morning, or later, Jesus came walking on the water. Having told them to stop being afraid, he assured them that he was no ghost. Only Matthew records Peter's disastrous attept to do as Jesus was doing, and many have seen in this a parable of pride, fall and restoration. The passage ends with the disciples' recognition of the divine Sonship of Jesus.

First Reading: *Isaiah 56.1,6-7*
The Jews had returned from their exile in Babylon and life had
been restarted in Jerusalem. The passage shows a remarkable
development in attitude to foreigners. The old exclusiveness was
breaking down. The problem arose because adherents to the
Jewish faith had returned with the exiles and further, some
foreigners had attached themselves to the remnant that had
never left Jerusalem. If these were loyal to the Jewish faith, they
should be part of it.

Responsorial Psalm: *Psalm 66.2-3,5-6,8*
The full version reveals the psalm as a harvest thanksgiving and
then the thought extends into the harvest of the world and this
idea is present in each of the three stanzas. God's concern for the
nations is recognised as a fact. This universal note echoes the
thought of the First Reading.

Second Reading: *Romans 11.13-15,29-32*
Still wrestling with the Jewish rejection of Christ, Paul asserts
that behind his mission to the pagans is the hope that his own
people will realise what they are missing. The recovery of the
Jews would mean blessing to all. God has never wavered in his
desire to save his people. The reading concludes with what has
been called a statement of "double predestination", the fact
that God has created situations in which men are disobedient, so
that in the long run, mercy may be shown to all.

Gospel: *Matthew 15.21-28*
In this story of healing, we observe that Our Lord breaks with his
previous practice of dealing only with his own people, so that
here there is the tiny beginning of the Universal mission. The
woman belonged to the ancient land of idolatry. The disciples
appeared to support her plea, but only to get rid of her. Our Lord
tests her faith by not yielding to her request immediately. This
faith is shown by a pretty turn of wit on the woman's part and
the healing she asks for is granted.

First Reading: *Isaiah 22.19-23*
The passage is unique in *Isaiah*, for nowhere else does the prophet denounce a person directly and show such authority that he can order a man out of office. Shebna held the highest rank in the royal household. Possibly his offence was that he tried to build himself a sepulchre of kingly proportions. There is a reference to the "key of the house of David". This was long and heavy and was actually carried on the shoulder. It represented the authority of Shebna's replacement.

Responsorial Psalm: *Psalm 137.1-3,6,8*
The psalmist gives thanks to God for his loving kindness and for his ready response to one in need. We do not know the cause of the writer's gratitude, only that it wells up with refreshing spontaneity. In the last line "work of your hands" is best taken as referring to the psalmist himself.

Second Reading: *Romans 11.33-36*
It could easily escape the reader's attention that Paul is still dealing with the problem of the Jews in relation to Christ, for this brief passage is a gem in itself, as Paul contemplates the mystery of God's knowledge and wisdom. It is as though in his speculation which we have set out in previous Second Readings he has reached the limit of man's ability to probe the divine purpose, reached in fact the point where man can only marvel at the wonder of God.

Gospel: *Matthew 16.13-20*
When asked by Our Lord, the disciples gave several views of his identity, all as it were, broken fragments of divine truth. It was Peter whose insight was like a flash of light that revealed the truth: "You are the Christ". No one had ever had such understanding. Then in the true fashion of old, he received a new name, as Abram became Abraham, no longer Simon bar Jonah, but Peter the Rock, for such was the meaning of his new name. Isaiah placed the "key of the House of David" on the shoulder of his appointee; in a similar way Our Lord denoted Peter's future authority. The place where all this occurred was once a centre of pagan worship.

First Reading: *Jeremiah 20.7-9*

Jeremiah was not by nature a prophet of woe, but was compelled by political circumstances to prophesy (i.e. preach) an unpopular message. As the power of Assyria waned, Judah looked to Egypt, but Jeremiah saw the folly of this. For advising submission to Babylon, he was immensely unpopular and put in the public stocks. In the reading we have part of Jeremiah's reflection on his plight. To be God's servant makes him an object of derision; not to speak, results in a fire burning within him.

Responsorial Psalm: *Psalm 62.2-6,8-9*

The psalm is a high water mark of spiritual development as seen in the Psalter. It is more profitable to concentrate on this than on the location of the psalm about which few agree. In the first stanza the writer sees his need for God as that of a parched land without water. Then in actual fact or in recollection, he is uplifted in the sanctuary. In the third stanza he looks ahead with confidence; finally, thinking of past spiritual experience inspires confidence for the present.

Second Reading: *Romans 12.1-2*

For many Sundays we have travelled along the peaks of *Romans*. Now we go down onto the level ground of every day experience as Paul takes his readers through the practical application of all that has gone before. Speaking metaphorically, he urges the Romans in the Second Reading to make a living sacrifice of themselves in a worship that accords with reason, as distinct from the sacrifice of animals that have no understanding of what is being done to and with them. Instead of conforming to the standards of society, the believer is to approach life with a mind transfigured, for this is the very word used to describe Our Lord's changed appearance on the Mount of Transfiguration.

Gospel: *Matthew 16.21-27*

The Gospel records Our Lord's first prediction of his impending Passion and Resurrection. No wonder Peter failed to understand and suffered the Lord's rebuke. The reading then gives the conditions of discipleship which involves so radical a change that the believer acts with total self-disregard. Once again the tenses of three imperatives makes it clear that the act of self-abnegation and the taking up of the cross of discipleship are single acts; the following goes on and on day after day. Criminals carrying the cross beam of their own execution would have been a common sight in Roman-occupied Judaea.

First Reading: *Ezekiel 33.7-9*

The *Book of Ezekiel* is difficult and presents great problems. It appears that Ezekiel was among the first to be deported to Babylon in 597 B.C. and that it was there he delivered the portion before us. In the role of watchman of his people, his function is to prepare them for the restoration of their city, but it will be only on the basis of their true repentance.

Responsorial Psalm: *Psalm 94.1-2,6-9*

This psalm was sung on the way to the Temple. In the sixth century S.Benedict required his monks to say it daily on waking. The approach to God is with a joyful noise in typical Oriental fashion. In the second stanza one feels the hush of awe and a pastoral note tells of the bond between God and his people. Finally mention of Massah and Meribah takes the reader back to desert experiences with Moses[1]

Second Reading: *Romans 13.8-10*

In Chapters 12 and 13 Paul deals with the principles that motivate Christian life and in the Second Reading the law of love is stated. Because love is an endless giving we must always be in this debt to others, but it is the only debt we may incur. All the commandments are gathered up in this one word, "love". Our Lord said it all in *Matthew 22.38-40*. When the *New Testament* was being written, a new word was needed, free from all the connotations of an erotic world and this word was on hand, almost unused, and ready to be filled with the new concepts, **agape** the love that is of the will, the love that is part of God's language.

Gospel: *Matthew 18.15-20*

Reconciliation is of the very heart of Christianity. Here in a passage found only in *Matthew*, Our Lord deals with the procedure for securing the reconciliation of those who within the Church are at variance with each other. The power of excommunication given to Peter in Ch.16.19 is here bestowed on all the disciples. We note again the rare use in the Gospels of "ecclesia" (church), the body of those "called out".

---

[1] See the First Reading and Notes Third Sunday of Lent, Year A.

First Reading: *Ecclesiasticus 27.30-28.7*
Ecclesiasticus was written about 200 B.C. and is part of what is
known as Wisdom literature. These writings cover a wide range of
topics such as the problem of suffering *(Job)*, advice on very
many life situations and the nature of Wisdom itself. She is
conceived as almost a person, "a clear flowing forth from the
Almighty". Among various warnings and precepts the writer
includes some profound remarks on forgiveness. This is the theme
of the First Reading.

Responsorial Psalm: *Psalm 102.1-4,9-12*
Thoughts of God's infinite love and goodness permeate the
psalm. The writer begins with a call to remember always the
blessings of God, and in the second stanza God's qualities are
stated, forgiveness, healing, redemption and love. In the last two
stanzas there are further assurances of God's love and redemption.
In the First Reading we see how man may react when wronged;
the Responsorial Psalm gives us God's reaction.

Second Reading: *Romans 14.7-9*
Chapter 14 begins with a plea for appreciation of other people's
point of view. Though some of the matters treated may seem
trivial to us, the principle of toleration still operates. In the
reading, Paul states that we influence each other, but that we
belong to Christ both in life and in death. This was made possible
by Christ's Humiliation and Exaltation. The Second Reading
two Sundays hence will echo this thought.

Gospel: *Matthew 18.21-35*
Peter who features often in this Gospel asks Our Lord how often
he should forgive. His generous seven times is extended to seventy
-seven (or seventy times seven in some manuscripts), in either
case a figure that confounds ordinary thinking. The Parable of
the Unmerciful Debtor brings into sharp contrast ten thousand
talents and one hundred denarii. Giving equivalents for ancient
money presents complex problems. Let it be simply said that the
first sum would have run into millions of dollars and the second is
about one five hundred thousandth of the first.

First Reading: *Isaiah 55.6-9*
These words are addressed to the exiles in Babylon and follow the invitation to the Messiah's banquet[1] . Here are words of earnest pleading, for many have grown cold and even sought heathen gods. But God is forgiving; his thoughts soar above the limits reached by man.

Responsorial Psalm: *Psalm 144.2-3,8-9,17-18*
This is the last of the alphabetical psalms and was probably rendered as a solo before the congregation. The greatness and the majesty of God are magnificently extolled throughout the psalm and in portions omitted in our Missals the writer "seeks to have a knowledge of God cover the earth". The kindness, love and justice of God emerge from the psalm as part of the writer's spiritual experience.

Second Reading: *Philippians 1.20-24,27*
The origin of the church at Philippi is set out in *Acts 16.12-40.* Paul wrote from prison, probably in Rome, to the Philippians to whom he was deeply attached, to thank them for their generosity to him. The letter begins with the usual greeting, followed by thanksgiving and prayers for the Philippians. He then explains how his imprisonment has actually helped to spread the gospel. In the Second Reading we see how it has affected Paul himself. His confident resignation suggests a preparation for martyrdom.

Gospel: *Matthew 20.1-16*
If the principles involved in the Parable of the Labourers in the Vineyard were applied to a modern industrial situation there would be uproar and the inevitable strike. But the parable does not illustrate a set of circumstances in which merit is a factor. Places in the Kingdom are not worked out by a formula; on the contrary they are given as acts of grace by an all-loving God to undeserving entrants. The parable is recorded only in *Matthew*.

---

[1] See Notes First Reading, Eighteenth Sunday in Ordinary Time, Year A.

First Reading: *Ezekiel 18.25-28*

King Zedekiah had dealt treacherously with Babylon to the hurt of his own people. Against this background Ezekiel sees the setting up of a new kingdom into which all nations will gather. But there will be principles by which this kingdom will be governed. The reading begins very abruptly. In the dialogue between prophet and people, the latter had objected to God's principle that past good cannot be set against present sin. From this, the argument of Ezekiel is developed. Renunciation of integrity means death; repudiation of evil brings life.

Responsorial Psalm: *Psalm 24.4-9*

Quite the neatest title devised by commentators on this psalm is "An Alphabet of Devout Prayers". In the first stanza the psalmist earnestly seeks the paths and ways of God. In the second there is a burden of guilt for which the sinner seeks God's mercy. Finally he seems to have emerged from his crisis and to have found absolution, and on the strength of the experience commends his God to others. The psalm should be considered in connexion with the First Reading.

Second Reading: *Philippians 2.1-11*

Having spoken of himself in prison, Paul deals with aspects of Christian life and then, in response to a local situation, makes a plea for unity. Into this setting he places what is generally agreed was an early Christian hymn designed to teach a basic understanding of the work of Christ. The hymn falls into two parts, Christ's Humiliation and subsequent Glorification. The Christ of the hymn is the pattern to emulate when unity is under attack.

Gospel: *Matthew 21.28-32*

When his authority was questioned by the chief priests and elders, Our Lord tried to elicit an answer to the question by whose authority John the Baptist acted. If they had given the obvious answer they would have condemned themselves. So Our Lord tells the Parable of the Two Sons which only Matthew records. By declaring that the son who said "no" and then changed his mind, really did his father's will, they cut the ground from under their feet. The passage abounds in variations in the text. One of these makes the chief priests and elders support the second son's reply, an exercise in perversity!

First Reading: *Isaiah 5.1—7*
The might of Assyria spread fear among its neighbours. Damascus and Israel, the northern kingdom of the Jews, formed an alliance and tried to force Judah, the southern kingdom to join, but Judah preferred the safety of being a tributary vassal of Assyria, turning a deaf ear to all the pleadings of prophets for moral reform. Against this background Isaiah prophesied. The First Reading is in the form of a parable, the point of which comes at the end with frightening effect.

Responsorial Psalm: *Psalm 79.9,12—16,19—20*
Under the familiar figure of a vineyard, the psalmist refers, most probably, to the northern kingdom of Israel which ceased to exist in 722 B.C. The first stanza reviews the bringing of the vine from Egypt and its planting in the Promised Land. Then follows a description of the desolation of the vineyard. In the last two stanzas the psalmist pleads with God to restore it, with the promise of the people's return of God.

Second Reading: *Philippians 4.6—9*
The *Letter to the Philippians* is drawing to a close. Paul, whose life was in the balance, urges his friends with whom the fear of persecution was always present, not to worry; they are to pray that the peace of God will garrison their hearts. The catalogue of virtues with which the reading concludes is quite remarkable; they are not Pauline words and read like a list from a pagan text book of ethics.

Gospel: *Matthew 21.33—43*
In the Parable of the Tenant-Farmers of the Vineyard there are three obvious elements, the owner, the owner's son and the tenants. The owner represents God who entrusts the farming to his chosen people who abuse the special power he has given them. The son is the Lord Jesus who will be the last emissary from God. The son who was put to death and mention of the rejected stone bring the parable to a striking conclusion.

First Reading: *Isaiah 25.6—10*

Scholars differ widely in their attempts to find a background for this prophecy. Coupled with the five verses that precede, it obviously celebrates the overthrow of a great city. But which one and when? Taking the First Reading, we see in it a Messianic banquet for ALL peoples, a celebration of the time when all will sit down at God's table; the note of immortality, rare in the *Old Testament*, is struck with vibrance; over all, to make everything possible, is the love of God for his people.

Responsorial Psalm: *Psalm 22*

The Shepherd psalm is unique in the Psalter and probably the best known. Into his image of the good shepherd, the writer, traditionally said to be David, projects all the qualities of the keeper of sheep on the hill side. What more could he do for his charges than is set out in the first two stanzas? Then the picture changes to a banquet where God is the host. The psalm ends with the feeling of security prompted by the Divine Shepherd. All we like sheep have gone astray and we find in this psalm the Shepherd who gently leads the lost back to the fold.

Second Reading: *Philippians 4.12—14,19—20*

There is in the Second Reading both a note of confidence and also of resignation. Using language from current mystery cults, Paul says that he has been through his initiation into hardship. Roman prisons were not noted for their amenities nor had his enemies over the years been gentle with him *(See II Corinthians 11.23—27)*. The portion before us shows his enormous spiritual strength and was designed to encourage his friends in Philippi. Paul does not doubt God's future provision for his friends.

Gospel: *Matthew 22.1—14*

Two parables have been combined to form the passage before us. The Messianic banquet in the First Reading was for all and so, finally, is the invitation to the king's wedding feast, but only after the elect have had and lost their chance. The universal note is clear in both passages; equally clear is the reference to the Jews as those who declined the invitation. Two points are noted: cross roads were points where people gathered and worshipped; the facts regarding the wedding garment are not altogether clear, but this is: to turn up without it was an insult to the host and a sign of not being prepared for the occasion.

First Reading: *Isaiah 45.1,4—6*

The captivity in Babylon began in 586 B.C. Among the exiles was the writer of *Isaiah 40* and following chapters. Called Isaiah, but only for convenience, he never lost hope of his country's restoration. Kingdoms rise and kingdoms fall and Babylon was no exception. Cyrus the Persian overran the city in 538 B.C. The prophet sees him as the liberator of the Jews and that is what the First Reading is all about. There is in this passage the typical Jewish view of history, God's shaping of international affairs to foster the progress or punishment of his people.

Responsorial Psalm: *Psalm 95.1,3—5,7—10*

This is one of a group of psalms that celebrate the Kingship of God and are known as Enthronement Psalms. In the first and second stanzas the writer declares that the psalm has been composed for the occasion; all Israel are invited to join in and reach out in song to all nations, whose gods have no reality for they are as nothing. Finally the people are invited to praise God in his Temple, to worship with an offering and to proclaim his kingship to all the world.

Second Reading: *I Thessalonians 1.1—5*

This is the first of five Second Readings from *I Thessalonians* which is probably the first book in the *New Testament* to be written. Thessalonike was a very important centre of trade and was capital of the province of Macedonia. *Acts 17.1—9* records the story of Paul's first contact with the city. *I Thessalonians* was written primarily to allay misplaced fears for those who died before the Lord's return. The brief reading shows one of the characteristics of the letter, Paul's affection for his converts.

Gospel: *Matthew 22.15—21*

The Pharisees, strict legalists, in an unholy alliance with the Herodians, adherents of Herod, try to trap Jesus on the question of the tribute payable to Rome. As devout Jews the Pharisees hated the tax, even refusing to look at Caesar's image, while the Herodians were pro-Roman. The tax was on a per capita basis, levied on all males over fourteen and females over twelve. Two points emerge: the suave approach to Our Lord, and the reply which he gave and which is echoed later in the letters of Paul and Peter, that civil authority must be recognised.

THIRTIETH SUNDAY IN ORDINARY TIME
YEAR A

First Reading: *Exodus 22.20—26*
The giving of the Ten Commandments is followed, in the *Book of Exodus,* by a long list of rules and injunctions covering many aspects of life. There are further instructions in the passage to be read: strangers, widows and children must be protected; lending money for interest (literally "biting") is forbidden; a garment offered to secure a loan must not be kept over night as it is the owner's only protection against the cold. Compassion is the keynote of these regulations.

Responsorial Psalm: *Psalm 17.2—4,47,51*
This psalm is almost identical with a psalm found in *II Samuel 22,* written to celebrate David's deliverance from "all his enemies and from the hands of Saul". It was probably used by other kings of David's line to celebrate their victories. In the first stanza the writer refers to several ways, mostly defensive, in which God has protected him and in the last stanza there is a repetition of some of these ideas. The psalm, as before us, can well serve as a personal thanksgiving.

Second Reading: *I Thessalonians 1.5—10*
Greece formed two Roman provinces, Achaia to the south and Macedonia to the north where Thessalonike was located. Paul thanks God for the spiritual development he sees in his converts. They are proof that his preaching was effective. Their Christian joy in spite of persecution *(Acts 17.5—9)* has made them an example in Macedonia and Achaia. Paul probably wrote from Corinth.

Gospel: *Matthew 22.34—40*
It is possible in the days of Jesus that an attempt was being made to find a simple basis for the whole Law. Also, some scribes recognised that some commandments were more important than others. The question put to Our Lord may echo these current modes of thought. His answer brought together, though possibly not for the first time, the *Shema* (Hear, O Israel) of *Deuteronony 6.4—9 and Leviticus 19.18:* "You must love the Lord your God". and "You must love your neighbour...", a principle and its application. There is a reference to the Sadducees, a wealthy sect of Jews consisting of a priestly aristocracy. They denied any belief in resurrection and angels.

THIRTY—FIRST SUNDAY IN ORDINARY TIME 89
YEAR A

First Reading: *Malachi 1.14—2.2,8—10*
Malachi is the last book in the *Old Testament*, but by no means
the latest. We know next to nothing about the writer, perhaps not
even his name, for Malachi means "my messenger". The Jews had
returned from exile; the Temple had been rebuilt, but all was not
well. The people were beset by many problems and to one of
these the reading is directed: the priests show indifference and
lack of reverence to God, thus laying themselves open to his curse.
The reference in the last sentence is to the custom of taking wives
from among foreign nations.

Responsorial Psalm: *Psalm 130*
This is one of the songs of Ascent[1]. The writer describes briefly,
but with telling effect, what he has discarded to reach peace with
God. Pride, haughtiness and things beyond his accomplishment
have yielded place to a peace like that of a child upon its
mother's breast.

Second Reading: *I Thessalonians 2.7—9,13*
This beautiful passage illustrates so well the basis for Paul's
affection for the Thessalonians. He reminds them that in helping
their growth in the faith he was like a mother caring for her
children. He recalls how when he lived among them he worked at
his trade of tent making — he did the same in Corinth — so that
he would not be a burden on them. This reads like a defensive
answer to some critics. Finally he expresses gratitude for the way
they accepted his preaching.

Gospel: *Matthew 23.1—12*
The essence of Our Lord's denunciation of the scribes and
Pharisees is their hypocrisy: "they do not practise what they
preach". The scribes were the scholars in the Law and as such
inherited Moses' authority. The Pharisees or separatists were
exclusive in their attitude to the common people; they took it
upon themselves to expound the minute details of the Law as
presented by the scribes. To distinguish themselves they wore
phylacteries or small leather boxes containing Hebrew passages
of the Law. The borders of their garments were made obvious by
tassels. The misuse of the word "Father" relates to the word
abba which is appropriate only to God.

---

[1] See Notes, Holy Family, Year A.

First Reading: *Wisdom 6.12—16*
The Book of Wisdom, written about 100 B.C. is divided into three sections: Wisdom and the destiny of man, the character of Wisdom and Wisdom in history. Wisdom is more than the quality of being wise; she is almost a person, an agent of creation , breath of the power of God. The First Reading is from the second section of the book and declares how readily Wisdom may be found.

Responsorial Psalm[1]: *Psalm 62.2-8*
The psalm represents a climax of spiritual development in the Psalter.   Deep longing for God and trust in his love are among its prominent features. In the first stanza the writer sees his need for God as that of a parched land without water. Then in fact or in recollection he is being lifted up in the sanctuary — was the writer, David in the wilderness?   Finally lying awake at night he thinks of God's mercy and protection and offers us a way to fill in sleepless hours.

Second Reading: *I Thessalonians 4.13—18*
In his preaching at Thessalonike, Paul laid great emphasis on the *Parousia* or Return of the Lord. His converts were living in intense anticipation of the event, yet some of the bretheren had died. This caused much concern among the Christian community for they were worried about the fate of the departed. Would they still share in the life to come? Paul writes to give instruction on this point and in so doing adds to the theology of the hereafter.

Gospel: *Matthew 25.1—13*
Chapter 24 of Matthew's Gospel has been called the Sermon on the End. The Parable of the Ten Bridesmaids follows Chapter 24; hence it is a message of preparedness for the Coming of Our Lord. The ten bridesmaids gather to welcome the groom on his way to the bride's father, before taking his bride to his own home. There was nothing amiss in their sleeping as they waited, for they all slept . Five brought additional oil and so were prepared when the time came. If they had shared their oil, they too would not have been able to escort the groom. The warning is clear: be prepared for the Lord's Coming, lest the door close with an awful finality.

---

[1] See Notes, Responsorial Psalm, Twenty-Second Sunday in Ordinary Time, Year A.

First Reading: *Proverbs 31.10—13,19—20,30—31*
Proverbs is part of the Wisdom literature of the *Old Testament.*
The book consists of several collections of sayings with dates of
composition spread over some centuries. *Proverbs* is a book of
searching for practical Wisdom and man's chances of success in
this endeavour are good. Chapter 31.10—31 which should be read
in full describes the perfect wife: she is virtuous, possessed of
many skills and a shrewd business woman. Yet she had hardly any
rights at law; her virtues were her own reward.

Responsorial Psalm: *Psalm 127.1—5*
This is one of the Songs of Ascent or Gradual Psalms (120—134),
sung by pilgrims ascending Zion's hill as they returned for one of
the great festivals. It sings the blessedness of the God-fearing man
in his family life: he will have enough to provide for his own; his
wife will bear him children and they shall be like shoots of the
spreading, evergreen olive *(Jeremiah 11.16).* A benediction brings
the psalm to its conclusion.

Second Reading: *I Thessalonians 5.1—6*
This passage from *I Thessalonians* follows on directly after the
Second Reading last Sunday and should be read in conjunction
with it; last Sunday there were details of the Lord's Coming; in
this Mass we are given two striking expressions of its suddenness,
the thief in the night and the onset of labour pains. When the
hour comes it will be too late to prepare for it. Advice what to do
now, is then given.

Gospel: *Matthew 25.14—30*
The parable of the Talents offers three sobering thoughts: the
Lord's Return though delayed, will come even although it be "a
long time after"; the Jews who were the repositories of God's
treasure did nothing with it and consequently have lost their
talent: finally, though the Greek word for "talent" means only an
immense sum of money (something weighed out), we can give the
parable a modern application by recognising our responsibility for
each of our gifts. To use them rightly is to share in the joy of the
Kingdom.

92   **LAST SUNDAY IN ORDINARY TIME**
OUR LORD JESUS CHRIST   UNIVERSAL KING
YEAR A

First Reading: *Ezekiel 34.11—12,15—17*

This section of *Ezekiel (Chs 33—39)* contains prophecies that deal with the redemption of God's people who are in exile in Babylon awaiting the rebuilding of their national hopes. In the First Reading the prophet thinks of rulers who have misused their kingly power and so have contributed to the state of the nation. Henceforth God himself will be the Shepherd of his people. In the reading, the duties of the shepherd are clearly seen.

Responsorial Psalm: *Psalm 22.1—3,5—6*

The Shepherd psalm is unique in the Psalter and probably the best known; this is the fourth time it has been used this year. Into his image of the good shepherd the writer, traditionally said to be David, projects all the qualities of the keeper of sheep on the hill side. What more could he do for his charges than is set out in the first two stanzas? Then the picture changes to a banquet where God is the host. The psalm ends with a feeling of security prompt-ted by the divine Shepherd. All we like sheep have gone astray, and we find in this psalm the Great Shepherd who gently leads the lost back to the fold.

Second Reading: *I Corinthians 15.20-26,28*

In the central part of this letter, Paul deals with various matters arising out of correspondence received from Corinth (Ch.7.1). He covers a wide variety of topics and finally in Ch.15 comes to grips with the question of resurrection. There was nothing in Greek thought to help the Corinthians in this matter; their kinsmen in Athens poured scorn on the idea *(Acts 17,32)*. So Paul states resurrection as a fact and using a favourite contrast between Adam and Christ, declares that the faithful departed will be brought to life in Christ who was the first of the harvest , to be followed by the full ingathering. Then he asserts what is central to this Mass: Christ reigns.

Gospel: *Matthew 25.31—46*

In this last Gospel for the year, Matthew gives us a magnificent climax to the work of Christ. He will return in glory with angelic hosts and separate his own from the pretenders, mixed in this age as sheep and goats are in an eastern flock. The reading sets out the principles on which the separation will take place and clearly asserts the fate of the two groups. While to some degree even an inspired writer is limited by the words he uses, the meaning of this passage is clear.

SUNDAY MASSES
Year B

First Reading: *Isaiah 63.16-17; 64.1,3-8*
The passage is difficult. A reading from near the end of *Isaiah*
ought to refer to a time after the exile. However everything
suggests that the Jews are still in exile in Babylon. The words
before us are part of a long prayer uttered by the prophet and
covering many themes: acknowledgement of the Fatherhood of
God turns into recriminations against him for their plight; a
contrite confession leads to a recognition that God is the potter
and they the clay.

Responsorial Psalm: *Psalm 79.2-3,15-16,18-19*
The psalm is a plea for help, to the Shepherd God whose throne is
supported by winged cherubim, symbols of his unapproach-
ableness. In the second stanza Israel is seen as a vine[1] imported
from Egypt and requiring God's special care. Finally, Israel,
the man of God's choice, seeks his protection and promises not
to fall away again.

Second Reading: *I Corinthians 1.3-9*
This short passage is the prelude to Paul's stern words covering
several topics. In it thanksgiving and hope are the main thoughts,
thanksgiving for the spiritual riches of his Corinthian converts
and the hope that comes with eager waiting for the Lord's
Appearing, a true Advent message.

Gospel: *Mark 13.33-37*
Mark is the Gospel for this year, the first to be written and the
shortest. It was composed about 65 A.D. in Rome and reflects
the influence of Peter. Its contents have been almost entirely
absorbed by Matthew and Luke. The passage before us is an
exhortation to chase sleep away; the Church is to be in constant
expectation of the Lord's Return. Then follows the Parable of
the Absentee Owner, who left each his allotted task, but with no
indication when he would return. So we are to keep awake
through all four watches of the night, ready for the great hour and
in the meantime, doing what has been assigned to us.

---

[1] See Notes, Twenty-seventh Sunday in Ordinary Time, Year A.

First Reading: *Isaiah 40.1-5,9-11*
The prophet Deutero - or Second Isaiah sees an end to the Babylonian captivity of the Jews. The reading falls into three parts: first it is made clear that enough is enough; the sins that brought the people to Babylon have been atoned for. Then a voice rings out. It is God who will bring his people back to Jerusalem and he shall be as an eastern potentate, for whose progress hills will be levelled and valleys filled in. Finally a messenger is bidden to go up to the vantage point of a high place and tell of God's coming in power, yet with the tenderness of a shepherd. Lovers of Handel's *Messiah* will hear the recitative *Comfort ye, comfort ye my people*[1].

Responsorial Psalm: *Psalm 84.9-14*
The psalmist is listening for God's voice and what he hears suggests the coming of a golden age. His glory will dwell in the land. The noblest virtues will flourish and material blessings will come from the earth. Peace, or the general well-being of all, will result from God's footsteps, his movement among his people.

Second Reading: *I I Peter 3.8-14*
The writer had evidently lived long — perhaps longer than many realise — after the time of Christ and in the reading he takes up the question of the Second Coming. God's ways of reckoning time are different from ours and in any case the delay gives many a chance they would not otherwise have had. The writer's description of cosmic convulsion reflects primitive ideas in the Church. The passage ends with a warning that is timeless: while we wait for the Lord's Return we must be ready and this cannot be better done than in the quality of our lives.

---

[1] *Messiah* is sung throughout in the Authorised or King James version of Scripture.

Gospel: *Mark 1.1-8*
Mark's Gospel begins so abruptly and with the omission of all
references to Our Lord's early life that many have thought that
the original beginning has been lost. Ancient writers took great
liberty with quotations. The verses before us are said to be from
Isaiah. In fact they are from *Malachi* and *Isaiah*. The words of the
latter have been altered and applied, not as in the original to God
bringing back his people, but to John the Baptist as the
forerunner of Christ who will bring people back to God. John's
repentance baptism that leads to forgiveness of sins is seen as
having special value in Advent.

First Reading: *Isaiah 61.1-2,10-11*

This passage which resembles the Songs of the Suffering Servant[1] and was used by Our Lord at Nazara (*Luke 4.18*) refers to the depressed condition in Jerusalem after the exile. Poverty, despair and submission to foreigners contributed to the gloom into which the prophet's message shines like a piercing light. His radiant hope draws on the joy of marriage and the verdant loveliness of spring.

Responsorial Psalm: *Luke 1.46-50,53-54*

Just occasionally the Responsorial Psalm comes from outside the Psalter and today is a case in point, as we turn to part of Our Lady's hymn, the *Magnificat,* so named from the first word of the Latin translation. Put together with phrases from the|psalms and resembling, but surpassing Hannah's song, the *Magnificat* is Blessed Mary's reaction to Elizabeth's congratulations. Whether it was her own compostiion or a hymn she had learnt as a girl, she has made it her own for all time.

Second Reading: *I Thessalonians: 5.16-24*

Having dealt with the state of the blessed dead which is the crux of the letter, Paul turns to the matter of the suddenness of the Second Coming and the need to be watchful. This leads into the practical exhortations of prayer and thanksgiving. The Spirit must not be suppressed – the old translation "quenched" retained the figure of fire. In a world flooded with crack-brained religions they were to test everything. The reading ends with a wish for the spiritual blessings of peace, holiness and a blameless life in readiness for the Lord's Appearing.

Gospel: *John 1.6-8,19-28*

From the profound theology of the Prologue to the Fourth Gospel, the reader is abruptly introduced to John the Baptist. He is shown in complete subordination to Christ, possibly because in some quarters he was given too exalted a position. He rejects the threefold suggestion regarding his identity and describes himself in Isaianic terms simply as a voice of preparation. His role is also to set the earthly scene for Christ's ministry. John's baptising with water is a prelude to the baptising of the Holy Spirit.

---

[1] See Notes, Baptism of the Lord, Year A and Second Sunday in Ordinary Time, Year A and Good Friday.

First Reading: *I I Samuel 7.1-5,8-12,14,16*
The message in the reading is simple and a perfect preface to
Christmas. David's warfare was accomplished, yet his conscience
was troubled because he was better housed than the ark of the
Lord. Through his prophet Nathan, God made it clear that
another would build for him, but that he would make a house
of David, a dynasty to endure for ever. In the Masses of Christmas
we shall be honouring him who is of David's line.

Responsorial Psalm: *Psalm 88.2-5,27,29*
The full version of the psalm is composite; the verses before us
reflect the facts of the First Reading. In the first stanza, the
writer declares his intentions of ever proclaiming God's love
which is as sure as the heavens. In the next stanza the permanence
of the Davidic covenant is affirmed. Finally the psalmist echoes
the conclusion of the First Reading in the words: "You are my
Father". So with sure hope we are being brought into the
Christmas season.

Second Reading: *Romans 16.25-27*
These three verses are the conclusion of Paul's great Roman
letter. Vibrant words, they form a doxology which is not Paul's
usual way of ending a letter. Placed in different positions in
different manuscripts they have provided scholars with a puzzle
of some dimension. You will hear the phrase "mystery kept
secret for endless ages". "Mystery" is not something insoluble,
but a secret long kept and finally revealed. And that is what this
time of the year is all about, the mystery of Christ.

Gospel: *Luke 1.26-38*
One of the most loved and most precious stories in the Bible, the
Annunciation is recorded only by Luke who is certainly using a
documentary source. Three points are offered: the link with
David's line is through Joseph; when Luke wrote "The power of
the Most High will cover you with its shadow", he used a rare
word which appears again in all accounts of the Transfiguration;
finally it is noted that Mary, unlike Zacharias in a lesser
annunciation, offered no protest, gave no thought to her social
position as pregnant and unmarried, but rendered total
submission to the will of God.

CHRISTMAS DAY: VIGIL MASS
See above p. 16

CHRISTMAS DAY: MIDNIGHT MASS
See above p. 17

CHRISTMAS DAY: DAWN MASS
See above p. 18

CHRISTMAS DAY: DAY MASS
See above p. 19

Sunday in the Octave of Christmas
THE HOLY FAMILY
OF JESUS, MARY AND JOSEPH
YEAR B

First Reading: *Genesis 15.1-6;21.1-3*
God's earlier promise (*Genesis 12.1-3*) to Abram seemed to have
come to nothing; in the reading Abram expresses his fears; he
may even have to adopt a slave of his household—the law allowed
this — to secure descendants. God assured Abram that his
descendants would be of his own flesh and blood. The conclusion
of the reading tells of the promise fulfilled. The words "who
counted this as making him justified" are the source of Paul's
doctrine of justification worked out in the *Letter to the Romans.*

Responsorial Psalm: *Psalm 104.1-6,8-9*
The psalm praises God as the God of the Covenant which he
made with Abraham. The full psalm shows the hand of God in all
the experiences of his people from Egypt onwards. He is the God
of history. The psalmist calls on his listeners to thank God and to
make his goodness known abroad.

Second Reading: *Hebrews 11.8,11-12,17-19*
The catalogue of heroes of faith set out in Ch. 11 was compiled
as an encouragement to the readers of this letter to stand firm
against persecution. The portion before us is a reminder how deep
an impression was made on not only the psalmist, but also on
the unknown writer of this letter by the story long ago of
Abraham, Sarah and Isaac and of Abraham's faith.

Gospel: *Luke 2.22-40*
The presentation of the Child Jesus in the Temple shows both the
poverty and the piety (*Leviticus 12.6,8*) of Mary and Joseph.
Revealed too is the fact that Jesus was under the Law. The story
of Simeon indicates the acute spiritual perception of holy men,
which in this case gave the Church the little gem we call *Nunc
Dimittis.* The first shadow falls across a mother's joy as she
catches a fleeting glimpse of her future role of *mater dolorosa.*
Finally across the scene comes Anna's gentle voice, Anna the type
of many an elderly nun, rich in years and wisdom.

SOLEMNITY OF MARY, MOTHER OF GOD

See above p. 21

6 January or
Sunday between 2 January and 8 January
THE EPIPHANY OF THE LORD

See above p. 23

Sunday after 6 January
BAPTISM OF THE LORD
(First Sunday in Ordinary Time)
YEAR B

First Reading: *Isaiah 55.1-11*

The author of the second part of *Isaiah* is writing to encourage his people who are still in exile in Babylon. The prophet issues an invitation to the Messiah's banquet, admission free. Through the basics of water, grain, wine and milk the needs of the spirit will be met. There is a promise of a new covenant and with it a command to return to God. The conclusion asserts the effectiveness of God's word, which is as sure in its working as the seasons are in promoting the sustaining powers of life.

Responsorial Psalm: *Isaiah 12.2-6*

The reading has been described as two small psalms sung by those who have been redeemed. It is considerably later than the part of *Isaiah* in which it has become embedded and should be read in connexion with the end of the previous chapter which speaks of times of deliverance. While not being specifically Messianic, it has a Messianic quality. The reading overflows with the joy of God's salvation which is like the inexhaustible springs of water from a well.

Second Reading: *I John 5.1-9*

The reading gives three signs of Sonship and three witnesses of Christ's Divinity. First the signs: we become God's children when we recognise Jesus as Christ; love of him means love of God and obedience to him. So we love one another and through our faith can oversome the world. The three witnesses are spirit, water and blood. With cautious steps in a field of great controversy, it is suggested that the spirit is the Spirit that descended at his Baptism, the water is the Water of Baptism and the blood is his Blood shed on Calvary.

Gospel: *Mark 1.7-11*

John the Baptist again acknowledging himself in a lesser role than Jesus, baptises him in the Jordan. In Mark's brief account we observe that the heavens "were being torn apart" — a more dramatic description than in the other Gospels — revealing the world Our Lord had left and to which he would return; that the Spirit descended like a dove, the symbol of peace and reconciliation (*Genesis 8.11*) and the Church's representation of the Holy Spirit; and that this voice was heard again at the Transfiguration and again when he prayed "The hour is come" (*John 12.23*). So began his ministry with a baptism that had every mark of divine approval.

See above p. 25

FIRST SUNDAY OF LENT
YEAR B

First Reading: *Genesis 9.8-15*

As is so often the case, the myths of early *Genesis* (Chapters 1-11)
embody profound truth. In the First Reading, the story of the
Flood and its aftermath gives the circumstances in which God
made his first Covenant with man, a Covenant to be followed by
others in the *Old Testament*. The Hebrew word expressing this
relationship between God and man affirms no equality between
the parties. God makes the promise and lays down the conditions.
The covenant was for ever; a new start was implied. In Lent we
think, against this background, of the New Covenant Our Lord
made before his death.

Responsorial Psalm: *Psalm 24.4-9*

Quite the neatest title devised by commentators on this psalm is
"An Alphabet of Devout Prayers". In the first stanza the psalmist
earnestly seeks the paths and ways of God. In the second there is
a burden of guilt for which the sinner looks to God's mercy.
Finally he seems to have emerged from his crisis and to have
found absolution, and on the strength of the experience
commends his God to others.

Second Reading: *I Peter 3.18-22*

The passage bristles with difficulties of interpretation, yet the
basic meaning is clear: Christ's victory over evil is the ground of
Christian confidence. The view is here taken amid enormous
variations of opinion that the preaching to the spirits in prison,
the *descensus ad inferos,* refers to Our Lord's visit to Paradise.
Typology, that is using events and people in the *Old Testament*
to foreshadow what is in the *New Testament* was common in
the early Church. There is an example in the reading where the
flood with its cleansing of the earth is a type of Christian Baptism
The letter was written to people facing persecution and the writer
braces them with the assertion that through Baptism they share in
the fruits of Christ's victory.

Gospel: *Mark 1.12-15*
The Spirit that descended with dove-like gentleness at Our Lord's
baptism now thrusts him out into the wilderness to do battle with
the forces of evil. Mark gives no details of the Temptation (for
which see *Luke 4.1-13*). The number "forty" recalls the years of
Israel's wanderings and Elijah's experience in the wilderness
(*1 Kings 19.8*). There is also the first mention in *Mark* of
Kingdom and repentance. The former suggests not only a
community, but also the royal rule; repentance is not just regret
for an action, but from the two components of the Greek word, a
change of heart or mind.

First Reading: *Genesis 22.1-2,9-13,15-18*

Isaac had been given to Abraham and Sarah, but now Isaac was required as a sacrifice. God's provision for a race more numerous than the stars or the sand on the shore seemed to have come to an intolerable contradiction. The Lord gives; the Lord takes away. Yet there was a solution and it lay in Abraham's complete obedience. As Paul said: "With any trial he will give you a way out of it (*1 Corinthians 10.13*)". So the Lenten theme of testing, obedience and victory goes on.

Responsorial Psalm: *Psalm 115.10,15-19*

This is one of the great Hallel (Hebrew:praise) or Egyptian Hallel Psalms (113-118[1]), traditionally sung while the Passover lambs were being slain and possibly sung by Our Lord and his disciples after the Last Supper. The psalmist has been rescued from some great peril. In his expression of gratitude there are two points: he makes a thanksgiving sacrifice — that was not uncommon — but he goes much further and offers himself with the words "Your servant am I". Then comes the second point: what he offers to God is to be done before all the people. It is his witness to all of God's mercy.

Second Reading: *Romans 8.31-34*

Over the space of eight chapters, Paul develops the idea that faith alone is necessary to secure the righteousness of God. The argument which does not always flow smoothly suddenly becomes a burst of great certainty. God who gave his own Son will withhold nothing; the ascended Christ pleads for us. The whole passage glows with hope.

Gospel: *Mark 9.2-10*

In addition to the Feast of August 6th., the Transfiguration is always celebrated on the Second Sunday of Lent. As Peter, James and John were the only witnesses and as Mark is the source of Matthew and Luke's Gospels, Peter is the obvious source of this material in the Gospels. From the days of the early Fathers the belief has been strong that Mark was Peter's interpreter. Three brief observations are offered: Our Lord's changed form revealed his godhead; Peter the impetuous had to say something so he suggested the three tents! The voice from heaven that had set the seal on Our Lord's ministry, now confirmed the way to the Cross.

---

[1] In the numeration of the *Jerusalem Bible*

First Reading: *Exodus 20.1-17*
The Ten Commandments were given to the Israelites as part of
their preparation for transition from a wandering to a settled life.
The second and third commandments require special
understanding. Catholics have often been objects of ill-informed
criticism regarding "carved images". The word means an image
hewn from wood or stone and refers to things worshipped in non-
Hebrew religions. The third commandment deals with the
Sabbath, that is our Saturday (*Sabbato* in modern Greek, as in
Italian). From the earliest times the Church has enjoined Sunday
worship as a celebration of the Resurrection. What then of the
Vigil Mass on Saturday? Many centuries ago the Church provided
Vigil Masses for certain greater festivals. More recently an
extension of the practice has been made to all Sunday Masses.

Responsorial Psalm: *Psalm 18.8-11*
This psalm, which is almost certainly two psalms blended
together, begins with a wondering look at the nightly sky and
ends with the psalmist's delight in observing the Law, that is, the
Mosaic law before the Pharisees converted it with their burdens
into a yoke. It is the latter portion of the psalm that will be read.
We turn from the grandeur of the heavens that make us feel
insignificant to the moral law which lifts man to his highest
dignity.

Second Reading: *I Corinthians 1.22-25*
Corinth was a Greek world in a nutshell. There were party
divisions in the Church; the community at large saw the
Crucifixion in widely differing lights, ranging from scandal to
madness. Into this seething cauldron of thought Paul casts his
own conviction that the death of Jesus was nothing less than the
power and wisdom of God.

Gospel: *John 2.13-25*
The selling of live stock and changing Roman money into Jewish
coinage was legitimate business. It is the abuse of the system, the
turning of the Temple into a brigand's cave, that aroused Our
Lord's anger. Though John places the incident at the beginning
of Jesus' ministry and the three synoptics place it at the end, the
difference lies in the fact that the Synoptic Gospels have their
material arranged in a time sequence, whereas John selects
incidents and makes them vehicles of his teaching. Attention has
been drawn to the "tragic irony" with which Our Lord's
reference to Herod's Temple was misunderstood. The Temple
which was completed about 64 A.D. was a truly magnificent
structure.

First Reading: *I I Chronicles 36.14-16,19-23*
The two *Books of Chronicles* trace the history of the Jews from
creation to their return from exile. The First Reading, which is
the last chapter in *Chronicles*, explains why the Jews were
deported and how Babylon was in time overwhelmed by the
Persian Cyrus who saw to it that the Jews returned home and
their Temple was rebuilt. The messengers mentioned early in the
reading are the prophets from Amos onwards. We note the typical
Jewish interpretation of history in God's controlling international
events to punish or promote his people.

Responsorial Psalm: *Psalm 136*
This psalm was written during the Jewish exile in Babylon where
the Jews were asked to sing some of the songs of Zion. Loyal to
the best in their past, they refused to debase their sacred songs by
singing them to entertain their captors. The rivers of Babylon are
the two great rivers Tigris and Euphrates.

Second Reading: *Ephesians 2.4-10*
Written from prison to churches in Asia Minor, the *Letter to the
Ephesians* is a circular letter considered by some, but not all, to
be Paul's finest epistle. The theme is God's plan to bring
everything together in Christ, to redeem Jew and pagan in him.
Into the story of God's redemptive love are woven phrases like
"brought to life with", "raised us up with", "gave us a place
with". Greek can build "with" into the structure of a word.
There are many examples in the letter of this concept of a shared
experience.

Gospel: *John 3.14-21*
Nicodemus, unknown outside the Fourth Gospel, represents the
quiet seeker, the best of the Jewish race. Our Lord tells him he
must be born again (or, from above) and in the first line of the
reading illustrates his meaning from *Numbers 21.9* with the story
of the bronze serpent which was an antidote to the bite of fierce
serpents in the desert. So the Son of Man, a title with origins in
the *Book of Daniel* and used by Our Lord of himself as the
Messiah, will, when lifted up on the Cross, be the remedy for the
poisonous sins of the world.

FIFTH SUNDAY OF LENT
YEAR B

First Reading: *Jeremiah 31.31-34*
Jeremiah, the most tragic of the prophets, walked closely with his God, felt the heartbreak of his people's sins and watched their headlong rush into events that brought them captivity in Babylon. He never ceased to love them or to spare them his denunciation. In the reading he sees the day of new life when God will make another covenant with his people, written not on tablets of stone, but on their hearts. God will forgive; God will rebuild.

Responsorial Psalm: *Psalm 50.3-4,12-15*
This is recognised as the greatest of all penitential prayers; it has a dubious association with David's sin in the company of Bathsheba. Through the years the psalm has helped penitents to find the forgiveness of God. In the portion before us a plea for mercy and a confession of sin lead into an expression of desire for restored communion. Finally, in the joy of a renewed relationship the penitent would go out and seek the lost.

Second Reading: *Hebrews 5.7-9*
Hebrews has been called the "Epistle of the High Priesthood of Jesus Christ". The brief reading sets out some of the qualities of the High Priest. He learnt obedience through his suffering and this is a source of power to save.

Gospel: *John 12.20-30*
The reading marks an important point in what the Fathers called the "Spiritual Gospel". Greeks want to see Jesus. Within a short time the Gospel would be received into the Greek world. Their language was to become the first medium of Christian expression. The death - life cycle of a grain of wheat becomes the basis of Our Lord's teaching about the higher life. We note, too, the third occasion in his life when the voice was heard from heaven.

PASSION SUNDAY (PALM SUNDAY)
See above pp. 31-34

HOLY THURSDAY: CHRISM MASS
See above p. 35

THE EASTER TRIDUUM

HOLY THURSDAY (Mass of the Lord's Supper)
See above p. 36

GOOD FRIDAY (Celebration of the Lord's Passion)
See above p. 37

EASTER VIGIL
See above pp. 38-42

THE SEASON OF EASTER

EASTER SUNDAY
See above p. 43

SECOND SUNDAY OF EASTER
YEAR B

First Reading: *Acts 4.32-35*
Luke, whose second volume is better known as the *Acts of the Apostles,* devotes the first eight chapters to early scenes in the Church at Jerusalem. The new life was expressing itself in a mission to the Jews and in sharing all with one another. This will now be described.

Responsorial Psalm: *Psalm 117.2-4,15-18,22-24*
The core of this difficult psalm is thanksgiving for deliverance from enemies and chastisement. First, the endless love of God is proclaimed; in the second stanza, it is God, not the individual, who has triumphed. Finally, the psalmist refers to that massive block of stone which was sunk in the ground and held secure the two meeting walls. Israel rejected its corner-stone which is now holding the Church together.

Second Reading: *1 John 5.1-6*
John who wrote the Fourth Gospel also wrote this letter. In both there is the same simple style expressing truth of great profundity The passage should be read privately, very slowly and thoughtfully, to grasp the nature of Christian love, its working and its victory. For the three witnesses see the notes on the extended passage in the Baptism of the Lord, Year B.

Gospel: *John 20.19-21*
The Resurrection appearance recorded in the reading serves a theological purpose, as the narrative does elsewhere in *John.* Coming through closed doors, Jesus gave his disciples his peace, a peace which covered the whole range of spiritual well being. The Risen Lord breathed on his disciples as the Father breathed on the world at its creation. They received their commission with priestly authority to forgive and to retain sins. The passage contains the only reference in the Gospels to the nails of the Cross.

THIRD SUNDAY OF EASTER
YEAR B

First Reading: *Acts 3.13-15.17-19*

Peter continues to dominate the early chapters of *Acts*. Fearless now, in the strength of his Lord's Resurrection, he makes two points in the passage to be read: it was a monstrous crime to have put the Holy One to death and a national repentance of the Jews would lead to a spiritual revival of Israel. Peter's hope was disappointed by their subsequent attitude to the new faith, because they continued to persecute the Church.

Responsorial Psalm: *Psalm 4.2,4,7,9*

The clear meaning of these verses is that the psalmist's faith in God does not waver, even in times of distress. In the full version of this psalm it emerges that the writer's joy in his God belongs to a time of famine when others were losing their faith. Not even this trial could suppress his spiritual satisfaction.

Second Reading: *I John 2.1-5*

While John recognises that God's love can come to perfection in us, he is also aware that we sin. He points to the sacrifice that takes away our sins, to him who is our Advocate with the Father. "Advocate" is a word used exclusively by John and means "one summoned to our side", not that God needs to be informed about us; rather it points to our own unworthiness to plead.

Gospel: *Luke 24.35-48*

Luke records only two Resurrection appearances, the one on the road to Emmaus and the account we are about to read. Our Lord appeared to his disciples to restore their faith and to make available to them that Resurrection power that would embolden their actions and colour their preaching. On this occasion he appeared to a group, and a large number is not likely to be in error. Listen for references to "hands", "feet", "bones" and "the act of eating". It was Luke the medical practitioner who recorded these facts, Luke for whom, as for all of us, the explanation lies beyond comprehension.

First Reading: *Acts 4.8-12*
There seemed no end to Peter's courage, for the reading is part of a speech he delivered before men whose wealth, power and intelligence were the greatest in the land and he was only a fisherman! The resurrection of Peter, now filled with the Holy Spirit, is one of the most compelling stories in the *New Testament*. We note the recurring reference to Jesus as the rejected stone, the cornerstone of the new structure.

Responsorial Psalm: *Psalm 117.1,8-9,21-23,26,28-29*
Thanksgiving for deliverance is at the heart of this psalm which appears to have been used at the Feast of Tabernacles, a harvest ingathering festival. The psalm was sung antiphonally. The first stanza covers a bitter experience with the declaration that only God is to be trusted. Then follows the reference to the massive block of stone, sunk in the ground to hold secure two meeting walls. The rejection of this stone was part of the psalmist's bitter experience at the hands of his enemies. The last stanza concludes with thanksgiving to God.

Second Reading: *I John 3.1-2*
God's love has been lavished on us, his children; all our future is not clear, but this is, that we shall eventually see him in all his glory. Set in this spiritual gem is a centre of darker hue; the world did not recognise Our Lord; it may well do the same to us.

Gospel: *John 10.11-18*
This is the third of the great "I am" statements of Jesus. All seven are found only in *John*, between Chapter 6.35 and 15.1. The salient features of the parable are: the hired man, often the object of attack in the *Old Testament (Jeremiah 23.1)*, represents the religious leaders of Our Lord's day; they cannot be trusted; the true shepherd will give his life for his charges; a time is envisaged when there will be one flock.

FIFTH SUNDAY OF EASTER
YEAR B

First Reading: *Acts 9.26-31*
Time had elapsed since Paul's dramatic conversion on the
Damascus road. Ready now to join those whom he had once
persecuted he found that they naturally distrusted him. Barnabas,
who has been described as one of the most lovable characters in
Acts, with great Christian charity took him by the hand (not "took
charge of him") and brought him into the company of the apostles.
We are told that the churches were left in peace. True, the arch-
persecutor had been converted!

Responsorial Psalm: *Psalm 21.26-28,30-32*
This psalm is one of great contrasts. It begins with the despairing
cry: "My God, why have you deserted me?" and was used on
Palm Sunday. However in the latter part, doubts vanish and the
psalmist sings of God's salvation. The second line in our Missals,
"the poor shall eat and have their fill" has more in it than meets
the eye. The poor – "meek", "faithful" would be a better word –
are his friends, invited to share in a sacrificial meal. We too have
a friend who invites us to share in such a meal.

Second Reading: *I John 3.18-24*
To be a child of God is to live the life of love, and this means
keeping God's commandments, believing in Jesus Christ and
loving one another. The phrase "quieten our conscience" arises
from a passage whose text, translation and meaning are uncertain.
The best sense seems to be a warning against the over-sensitive
conscience that can climb mountains and just as easily slip into
deep valleys of despair, when all the time the assurance of God's
love should lead us over level plains.

Gospel: *John 15.1-8*
This is the last of John's "I am" parables; they are all claims for
that divine status which belonged to the "I am who I am" that
spoke to Moses from the burning bush *(Exodus 3.14). Jeremiah
(2.21)* and others in the *Old Testament* use the vine as a figure of
Israel. Here Our Lord uses the image of the vine to express the
oneness of himself and his disciples, a unity as indissoluble as
branch and stem. The lesson of growing, pruning, discarding and
bearing fruit presents a forceful picture.

First Reading: *Acts 10.25-26,34-35,44-48*
Chapter 10 in *Acts* is a very important point in the developing story of the spread of the faith. Cornelius, a non-commissioned officer in the Roman army at Caesarea, was one of many serious - minded men who were dissatisfied with their native religion and had had some contact with Jewish faith. The reading tells of his admission into the Church through the sacrament of Baptism. From now on the missionary activities become world orientated.

Responsorial Psalm: *Psalm 97.1-4*
The psalm had its origin in some great deliverance. The psalmist turns the occasion into an opportunity for God to show the nations his concern for his people. The writer uses the term "new" because his psalm is another in the enthronement series, or because it is a special occasion, possibly deliverance from Babylon. All the earth is invited to rejoice in what God has done for his people, to rejoice in his saving and rescuing power.

Second Reading: *I John 4.7-10*
John's teaching here is that love belongs to the very nature of God and when we feel Christian (i.e. Christ's) love for one another, a new birth has taken place in us. Twice in this brief portion John speaks of God sending his Son into the world. Thus he echoes a theme presented more than twenty times in the Gospel.

Gospel: *John 15.9-17*
The reading follows on from where the Gospel ended last week. In it was revealed how the disciples are united to Christ as branch to stem; today we see how the disciples are united in love in Christ to one another. Towards the end of the reading are the words "The Father will give you anything you ask in my name". This is stated frequently in *John* and calls for careful understanding. The phrase "in my name" suggests an asking that only Our Lord would make. By this criterion what a host of petitions fail before they are uttered!

First Reading: *Acts 1.1-11*
The reading begins with a reference to "my earlier work", which
is Luke's Gospel, and to "Theophilus", who is anybody's guess.
The writer then mentions in general terms Our Lord's
Resurrection appearances. The promise of the gift of the Holy
Spirit — *Acts* has been called the Book of the Holy Spirit — is
repeated; questions about the political future of Jerusalem are
not answered and with that the earthly ministry of Our Lord ends
in his Ascension.

Responsorial Psalm: *Psalm 46.2-3,6-9*
This is one of the Enthronement Psalms used to celebrate the
Kingship of God, possibly in association with the festival of the
New Year. While there may be references to some great
deliverance, more probably the writer in this psalm looks towards
God's future universal rule. The psalm has a traditional
association with Ascension Day.

Second Reading: *Ephesians 1.17-23*
Paul's *Letter to the Ephesians*, written from prison, was a circular
letter to the churches of Asia Minor; it represents his spiritual
genius in full flower. The theme is the Church as the Body of
Christ, embracing Jews and pagans without distinction. The
reading deals with Christ's supremacy and sets out what he who
has triumphed over angelic and demonic hosts will confer on
believers.

Optional Second Reading for Year B: *Ephesians 4.1-13*
Passing from his doctrinal teaching on the unity of all things in
Christ, Paul comes, as elsewhere, to the practical application.
From prison he implores his various readers to preserve the unity
of the Spirit. But unity does not mean identity, as the conclusion
of the reading shows. There are two acute problems in the middle
of the passage: a quotation from the psalms referring to God as a
conqueror in war, has been altered or misquoted to refer to
Christ; does "he descended" refer to the Incarnation or to the
descent to Paradise?

Gospel: *Mark 16.15-20*

Attention[1] has been drawn to the abrupt beginning of Mark's gospel. The traditional ending with the words "for they were afraid", has led many to suspect that some chapters have been lost. The early Church also had its suspicions and an unknown hand has made up the deficiency and part of this is before us now. The importance of the reference to the Ascension in this document is that the Church realised the full significance of the Ascension in the story of Our Lord's life and work.

---

[1] See Notes, Second Sunday in Advent, Year B.

First Reading: *Acts 1.15-17,20-26*
The passage deals with the election of a successor to Judas, whose death by a different means is told in one of the omitted verses. Two points deserve mention: of all those who heard Our Lord, only one hundred and twenty assembled for the election; yet this tiny number was the nucleus of preaching that extended to the ends of the earth. Second, Matthias emerged as the replacement. Nothing is known of his earlier life; he may have been one of the seventy-two disciples mentioned in *Luke 10-1;* he is said to have taken the Gospel to Ethiopia. The Church remembers him on 14 May.

Responsorial Psalm: *Psalm 102.1-2,11-12,19-20*
The psalm is dominated by thoughts of God's infinite goodness and love, as shown by his longsuffering and patience towards sinful humanity. The portion before us begins and ends with a call to thankfulness. It is one of the unique contributions of Hebrew thought that God is a God of love.

Second Reading: *I John 4.11-16*
The concept of a loving God is continued and expanded. He is not distant and beyond our experience. In fact, he is within us, part of our being, if we practice Christ's love towards one another. John brings the psalm down from the heights of heaven and sets its application in our lives.

Gospel: *John 17.11-19*
The priestly prayer of Jesus in *John* Chapter 17 has been described as "One of the most sacred passages in the *New Testament"*. His arrest imminent, he prays for his disciples that God will watch over them as they work out their destiny in a hostile world. He prays too for their consecration in the truth. The verb "to consecrate" has a history of hallowed usage. It is used in the Greek version of the Old Testament to describe God's consecration of Moses, Jeremiah and the chosen people.

See above p. 52

MASS DURING THE DAY
YEAR B

First Reading: *Acts 2.1-11*

Pentecost was originally a festival of the crops. The reading tells how it became one of the greatest occasions in history when God the Holy Spirit burst into human affairs. In all great religious experiences words become inadequate. In spite of his mastery of language, Luke can only say that the coming of the Holy Spirit was **like** a powerful wind and **like** tongues of fire. There is mention of people from many places. These were Jews, citizens of the countries into which, over the years, they had been scattered, but always Jews; who returned to Jerusalem for the festival of Pentecost and now found themselves caught up in the outpouring of the Spirit.

Responsorial Psalm: *Psalm 103.1,24,29-31,34*

Gathering thoughts from various accounts of creation that circulated in other lands, the psalmist has put together a magnificent hymn of praise to God the Maker of all things. Our Missal quotes only a fragment of the whole which, seen in its full form, shows how poetry can be used in praise.

Second Reading: *Galatians 5.16-25*

Paul's Galatian converts were stultifying their own spiritual growth by reverting to a form of legalism which gave no freedom and did, in fact, enslave them. The writer urges his readers to live in the Spirit and so escape the tyranny of their baser selves. Life in the Spirit produces the noblest of human characteristics. Listen for the gifts of the Spirit as set out in the reading.

Gospel: *John 15.26-27;16.12-15*

Continuing his farewell discourse, Jesus returns to his teaching about the Holy Spirit, the Advocate, the One called to our side. He realised that with events closing in on him there was not time to give all the instruction he would have wished. This would now be done by the Holy Spirit. The fact that on four occasions in this long discourse, he refers to the Holy Spirit, illustrates how important it is for us to grasp what we can of this vital element in Christian doctrine.

Sunday after Pentecost
THE MOST HOLY TRINITY
YEAR B

First Reading: *Deuteronomy 4.32-34,39-40*
Deuteronomy begins with a statement of the mighty acts of God performed for the good of his people. The passage before us comes at the end of the first of three addresses and is designed to explain the uniqueness of Israel's God. Other contemporary nations had their gods, but they are only the creations of men's hands and minds. Scripture makes Israel's position clear: "The Lord is God indeed....there is no other".

Responsorial Psalm: *Psalm 32.4-6,18-20,22*
God is praised in this psalm for his perfect qualities. He is faithful; his love never varies and he is the Creator of the ends of the earth. He is active in the affairs of men and is ready to extend his saving power. The psalm, originally in commemoration of a great deliverance, reveals the greatness of God and how our needs are met.

Second Reading: *Romans 8.14-17*
In all Scripture, there is nothing comparable to the eighth Chapter of *Romans* for guidance on the doctrine of the Holy Spirit. In the passage before us we discover how the Spirit bonds us to God in a relationship so close that we are in fact God's children. To be the adopted children of God would have meant so much to the Romans in whose society, from the highest levels down, adoption was a way of life. The adopted enjoyed the most elevated status.

Gospel: *Matthew 28.16-20*
All our thoughts in the Mass for Trinity Sunday are gathered up in the Lord's words: "Baptising them in the name of the Father and the Son and the Holy Spirit". Nowhere else in the *New Testament* do we find the Trinitarian baptism formula. This bringing together of the Three Persons of the Trinity shows how early in its life the Church was evolving its basic teaching.

First Reading: *Exodus 24.3-8*
Earlier in *Exodus*, God had given his people, through Moses, the details of their new way of life. Now we are to hear how this covenant was ratified. There is an altar which represents God. Moses stands between the altar and the people. The Covenant is read, the people assent and Moses scatters sacrificial blood over the altar and the people. Life is taken from the victims and used to bind God and people together, for the life is in the blood. The reference to blood provides the link with Corpus Christi.

Responsorial Psalm: *Psalm 115.12-13,15-18*
This is one of the psalms traditionally sung while the Passover lambs were being slain and possibly used by Our Lord and his disciples after the Last Supper. The psalm expresses the thanksgiving and vows of one delivered from a great distress. "The cup of salvation" is a reference to the pouring of a drink offering at the time of sacrifice. The last stanza declares that what was vowed in distress has been paid.

Second Reading: *Hebrews 9.11-15*
The unknown writer of this letter aims to show from the very first page that the Christian dispensation is superior in every way to the Old Covenant of Judaism. In the passage to be read there are two ways in which the New is superior to the Old: Christ's Ascension into the presence of God is superior to the priest's entry into the sanctuary; his blood has a power greater than that of sacrificial victims.

Gospel: *Mark 14.12-16,22-26*
Few words of Scripture are better known than this portion of Mark's Gospel. Here the institution of the Eucharist is described and in these words we are brought to the very heart of Catholic worship, to the celebration of the Mass. The Eucharistic Prayers echo phrases from the Gospel. Though we know the passage almost by heart, we never tire of hearing it afresh.

Friday after the Second Sunday after Pentecost
THE SACRED HEART OF JESUS
YEAR B

First Reading: *Hosea 11.1,3-4,8-9*

Hosea is a sad figure. Married to an unfaithful wife, he belonged
to the northern kingdom which he calls Ephraim. Standards of
morality were low; idolatry was rife. The tragedy of the prophet's
life is reflected in the references to marriage, and here, to what
could be a tender family scene. Under the image of father and
infant son we see what has been called the "Fatherhood and
Humanity of God". Ephraim deserved God's rejection, but God
cannot let him go. Admah and Zeboiim were cities destroyed for
the same reason as Sodom and Gomorrah.

Responsorial Psalm: *Isaiah 12.2-6*

The reading has been described as two small psalms sung by
those who have been redeemed. It is considerably later than the
part of *Isaiah* in which it has become embedded and should be
read in connexion with the end of the previous chapter which
speaks of times of deliverance. While not being specifically
Messianic, it has a Messianic quality. The reading overflows with
the joy of God's salvation which is like the inexhaustible springs
of water from a well.

Second Reading: *Ephesians 3.8-12,14-19*

Ephesians is a circular letter sent to the churches of Asia Minor,
not corrective of errors in the recipients' faith, but Paul's genius
in full flower, in some opinions his greatest work. The central
theme is the unity of all in the Church, Christ's Body. The
reading is in two parts, a statement of the writer's commission
and a prayer for his readers'enlightenment with Christ in their
hearts.

Gospel: *John 19.31-37*

In the tragedy and the triumph of which we are to read, the *Old
Testament* keeps coming to the surface. The body of a man hung
on a tree had to be removed before nightfall (*Deuteronomy 21.
22*). In *Exodus (12.46)* the injunction to eat the Passover lamb
with its bones unbroken, clearly suggests a Pascal significance in
the fact that Our Lord's legs were not broken. The very difficult
verse in *Zechariah 12.10* – the text is uncertain – is made to refer
to the soldier's piercing of Jesus' side. Thus two of John's three
witnesses are brought together in the Gospel narrative [1].

---

[1] See Second Reading and Notes, Second Sunday of Easter,
Year B.

First Sunday in Ordinary Time
BAPTISM OF THE LORD
YEAR B

See above page 102

First Reading: *I Samuel 3.3-10,19*
The Prophets were a unique feature of Hebrew religion. The
passage to be read is much more than the lovely familiar story
of a child's obedience to the voice of God. In fact, it records
the call of one destined to found the Prophetic Order which
endured through the exile and into the years following the return
from captivity. (See *Acts 3.24*). What better could we do so
early in the year than listen to God calling Samuel?

Responsorial Psalm: *Psalm 39.2,4,7-10*
In the portion before us there is an expression of gratitude for
recovery from illness. The psalmist had been ill for a long time,
but God heard his cry. In the second stanza the futility of
sacrifice is recognised; only the willing heart prevails with God.
The reference to the "scroll of the book" is not clear. Ready to
do the will of God, the psalmist feels he must speak out to
others of the justice of God.

Second Reading: *I Corinthians 6.13-15,17-20*
The church in Corinth was set in what has been called the Vanity
Fair of the Greek world. The Greeks who took a great deal of
moral liberty for granted, even had a word meaning "to live like
a Corinthian". When Paul received news of immorality in the
Corinthian church (Ch.5), he reacted sharply and in the Second
Reading goes to the heart of the matter: sexual licence is sin
against the body which is the temple of the Holy Spirit.

Gospel: *John 1.35-42*
The First Reading told of a child's response to the voice of God.
The Gospel records the reactions of grown men to the unspoken
call of God's Son. Two words invite comment: when "John
stared hard at Jesus" a word is used that suggests the
concentrated gaze in the theatre, at the drama on stage; and again
when Our Lord called Peter, he gave him the name "Cephas"
which in his native tongue Aramaic, means "rock".

First Reading: *Jonah 3.1-5,10*
Few parts of the *Bible* have been more misunderstood than the
Book of Jonah in which the whale has, with some, become
almost an article of faith. The book belongs to the period after
the exile when two views were current regarding the saving work
of God. The general opinion was that his mercy and love were
centred on the Jews alone; a few more enlightened thinkers
declared that his concern was for all mankind. Set possibly four
centuries back in the past with a once upon a time story effect,
the book tells of Jonah who was punished for not calling the
pagan city of Nineveh to repentance; then in the First Reading
a repentant Jonah does as he was told to do and Nineveh was
saved. Thus with telling effect the book expresses the two views
of God's saving work.

Responsorial Psalm: *Psalm 24.4-9*
Quite the neatest title devised by commentators on this psalm
is an "Alphabet of Devout Prayers". In the first stanza the
psalmist earnestly seeks the paths and ways of God. In the
second, there is a burden of guilt for which the sinner looks to
God's mercy. Finally he seems to have emerged from his crisis
and to have found absolution, and on the strength of the
experience commends his God to others.

Second Reading: *I Corinthians 7.29-31*
The reading is difficult, but if we recall how Paul had given up
everything for Christ and if we try to think ourselves into the
position of one who believed the Lord's Return was imminent,
the passage begins to make sense. Years later, at the end of his
life when the Second Coming was less evident in his thoughts
he could write to the Ephesians of marriage as a symbol of
Christ's relationship with the Church.

Gospel: *Mark 1.14-20*
Mark is the Gospel for the year and the use of it begins in earnest
now. It is the shortest of the Gospels though it may have lost
its beginning and end. It was the first of the four and was written
in the late 60's A.D., probably in Rome. An early Father of the
Church declares that "Mark was a disciple and interpreter of
Peter". There are 105 sections in *Mark*; all but four have been
absorbed into *Matthew* and *Luke*. The central theme is the
coming of the Kingdom and this emerges in the Gospel for
today.

First Reading: *Deuteronomy 18.15-20*
In setting out the terms of the Covenant between God and his people, Moses is speaking in the context of religious observances. After warning against the dangers of imitating native practices of seeking the will of God, Moses reminds his listeners that at Horeb they asked for an intermediary between themselves and God; now it is stated that prophets will be raised up in their midst to carry on the spiritual work of Moses.

Responsorial Psalm: *Psalm 94.1-2,6-9*
This psalm was sung on the way to the Temple. In the sixth century S.Benedict required his monks to say it daily on waking. The approach to God is with a joyful noise in typical Oriental fashion. In the second stanza one feels the hush of awe and a pastoral note tells of the bond between God and his people. Finally, mention of Massah and Meribah takes the reader back to desert experiences with Moses.

Second Reading:[1] *I Corinthians 7.32-35*
The passage must be seen in the same context as the Second Reading last Sunday. Paul's conviction that the Second Coming was imminent continues to colour his thoughts. While pleading for universal dedication to the affairs of the Lord, he appears to be carried away by his own thoughts. We should each take from these instructions as much as can be applied to our own situation.

Gospel: *Mark 1.21-28*
The Galilean ministry had begun. Fresh from the desert victories over Satan, Our Lord began to gather a band of followers and in Capernaum, a large town by the lake, he so impressed people with the power of his preaching that in the words of one eminent scholar "the hearers were astonished because the voice of prophecy had long been silent in Israel". Jesus then showed his power in another way by healing the man with the unclean spirit. With greater medical knowledge, we describe these afflictions in more modern terms. The spirit is vividly rebuked with the Greek word: "Be muzzled".

---

[1] See Notes on Second Reading, previous Sunday.

First Reading: *Job 7.1-4,6-7*
Great literature is the product of its times. *The Book of Job* reflects serious concern, after the exile, with the problem of suffering, how to reconcile the misfortunes of the righteous with the justice and love of God. The view, often found in the psalms, that suffering is the result of sin no longer satisfied seeking minds. So in a story mostly in poetic form, Job suffers while his friends try to interpret his suffering. In the reading Job's miseries are just beginning. The book represents the pinnacle of the Wisdom literature.

Responsorial Psalm: [1] *Psalm 146.1-6*
Praise continues throughout the twenty verses of this psalm. In the three stanzas before us, God is praised for rebuilding Jerusalem after the exile. The psalm reflects the great sufferings of the people, but more than that it declares confidence in the God who is Lord of nature, that he will "bind up all their wounds".

Second Reading: *I Corinthians 9.16-19,22-23*
From the beginning of this chapter, Paul has been defending his apostolic position almost in answer to some who may have doubted it. As God's slave, a status often declared, he is under compulsion to preach the Gospel without personal reward. So he claims his reward from men, to be allowed to serve them for nothing. His reward lies in the blessings of the Gospel.

Gospel: *Mark 1.29-39*
The ministry of healing continues to demonstrate the power of Our Lord amid the needs of a suffering world. From the beginning and the end of the passage, two compelling points emerge: "straight" i.e. "immediately" is a word used more than forty times in *Mark*, making urgency one of the keynotes of this Gospel; the last paragraph of the reading stresses the source of Our Lord's power. His spiritual resources needed to be replenished in communion with his Father whom he sought before the day began, in some lonely place.

---

[1] See Notes, Third Sunday of Advent, Year C.

First Reading: *Leviticus 13.1-2,44-46*

The *Book of Leviticus* purports to deal with laws to regulate the religion and worship of the Israelites during their forty years of wandering. It is also concerned with various aspects of cleanliness. Actually *Leviticus* is one of the latest strands in the first five books of the *Old Testament* that are so often called the *Pentateuch*. Composed after the exile, it reflects the fully developed religious life of the Jews. The reference in the reading to leprosy prepares us for the Gospel of the Mass.

Responsorial Psalm: *Psalm 31.1-2,5,11*

This psalm is the second of seven great penitential psalms in the Psalter. The sinner convicted of his sin, finds happiness and peace with God. The nature of the sin is not told, but many connect this psalm with David and his dealings with Bath-Sheba, wife of Uriah. Augustine found great comfort in this psalm in his last hours.

Second Reading: *I Corinthians 10.31-11.1*

Butchers' shops in Corinth were supplied with meat from pagan temples where it had been offered to idols. Many Christians were worried and sought Paul's advice. He replied that because idols were nothing the meat could therefore be eaten provided no one was offended. If anyone was offended, the meat should not be eaten lest a brother be distressed.

Gospel: *Mark 1.40-45*

Three points come quickly to the surface in this reading. The leprosy mentioned here is not the disease which manifests itself in such distressing forms today, but rather a skin complaint described in the First Reading. The word "sternly ordered him" comes from a difficult word used of horses snorting and so conveys the idea of strong emotion. (See *John 11.33*). The frequent injunction to keep silent about Our Lord's activity arose from his desire to reveal his true identity in his own time.

First Reading: *Isaiah 43.18-19,21-22,24-25*
The writer of Second Isaiah [1] shared the exile in Babylon with his compatriots to whom his prophecies were delivered. The First Reading is part of a section (Chs. 41-48) dealing with God's plans for Israel. Just as of old God led his people from captivity in Egypt, so now with the fall of Babylon imminent, there will be another exodus. The passage closes with a plea by God to his people to call upon him.

Responsorial Psalm: *Psalm 40.2-5,13-14*
Deep personal experience lies behind this psalm, perhaps a serious illness. The writer sees a right attitude to the poor and the defenceless as the true basis for happiness and as an assurance of God's help in his own need. From this tranquil thought he turns to self examination and a confession of sin and this restores his confidence. The psalm concludes with a simple doxology.

Second Reading: *I I Corinthians 1.18-22*
This is the first of eight readings from *I I Corinthians,* a difficult book of which it has been said that it has contents, but no plan. Possibly three letters, or parts of them have been joined together to form *I I Corinthians*. Apparently Paul's itinerary had been changed and his enemies were quick to call his religion a "yes" and "no" affair. Paul asserts the positive quality of Christ. Two interesting words are used in the last sentence: briefly, a **seal** indicates ownership; **pledge** denotes a down payment, a deposit that validates the agreement. A derivative of the word comes down into modern Greek meaning "a girl engaged to be married".

Gospel: *Mark 2.1-12*
Mark's gift for vivid narrative is well exercised in this passage. Events move quickly, with a sense of determination and urgency. The roof consisted of beams; the interlacing branches were covered by trampled earth. Through this they literally dug their way. The word "forgive" is rich in meaning; basically meaning "to send away", it had *Old Testament* overtones *(Leviticus 16.21)*. Our Lord's claim to forgive sins which so incensed his critics is tied to the first of many uses in *Mark* of the Messianic title "Son of Man".

---

[1] See Notes Twenty-ninth Sunday in Ordinary Time, Year A.

First Reading: *Hosea 2.16-17,21-22*

The tragedy of Hosea's married life colours his prophetic utterances. The reading begins with the lovely word picture of Hosea's seeking to woo his errant wife [1] again and of her responding in love. The prophet's thought turns to Israel and its apostasy and the possibility of being wooed again by God as from a second Egypt. Like lost love renewed, the relationship will be as a second betrothal.

Responsorial Psalm [2]: *Psalm 102.1-4,8,10,12,13*

This is the fifth use in the Missal of *Psalm 102* and not the last. It reflects the writer's long communion with his God and how from the needs of his own soul he has found the many responses of the divine, forgiveness, healing, redemption, mercy and the gift of long life. A date has been assigned to the psalm, but it is also in a sense, timeless, Everyman's theology of God.

Second Reading: *II Corinthians 3.1-6*

If *II Corinthians* is a letter of bits and pieces, this portion (Chapters 1-9) could be a letter of reconciliation after the big row between Paul and the Corinthian Church. In this reading Paul is aware to what extent he has had to assert himself in dealing with the Corinthian Church and offers a corrective by declaring that the Corinthians are his best commendation. God is the source of his qualifications to administer the New Covenant.

Gospel: *Mark 2.18-22*

The passage contains two separate thoughts. The question of fasting arose and seeking, as usual, to trap him, "some people" pointed out that his disciples did not in fact fast, as was the custom. Our Lord uses his critics to teach what is in effect a simple rule: there is a time and place for everything. The references to the old and the new make it clear that his teaching involves a new order, not a patched-up version of the old.

---

[1] See Notes, Tenth Sunday in Ordinary Time, Year A and Sacred Heart Year B.
[2] See Notes Sacred Heart Year A, Twenty-fourth Sunday in Ordinary Time Year A and Seventh Sunday of Easter, Year B.

First Reading: *Deuteronomy 5.12-15*
The basis of Sabbath observance in this reading differs from
that recorded in *Exodus 31.12-17*. We observe the characteristic
humanitarian note in *Deuteronomy*; in both accounts rest and
worship are stressed. We need to ask ourselves what day the
Sabbath is. Clearly there can be only one answer and that is
Saturday. The modern Greek for Saturday is *Sabbato.* Our
Lord's attitude to the Sabbath is recorded in the Gospel for the
Mass and should be carefully considered.

Responsorial Psalm: *Psalm 80.3-8,10-11*
The abridged form of the psalm before us is clearly much easier
to handle than the full version. It begins with a call to praise
God at some festival. The second stanza gives the reason for
observing the feast and refers to God's punishment of Egypt for
what was done to his people. Stanza three recalls that God
lifted the burden from the shoulders of his people in Egypt. The
psalm concludes with a plea, ever necessary, to thrust out foreign
gods from their land.

Second Reading: *I I Corinthians 4.6-11*
The passage opens with a paragraph of radiance that continues
on from the end of Chapter 3. Then the writer's mood changes:
his life is held in the meanest of containers, an earthern jar; he
has suffered greatly – how greatly, may be seen in Chapter 11.23
-29 – for Christ, so that in Paul's body the light of his Lord may
be seen.

Gospel: *Mark 2.23-3.6*
Pharisaic additions to the Law were often ludicrous. The Lord's
disciples were not acting wrongly in picking the corn
(Deuteronomy 23.25), but by rubbing the corn they were
threshing it and so, working on the Sabbath! The reference to
David may be found in *I Samuel 21.1-8.* How far Our Lord had
moved from the basic idea of *shabbath* — to sit down and be
still— is clear from his remark that "the Sabbath was made for
man...." But what did he mean? That is for each of us to work
out for himself in the light of what *Mark* records of Our Lord's
activity on the Sabbath.

First Reading: *Genesis 3.9-15*
The reading seeks to explain through one of the earliest strands in *Genesis* how man, created in the first instance by God for his fellowship, fell from that state of bliss. We observe how the blame was first placed on the woman and then how she attributed her plight to the serpent and finally how the serpent, identified in later thought with Satan *(Wisdom 2.24)* was cursed for his part in the Fall. The last two lines of the reading have long been regarded by some as a Protevangelium or first intimation of redemption through Blessed Mary's Son.

Responsorial Psalm: *Psalm 129*
This is one of the Gradual Psalms or songs sung by pilgrims ascending Mount Zion; it is also, and more pertinently, a penitential psalm. The deep emotion of the penitent is reflected in the irregularity of the Hebrew verse. First there is a long cry of distress in which, as we say in English, the psalmist is in deep water. The second half reveals a mood of expectancy as he waits for deliverance and forgiveness.

Second Reading: *I I Corinthians 4.13-5.1*
Paul has discovered that the more one is active for Christ the greater are the trials[1]. Yet he presses on and amid physical weakness is constantly renewed in his inner life by the hope of future glory. At the end of the reading the frailty of our tent-like dwelling on earth is contrasted with the solid structure of the heavenly home.

Gospel: *Mark 3.20-35*
Into this Gospel are compressed three tremendous facets of the Lord's teaching. First, he refutes those who declare him to be devil - possessed by asserting in effect that if the claim were true there would be warfare in the demon world. Then comes the reference to the unforgivable sin, which seems to be the state of him whose values are so perverted that he sees evil as good. Anyone thus guilty would have no awareness of his state. Finally there is the magnificent sweep of spiritual vision that takes in all those who do God's will as members of Our Lord's family.

---

[1] See the previous Second Reading and the Notes.

ELEVENTH SUNDAY IN ORDINARY TIME   133
YEAR B

First Reading: *Ezekiel 17.22-24*
Ezekiel delivers his prophecies in allegorical form; that is, he uses
symbols to convey his thought. The present reading is a good
example of this form of expression. Zedekiah's treachery towards
Babylon had resulted in the deportation of the Jews to that city.
In characteristic form, Ezekiel prophesied that God would plant
a cedar twig which would grow into a large tree sheltering the
birds and overtopping all other trees, a prophecy of a restored
and greater Jerusalem.

Responsorial Psalm: *Psalm 91.2-3,13-16*
In the full version, the psalmist grasps the nettle of goodness and
evil in relation to prosperity and suffering and thinks that he has
disposed of it! Before us is only the picture of the godly man;
omitted verses give the fate of the wicked. The writer uses the
morning and evening services to thank God for his position. He
likens himself to the fruitful date palm and the lovely cedar tree
which is the symbol of strength and long life.

Second Reading: *I I Corinthians 5.6-10*
Paul uses the ideas of exile and living at home to express the
contrast between earthly life and finally being with the Lord. To
appreciate fully the sharpness of this antithesis it must be
remembered that in the ancient world exile was a devastating
experience. While saying little about the hereafter, Paul does lay
stress on the future judgment.

Gospel: *Mark 4.26-34*
Here we have Parables of the Kingdom, many only hinted at. The
first declares that the growth of this Kingdom resembles the
mysterious processes of nature; so too the growth of the
Kingdom is equally mysterious, as God's ways always are. A
second parable, that of the Mustard Seed, stressed the enormous
potential of the Kingdom in spite of its tiny beginning. A parable,
from the Greek meaning "laid alongside", has been called "an
earthly story with a heavenly meaning".

First Reading: *Job 38.1,8-11*[1]
The *Book of Job* is not history, but the story of man's struggle with the problem of suffering. Three friends have had their say and added little to the solution of the problem. God then speaks, ranging over many aspects of his almighty power. The problem is not resolved. Job accepts the greater wisdom of God. In the First Reading we shall hear how God has, in his power, set bounds to the limit of the ocean.

Responsorial Psalm: *Psalm 106.23-26,28-31*
The psalm begins with thanksgiving and concludes with a meditation on God's providence. There is a long section in the middle devoted to the rescue from peril of desert - travellers, exiles, the sick and seafarers. The psalm belongs to a period about 300 B.C. when the Jews were scattered over the ancient world for the purpose of trade. It was probably sung at one of their annual returns to Jerusalem. The portion of the psalm in our Missals deals with seafaring men and forms an ideal introduction to the Gospel.

Second Reading: *II Corinthians 5.14-17*
Personal explanations are once again finding expression. Paul begins by showing how life may be given a new direction. At the beginning of the Mass we read: "turbulence can become the birth-pangs of a new creation". How that may be so is set out in the last paragraph of this reading. The words "There is a new creation" can be just as well translated: "He is a new creature".

Gospel: *Mark 4.35-41*
This vivid description of a storm at sea, a common feature of Lake Galilee, suggests the account of an eyewitness, undoubtedly Peter whose voice is often heard in Mark's narrative. As vivid as the description is the Greek word behind "Be calm". This is the language of exorcism, used earlier by Our Lord in casting out an unclean spirit (Ch.1.25). This one Greek word means "Be muzzled and stay that way".

---

[1] See Notes, Fifth Sunday In Ordinary Time, Year B.

First Reading: *Wisdom 1.13-15,2.23-24*[1]

In the main, the idea of life after death is shadowy and ill-developed in the *Old Testament*. The departed go down to Sheol or Hades where they are separated from God. In later Hebrew times there was some development in these ideas. On the other hand, the First Reading which was written about 100 B.C. reflects the ideas of the early part of *Genesis*[2].

Responsorial Psalm: *Psalm 29.2,4-6,11-13*

The psalm is a personal thanksgiving for recovery after an illness during which the writer nearly died. Listen for the words: "Lord, you have raised my soul from the dead". Not to be taken literally, the words mean that God rescued him as he was going down to Sheol. He calls on others who love God to join him in his overflowing joy. A true chord of life is struck in the words: "All night there are tears, but joy comes with dawn".

Second Reading: *II Corinthians 8.7,9.13-15*

We meet Paul in many roles, here as fund-raiser for the impoverished Mother-Church in Jerusalem. The scheme was being administered by Titus who was about to approach the Corinthian church. Paul therefore addressed to the Christians in Corinth words that serve as a model for such purposes. Chapters eight and nine have been called a "Philosophy of Christian Giving".

Gospel: *Mark 5.21-43*

The Gospel deals mainly with the restoration to life of a little girl of twelve. We hear again the voice of Peter on whom the occasion made so strong an impression that he remembered what Our Lord said in his native tongue, Aramaic, "Talitha kum". "Talitha" is a term of affection meaning "pet", "dear". He who claimed to be the Resurrection and the Life could also say: "Give her something to eat". The story is interrupted by the account of the healing of the woman with the hemorrhage. An eminent scholar ascribes the cure to "faith energized by the personality of Jesus".

---

[1] See Notes, Thirty-Second Sunday in Ordinary Time, Year A.

[2] See the end of the First Reading and the Notes, Tenth Sunday in Ordinary Time, Year B.

First Reading: *Ezekiel 2.2-5*
The reading tells of Ezekiel's call to the role of prophet. The time
is 592 B.C. Though the Jews were bonded to Nebuchadnezzar,
King of Babylon, some were playing dangerous political games
with Egypt. Social and religious life was at an all time low.
Against this background, Ezekiel was called to prophesy, that is
to preach to his people. He is not required to get results, only to
deliver the word of God. The title "son of man", used very often
by Ezekiel, means no more than "man" and is not to be confused
with the same phrase in the Gospels.

Responsorial Psalm: *Psalm 122*
This psalm is one of the Songs of Ascent[1]. In this case the pilgrims
are from abroad where they have experienced, as Jews often did,
the spite of those about them. The third stanza clearly points in
this direction. The first two stanzas reflect the joyful devotion
with which the pilgrims are returning to their native Jerusalem.

Second Reading: *I I Corinthians 12.7-10*
The readings from *I I Corinthians* conclude with a well known
passage in which there is mention of Paul's thorn in the flesh. It
follows, almost as the other side of a coin, a passage in which
Paul has been singing his own praises (Chapter 11). The nature
of the "thorn" has given rise to much speculation, both ancient
and modern; that it was physical, acute ophthalmia, epilepsy etc.
seems the general, but by no means universal view. Thoughts
naturally turn to *Galatians 6.17*. More important than the nature
of the thorn is the way Paul turns it to the glory of God.

Gospel: *Mark 6.1-6*
Jesus was by now well known and on returning to Nazareth, was
invited to take part in the synagogue service. His manifest power
and authority aroused envy and spite. Even his own could not
accept him. Who were his brothers, his sisters? In the Greek
version of the Old Testament, *Genesis 13.8* and elsewhere
"kinsman" is the meaning of the word usually translated
"brother".

---

[1] See Notes, First Sunday in Advent, Year A.

First Reading: *Amos 7.12-15*

Amos, who lived in the middle of the eighth century B.C., was the first of the canonical prophets and came from the land, with no prophetic training or experience. His voice was loud in condemnation of social evils[1] and when ordered from Bethel, the national sanctuary with its religious leaders, he fearlessly stood his ground, for God had called him to speak out; he would not be silenced.

Responsorial Psalm: *Psalm 84.9-14*[2]

Having spoken of past mercies and the needs of the present, the psalmist delivers a prophetic message which forms the part of the psalm in our Missals. A state of righteousness, peace and happiness is depicted in the land. Prophetically he sees a reign of God on earth with its attendant prosperity, a line which the Hebrew mind cannot escape.

Second Reading: *Ephesians 1.3-14*

Paul's *Letter to the Ephesians*[3] which will be read on successive Sundays, was probably a circular letter written to churches in Asia Minor. Along with *Colossians*, it has its own distinctive structure; the first part is doctrinal while the latter portion consists of practical applications. In the section before us, one of Paul's noblest utterances, there is set out God's plan for us in Christ.

Gospel: *Mark 6.7-13*

The disciples had already responded to the Lord's first call, "Come". Now they must "Go", as the second phase of their ministry. All the instructions suggest the urgency of the time, for the Kingdom was at hand. They must take what comes when it comes; they must travel light; through a ministry of healing, minds would become receptive of the new sense of values which is the essence of repentance. The world must see that personal convenience is not part of the missionary's equipment. Indeed it was the Lord's charge to the Twelve that won S.Francis of Assisi to accept "Lady Poverty".

---

[1] See Reading and Notes, Twenty-sixth Sunday in Ordinary Time, Year C.

[2] See Reading and Notes, Nineteenth Sunday in Ordinary Time, Year A.

[3] See Notes Second Sunday after Christmas.

First Reading: *Jeremiah 23.1-6*
The Jewish nation (or Judah, which was all that was left of it)
was increasingly being lured into intrigue with Egypt, whereas in
fact the country was vassal to Babylon. The setting is about 600
B.C. Moreover the social and moral fibre of the country was
rotten. The reading looks out over this scene; the leaders who are
called shepherds will be removed; God will regather his people
under a real king in place of the weak rulers of Jeremiah's day.
The latter part of the reading is clearly Messianic.

Responsorial Psalm: *Psalm 22.*
The Shepherd psalm is unique in the Psalter and probably the
best known. Into his image of the good shepherd, the writer,
traditionally said to be David, projects all the qualities of the
keeper of sheep on the hill side. What more could he do for his
charges than is set out in the first two stanzas? Then the picture
changes to a banquet where God is the host. The psalm ends with
a feeling of security prompted by the divine Shepherd. All we
like sheep have gone astray and we find in this psalm the Great
Shepherd who gently leads the lost back to the fold.

Second Reading: *Ephesians 2.13-18*
With unity as the theme of the letter, Paul deals with the
reconciliation of Jew and pagan in Christ to form a "single new
man". "The barrier" refers to the fence which marked the limit
to which pagans might go in the Temple. Look for the references
to the two that are to be brought together; they include "you
who were far away" (the pagans) and "those who were near at
hand" (Jews).

Gospel: *Mark 6.30-34*
None of the Evangelists records any comment by Jesus on what
the disciples had done during their mission (See Gospel last
Sunday). He was more concerned that their spiritual resources
had been depleted and that a retreat was necessary. But it was not
to be. The crowds gathered and because he saw them as sheep
without a shepherd, their needs came first and with great
compassion he ministered to them with extensive teaching.

First Reading: *I I Kings 4.42-44*

Before the canonical prophets, those whose utterances are on record, there was from the days of Samuel a Prophetic Order[1]. Elisha belonged to these men of God. The practice of making an offering to the prophets is attested in *I Samuel 9.7.* In any case, there was an obligation to bring the first fruits to the Lord. The food both in this miracle and its parallel in the Gospel for today had a sacramental quality, touched in one case by a man of God, and in the other, by the Son of God.

Responsorial Psalm: *Psalm 144.10-11,15-18*

Rendered as a solo before the congregation, this psalm has been described as "one of the most inspiring in the Psalter". Its author must have had a deep experience of God. It is the last of the alphabetical or acrostic psalms — it should be seen in the *Jerusalem Bible* — in which each verse begins with a succeeding letter of the Hebrew alphabet. First God is praised for his beneficent rule; in the second stanza the psalmist sees God's rule as universal and the dependence of all people on him. The psalm closes with a declaration of God's justice and loving kindness.

Second Reading: *Ephesians 4.1-6*

Passing from his doctrinal teaching on the unity of all things in Christ, Paul comes to the practical application. From prison he implores his readers to preserve the unity of the Spirit. The virtues that must be practised to achieve this end, are set down. The reading closes with the doctrinal basis for unity, one faith, one baptism, one God.

Gospel: *John 6.1-15*

For this and the next five Sundays attention moves to *John* with its teaching on the Eucharist. The miracle of Feeding the Five Thousand is the only one recorded in all our four Gospels. In this graphic account with its touches of realism and colour — the extensive area of grass where they all sat down — we observe Andrew's bewilderment and the Lord's complete control, the use of the apparently insignificant to serve a tremendous purpose and the surplus that went beyond all needs. So lavish is the divine economy.

---

[1] See Notes, Second Sunday in Ordinary Time, Year B.

First Reading: *Exodus 16.2-4,12-15*

A month out into the desert, the novelty of their journey had
worn off and the Israelites began to grumble. Complaints are
often irrational; what they ate in Egypt can hardly be as they
claimed. No despite is done to the story of the manna by seeking
to explain it — and much has been written — by describing it as a
sweet deposit left on tamarisk bushes or as a kind of lichen. It is
characteristic of God's working to have provided for his people
from the natural resources of the desert.

Responsorial Psalm: *Psalm 77.3-4,23-25,54*

This long psalm of over seventy verses raises issues that cannot
even be mentioned here. In the first stanza the teaching is very
clear that future generations will profit from the past. Then in
the next two stanzas, that part of the journey in the wilderness
that is relevant to the First Reading is told. Outside the portion
in the Missal, the psalmist comments: "Despite all this, they
went on sinning".

Second Reading: *Ephesians 4.17,20-24*

For this Sunday and another three the practical applications of
Ephesians Chs. 1-3 continue. Faith in Christ imposes a new order
that will mark the readers off from the aimless life of the pagan
world. Paul describes this new order with a metaphor of which he
is very fond, the taking off of a garment and the putting on of
another, in this instance nothing less than the removal of the old
self.

Gospel: *John 6.24-35*

Between the end of this reading and Ch. 15. 1 are the seven great
"I am" declarations of Jesus regarding his identity. It is worth
searching them out and meditating on them. The passage opens
with a warning that to follow Jesus only for material benefit will
result in blessing being lost. When Our Lord refers to the Bread
of Life, we are drawn into the very heart of Catholic worship, the
celebration of the Eucharist in the Mass. So simply stated, it has
a depth we never really plumb.

First Reading: *I Kings 19.4-8*
Ahab, king of Israel, married Jezebel, a Phoenician woman who introduced worship of Baal into the country. This led to the well known contest on Mount Carmel and the defeat of the prophets of Baal. Jezebel vowed to be avenged with Elijah's death and so he fled into the wilderness only to find how God provides for his own, this time with a cake baked on hot stones in the ashes and with a jar of water. Thus provided, he travelled on to reach God's holy mountain.

Responsorial Psalm: *Psalm 33.2-9*
The psalm is intensely personal; "I", "my" and "me" are prominent in the first two stanzas. The writer's profound belief in God seems to be based on some deliverance. In and through his faith is woven another thread, a desire that others should share in his joyful experience of God. Taste and sight, faculties of daily living, become means of spiritual perception.

Second Reading: *Ephesians 4.30-5.2*
The letter began on heights almost beyond our view; here Paul comes down to the commonest practicalities of every day, our shortcomings and failures, grudges, bad temper, anger etc. They are all contrary to the spirit of unity which Paul is enjoining on his readers. Imitation of Christ is the way to combat these frailties.

Gospel: *John 6.41-51*
Continuing to expound on the subject of the Bread of Life, Our Lord adopts the policy that attack is the best method of defence for when under criticism about what he had already said (See the Gospel for last Sunday) he carried his teaching still further. Not only are he and spiritual bread one; he now asserts that he will raise up at the last day those whom God has committed to him and only thus can men and women come to Christ.

TWENTIETH SUNDAY IN ORDINARY TIME
YEAR B

First Reading: *Proverbs 9.1-6*
Wisdom is very much more than the quality of being wise. She
(so designated in Hebrew), is the first of God's creation, a flowing
forth from him[1]. The concept belongs to the period after the
exile. *Proverbs* Ch. 8 is full of enlightenment. In the reading,
Wisdom is represented as a lady with a luxurious house where she
has prepared a banquet for her guests. The foolish are specially
invited so that they may become wise.

Responsorial Psalm: *Psalm 33.2-3,10-15*
Different verses of this psalm were used last Sunday. In the
portion before us, the psalmist becomes a teacher passing on to
others whom he affectionately calls "children", what fear of God
involves and how it brings long life and prosperity, a nexus that
is strong in the psalms. The last stanza echoes the Second Reading
of last Sunday.

Second Reading: *Ephesians 5.15-20*
Paul continues his practical application of the earlier teaching on
unity and here deals with matters of conduct vital to Christians.
Two thoughts stand out: "Your lives should redeem it" is a very
difficult sentence which "commentators ancient and modern
have wrestled with". If this translation is correct, it could denote
purchase from a slave market. Or the words could mean "making
the most of the time", The reference to hymns reminds us of the
lost treasures of the early Church. These notes draw attention,
whenever possible, to hymns that are embedded in the *New
Testament*[2].

Gospel: *John 6.51-58*
Simple words and simple writing express some of Our Lord's
most profound teaching. How we receive him into ourselves in
the sacred mystery of the Mass is set out. It can be appreciated
how difficult then (*Leviticus 17.14*) and now it must be for
non-believers to accept this doctrine. The use of "flesh" rather
than "body" is seen as being due to a desire to emphasise Our
Lord's humanity.

---

[1] See Notes Thirty-third Sunday in Ordinary Time, Year A.
[2] See Notes Second Reading, Fourth Sunday in Lent, Year A and
Twenty-sixth Sunday in Ordinary Time, Year A.

First Reading: *Joshua 24.1-2,15-18*
The *Book of Joshua* deals with the conquest of the Promised
Land and its division between the tribes of Israel. Final addresses
follow and before us is the ratification of the Covenant between
God and Israel by a definite choice on the part of the people.

Responsorial Psalm: *Psalm 33.2-3,16-23*
We have a situation unique in the Missal; the same psalm has been
used in different portions on three successive Sundays. The first
four stanzas contain statements that do not always accord with
the inescapable facts of life, for the psalmist overstresses the
deliverance of the good and the destruction of the wicked. While
the psalmist concedes that the good do suffer, their ultimate
triumph is not always a fact, at least not in this life. The writer's
faith in the justice of God is unshakable.

Second Reading: *Ephesians 5.21-32*
Paul's practical applications continue and are now directed to
the relationship between husbands and wives. The indivisibility
of man and woman in marriage is affirmed and related to Christ
and the Church. Against the background of the times, Paul was
imposing a new image on marriage. In the middle of the passage
there is a clear reference to baptism; "with a form of words"
strongly suggests the recitation of a baptismal formula at the time
of the sacrament.

Gospel: *John 6.60-69*
Our Lord's teaching on the subject of the Eucharist caused a split
among his followers, with the Twelve, now more strongly bonded
to him, standing firm. If only those who turned away from him
had heard, when he went on to refer to his Ascension, that the
eating of his flesh was not meant to be physical, the scene might
have been different. As it was then, so always, people harden
their hearts and turn away from God's salvation.

First Reading: *Deuteronomy 4.1-2,6-8*
Deuteronomy begins with a statement of the mighty acts of God, performed for the good of his people. The reading comes near the end of the first of three addresses given by Moses: Israel must adhere strictly to the laws given by God; if obeyed, they will place Israel above all other peoples in the land they were about to enter, the Promised Land. The instruction to add nothing to the Law has special pertinence in the Gospel for the day.

Responsorial Psalm: *Psalm 14.2-5*
The first line of the psalm (omitted in the Missal), "God, who has the right to enter your tent?", explains all. Pilgrims asked this question and a priest gave them this psalm for an answer. There is emphasised throughout a strong link between religion and conduct. In the last stanza we are reminded that Jews were forbidden to lend to each other at interest *(Leviticus 25.36)*; it amounted to profiting from another's distress.

Second Reading: *James 1.17-18,21-22,27*
This is the first of five readings from the *Letter of James* which may possibly have been the first part of the *New Testament* to be written. Variously assessed as a "string of pearls" and a "bundle of straw" (Luther), its rapidly changing themes could suggest topics on which advice had been sought. The reading has three main thoughts: we are the children of the unchanging God who is the source of all light, sun, moon and stars; as in the First Reading there is an injunction to accept God's saving word; the reading concludes with a definition of pure religion.

Gospel: *Mark 7.1-8,14-15,21-23*
Jesus' disciples, by their failure to conform to the minute regulations of the Pharisees attracted critical attention. The reading cites many examples of Oral Tradition, the additions to the Law forbidden in the First Reading. With trenchant penetration, Our Lord gives a list of ways in which the keepers of the Law do in fact break it. The quotation is from *Isaiah 29.13* in which the prophet attacks the attitude of his countrymen in the days before the exile.

First Reading: *Isaiah 35.4-7*
Isaiah, setting aside the gloom and fear of the current political situation, looks to a Golden Age when God's salvation will transform everything. There are two main thoughts in the reading, the second in two parts: first, there is a call to courage; "vengeance" in Hebrew suggests God's act of vindication, i.e, salvation; life's wounded ones will be healed and the deprived places of nature will blossom. Thus Isaiah encourages his people in difficult days.

Responsorial Psalm: *Psalm 145.7-10*
This is the first of the Alleluia psalms, so called because they begin and end with Alleluia. The thought in the portion before us echoes the First Reading. The psalmist repeatedly places "The Lord" at the beginning of its sentence, a position more emphatic than in English. The psalm is full of hope for the deprived; their God rules for ever. The psalm was used each morning in the services of the synagogue.

Second Reading: *James 2.1-5*
From thoughts of pure religion and the underprivileged the writer turns to the need to show equal respect to all. One feels that the abuses under attack were actual occurrences known to the writer. The last paragraph is a reminder that possession of this world's wealth is no indication of the depth of a person's faith. It was the lower classes in society that from the beginning were attracted to the Christian way of life.

Gospel: *Mark 7.31-37*
The healing of the deaf mute, which is recorded only in *Mark*, shows Our Lord's compassion reaching out to a pagan. The vivid description of the incident is in keeping with Mark's narrative skill. We observe also that Our Lord spoke his own native Aramaic, for to this language the word "Ephphatha" belongs. Finally, as noted before, the injunction to keep silent about the cure was to avoid giving a false impression of his mission.

First Reading: *Isaiah 50.5-9*

In *Second* or *Deutero-Isaiah* there are four Songs of the Suffering Servant and here we have the third. In the first stanza the Servant is wholly submissive to the wickedness of his tormentors. The scene then changes to a court room in which the Servant is supported by God. There has been interminable discussion regarding the identity of the Servant whom many have seen as Christ. The prophet is delivering a message of comfort to the Jews exiled in Babylon.

Responsorial Psalm: *Psalm 114.1-6,8-9*[1]

This is one of the psalms traditionally sung while Passover lambs were being slain, and possibly used by Our Lord and his disciples after the Last Supper. The psalmist describes in vivid terms the seriousness of an illness from which, by the goodness of God, he was restored to health. The psalm was one of the Hallel or Hymns of Praise (113-118 in the *Jerusalem Bible*) used at various great festivals.

Second Reading: *James 2.14-18*

This well known passage has attracted a lot of comment, some of it not always accurate. Paul declared that "salvation is by faith alone"; James asserts that faith without works is dead. There is no conflict in these two statements. They are in fact complementary. It could well be that this was one of those topics presented to the author for a ruling.

Gospel: *Mark 8.27-35*

Clearly there had been intense speculation about Our Lord's identity. Aware of this, he brings the matter before his disciples. Peter's reply "You are the Christ" indicates the progress of the Master's teaching. Now for the first time Jesus spoke of his Passion, but to Peter the idea of a suffering Christ was intolerable and so he was sternly rebuked. Greek can often express in the very form of a word what it takes a whole sentence in English to convey. There is an example of this when Our Lord goes on to define the nature of discipleship. Self denial and taking up one's cross are single, once and for all actions; following him, on the other hand, goes on and on.

---

[1] Number 116 in the *Jerusalem Bible*

First Reading: *Wisdom 2.12,17-20*[1]

The first part of the *Book of Wisdom* contrasts the destinies of virtuous and godless men. In Chapter 2 the philosophy of the latter is stated and as part of it, the First Reading brings out the hostility of evil men to the good whom they see as obstructing their way of life. They unashamedly seek their death.

Responsorial Psalm: *Psalm 53.3-6,8*

The psalmist is in great distress which could have been the sort of situation provided by the persecution of godless men mentioned in the First Reading. He does not doubt that God's help will come; "name" in stanza one is more evocative than the English word, for it denotes the whole personality, character and power of God. The psalmist, almost on a *quid pro quo* basis, offers to sacrifice in return for help.

Second Reading: *James 3.16-4.3*

This passage is a remarkable reiteration of the First Reading. Clearly, the "wisdom that comes down from above" is the wisdom that *Old Testament* writers have described in various First Readings. These virtues are now seen through Christian eyes. The passage before us could be summed up as kindness, love and consideration set over against greed in all its manifestations.

Gospel: *Mark 9.30-37*

The reading opens with a reference to "leaving the mountain". This is none other than the Mount of Transfiguration. They had come down onto the plain, back to the realities of life. The passage contains the second and more specific reference to Our Lord's Passion. Yet even now the disciples were squabbling over precedence, and Our Lord took a little child to explain what so far seemed to have eluded them. There is a tradition that this child grew up to become Ignatius, famous bishop and martyr whom we remember on October 17th.

---

[1] See Notes Thirty-second Sunday in Ordinary Time, Year A.

First Reading: *Numbers 11.25-29*
Much of the *Book of Numbers* is devoted to the wanderings of
the Israelites in the wilderness. In fact the Hebrew title is "In
the Wilderness". The grumbling of the people filled Moses with
despair and he complained to God that his burden was too great.
To this God replied with the instruction to gather seventy elders.
The reading tells how the Spirit was given them for their work of
helping Moses. Their prophesying was not foretelling the future,
but acting in the Spirit as the early prophets had done. The
concluding reference to Eldad and Medad is reminiscent of Our
Lord's remark: "Anyone who is not against us is for us" (*Mark 9.
40).*

Responsorial Psalm: *Psalm 18.8,10,12-14*
This psalm which is almost certainly two psalms joined together —
even the metre of the two parts is different — begins with a
wondering look at the nightly sky and ends with the psalmist's
delight in observing the Law. It is the latter portion of the psalm
that will be read. We turn from the grandeur of the heavens
that make us feel insignificant to the moral law which lifts man
to his highest dignity.

Second Reading: *James 5.1-6*
In this, the last look at the *Letter of James*, there is a scathing
condemnation of the oppressive rich. It is generally agreed that
the writer here has in mind men of trade and business who were
outside the Church. The passage suggests the utterances of the
pre-exilic prophets, especially Amos. James stresses the
corrupting power of wealth and a retribution to come. Again it is
felt that the writer knows at first hand the things of which he
speaks.

Gospel: *Mark 9.38-43,45,47-48*
Our thoughts go back to the latter part of the First Reading.
There is a call for toleration in Christian work. From acts in
which others are hurt Our Lord turns to the injuring of ourselves
and brings home his point with three examples of Semitic
exaggeration, a device often used to enforce a point with almost
frightening effect. The "hell" mentioned near the end is Gehenna,
the ever burning rubbish dump outside Jerusalem, a symbol of
utter destruction.

First Reading: *Genesis 2.18-24*

Man found no companionship in the created order, and according to this very ancient element in *Genesis,* God created woman. There is the same play on the words man and woman in Hebrew as in English. Made from one, they were destined to become one in marriage. Two special thoughts come to mind: the *Jerusalem Bible* brings out fully the nature of woman's creation; the rib was built, not just made, into a woman; there is a note of ecstasy in the man's cry when he saw her, a cry that is not easy to put into a translation.

Responsorial Psalm: *Psalm 127*

This is one of the Songs of Ascent or Gradual Psalms (120-134), sung by pilgrims ascending Zion's hill as they returned for one of the great festivals. It sings the blessedness of the God-fearing man in his family life; he will have enough to provide for his own; his wife will bear him children and they shall be like shoots of the spreading, evergreen olive (*Jeremiah 11.16*). A benediction brings the psalm to its conclusion.

Second Reading: *Hebrews 2.9-11*

Hebrews will provide the Second Readings for the remaining Sundays in Ordinary Time this year. Centuries of speculation have failed to provide a convincing solution to the authorship of *Hebrews*. We cannot be certain where, to whom or when the letter was written. The letter asserts the unique nature of Christ, though in the passage before us his brief inferiority to angels during his earthly life is stated. Then the writer declares that Christ took our nature, was perfected through suffering and so was able to call us brothers.

Gospel: *Mark 10.2-16*

Our Lord is quite uncompromising in the matter of divorce. Jewish law allowed a man to divorce his wife, but the reverse was not permitted. Jesus is therefore protecting defenceless women against a situation that could be very cruel as opinions differed regarding permissible grounds for divorce. Our Lord stands firm on the indivisibility of one flesh. The Gospel concludes with another example of a child used as teaching regarding the Kingdom.

First Reading: *Wisdom 7.7—11*
In the second part of the *Book of Wisdom*[1] , Wisdom speaks,
setting forth her virtues and what she confers on those who seek
her. In Chapter 7, Solomon, proverbial for his wisdom, appears
and declares that he was born as an ordinary man. Then in the
First Reading he tells how he prayed for Wisdom and how he
valued her above all treasures.

Responsorial Psalm: *Psalm 89.12—17*
A wistful note runs through this psalm. God is eternal; man's
life is a fleeting thing; his sin is the cause of God's anger. The
reading opens with a plea for Wisdom so that we may be aware of
God's anger and realise how short life is. Various petitions are
directed to God's favour and success is sought for "the work of
our hands", a connection noted previously.

Second Reading: *Hebrews 4.12—13*
The writer has already indicated that because of disobedience, the
Israelites, who were led from Egypt, found no rest; but God has
provided a rest for his own through Christ. The reading sounds a
warning to those who may wrongly seek to enter this rest. We
cannot deceive God; his word has a penetrating and discerning
power and false claims to enter his rest will be recognised.

Gospel: *Mark 10.17—30*
The reading contains three elements: the story of the rich young
man speaks of wealth that must be surrendered because it was an
obstacle to spiritual development; in the second section, futile
and unnecessary attempts have been made to explain the "eye of
the needle", an example of Semitic exaggeration to enforce a
point; in the last section Peter is told the cost and the rewards
of discipleship.

---

[1] For the first part, see the Twenty-fifth Sunday in Ordinary
Time Year B and the Notes.

First Reading: *Isaiah 53.10-11*

As noted elsewhere, *Second* or *Deutero-Isaiah* contains four Songs of the Suffering Servant, and before us now is portion of the last of these. Set against the time of exile in Babylon, the Servant appears first humiliated and suffering and then triumphant. Who was the Suffering Servant? An individual? Israel? A faithful remnant? The Church has found the full expression of the Servant in Christ.

Responsorial Psalm: *Psalm 32.4-5,18-20,22*

The psalm appears seven times in the Missal in various forms. The first line in the full text contains the key-note: "Shout for Joy", a ringing cry of joy probably for some deliverance. The three stanzas before us give some of the reasons for the joyful outburst: God's moral qualities embrace the noblest that man can imagine; in the second stanza his care of his own is stated; finally the psalmist can look to God's protection in the future with confidence.

Second Reading: *Hebrews 4.14-16*

In his theme of Christ, greater than all the *Old Testament* offered, the writer declares that Jesus is superior to the Levitical high priests because in his triumph he has not only passed into the Holy of Holies, but into the very presence of God. He was tempted (and tested, for the Greek has both meanings) in every way, yet sinless, and can therefore come to our help. So we are able to approach him with confidence. There are good reasons for thinking that the letter was written to Christians undergoing persecution.

Gospel: *Mark 10.35-45*

James and John, Sons of Thunder, impetuous and, it seems, impervious to Our Lord's teaching, make an impossible request for precedence. The reply reverses the world's standards in matters of priority. There are references in the *Old Testament* to the cup of suffering, e.g. *Psalm 75.8.* One senses in the reference to the cup, the lengthening shadow of the Cross.

First Reading: *Jeremiah 31.7-9*

Scholars have difficulty in giving this passage an historical
setting which accords with the times of Jeremiah. What matters
to us is that here we have an ingathering of God's people and a
promise of his comfort which is eternal. The passage shows the
range of God's concern. Blind people, the lame and the pregnant
are not ones who usually make journeys, but they will be part of
this great return to God.

Responsorial Psalm: *Psalm 125*

This is one of the fifteen Songs of Ascent sung by pilgrims on
their way up to Jerusalem for the great festivals. The first two
stanzas reflect the anticipated joy of return from Babylon to
Jerusalem; even the pagan nations marvelled, but like a dream
there was unreality in it. This is apparent in the last two stanzas
which refer to the many difficulties which faced them on their
return, but hope breaks through this second barrier.

Second Reading: *Hebrews 5.1-6*

Christ is our High Priest. The superiority of his Priesthood to the
Levitical holders of that office is developed in the reading around
the appointment and compassion of the priest. The sinlessness
of Christ is, by implication, contrasted with the earthly high
priest who has to offer sacrifice for his own sins. For
Melchizedek, see *Genesis 14.18* [1].

Gospel: *Mark 10.46-52*

All three Synoptic Gospels record this miracle, but with minor
differences. For all his physical blindness, Bartimaeus had
great perception: he knew who Jesus was and addressed him as
"Son of David"; his persistence suggests that somehow he sensed
that this was his only chance to meet Jesus. In addressing Jesus
as "Son of David" he recognised him as Messiah. Jesus did not
disallow the title. It is not coincidental that in the next chapter
Mark records the triumphal entry into Jerusalem.

---

[1] See also Body and Blood of Christ, Year C.

First Reading: *Deuteronomy 6.2-6*
The Israelites were on the east side of the Jordan and about to enter the Promised Land. Moses had given the Ten Commandments to the people and in the reading are recorded the principles on which the Commandments had been put together: Israel must show reverence for God's laws and observe them; in return there will be rewards and blessings; love for God — "love" in Hebrew ranges as widely in meaning as in English — is solemnly enjoyed. The idea of milk and honey as representing the choicest of food and drink probably came from the desert Bedouins.

Responsorial Psalm: *Psalm 17.2-4,47,51*
This psalm is almost identical with a psalm found in *II Samuel 22*, written to celebrate David's deliverance from "all his enemies and from the hands of Saul". It was probably used by other kings of David's line to celebrate their victories. In the first stanza the writer refers to several ways, mostly defensive, in which God has protected him and in the last stanza there is a repetition of some of these ideas. The psalm, as before us, can well serve as a personal thanksgiving.

Second Reading: *Hebrews 7.23-28*
The unknown writer of the *Letter to the Hebrews* continues the theme of the last Second Reading. The Levitical priesthood was not permanent in its personnel as death constantly intervened. Christ, our High Priest is eternal. The moral qualities of our High Priest are then stated and are set over against those of the Levitical order. Christ's supreme purpose, as seen by the writer, is to reconcile man to God.

Gospel: *Mark 12.28-34*
The scene has now moved inside the sacred city which Our Lord will leave finally for his crucifixion. Much is recorded of what he taught in this brief period. Its diverse nature may be found in *Mark Chs 11-13*. In this reading, we note three points: the "commandments" may denote the "Ten" or may include the mass of Pharisaic additions. The Greek here for "love" is the word of special Christian usage, denoting love as an exercise of the mind and the spirit. Finally, the reference to the First Reading is obvious; every pious Jew recited three times daily the "Listen, Israel". It was called the "Shema" for that is the first Hebrew word in the quotation.

First Reading: *I Kings 17.10-16*

The *Books of Kings* trace the history of Israel and Judah from the accession of Solomon to the fall of Jerusalem in 598 B.C. The narrative is often dull, but is enlivened by the appearance of Elijah, one of the greatest Hebrew prophets. Having warned King Ahab of an impending drought, an expression of God's anger, Elijah left for the Wadi Cherith where ravens fed him. Then he lodged with the widow in Phoenicia. The reading begins with a picture of abject misery in drought-stricken country and ends on the note of God's providence and the widow's reward.

Responsorial Psalm: *Psalm 145.7-10*

This is part of an Alleluia psalm, those which begin and end with Alleluia. After decrying the value of trusting in people, especially in high places, the psalmist praises God who makes the socially deprived his special care and concern. God's rule, unlike an earthly king's, is for ever. In Hebrew the verb is usually placed at the beginning of a sentence. Five times in this psalm "The Lord" occupies that position of special emphasis.

Second Reading: *Hebrews 9.24-28*

In this reading everything revolves around the thought that Christ made only one offering of himself. The high priest entered the sanctuary once a year; Christ made one sacrifice because to have sacrificed himself more than once would have meant that each sacrifice was less than perfect. To die more than once is contrary to nature. The writer passes from the false idea of Christ's dying a second time to his Second Coming.

Gospel: *Mark 12.38-44*

Our Lord often turned social values upside down and nowhere more forcefully than in this reading. The ostentation of the religious leaders is set in stark contrast with the devout humility of the poor widow who gave her all. The treasury consisted of thirteen trumpet shaped metal receptacles into which the rich could throw their coins — there was no paper money — with an attracting rattle. The widow's offering was made with the smallest of Roman coins. The true value of a gift can be measured only in the cost to the donor.

First Reading: *Daniel 12.1-3*
Like the *Book of Jonah* [1], *Daniel* is set back in the past. It was, however, written about 165 B.C. during times of terrible persecution under the rule of Antiochus 1V. The *First Book of the Maccabees* deals with this period. In the reading there is a warning of a fearful time that is coming. But Michael, the patron angel of the people, will be present. The writer sees a resurrection to rewards and punishments.

Responsorial Psalm: *Psalm 15.5,8-11*
The writer lives near to his God and finds joy in his oneness with him. First, he states what is almost a creed; then comes confidence that he will be spared untimely death, for contemporary ideas of the hereafter were undeveloped and offered little consolation. Finally, the psalmist sees himself enjoying a life guided by the hand of God. In the first stanza, "portion" is almost a technical term, for it means the allotment made to a tribe in the Promised Land.

Second Reading: *Hebrews 10.11-14,18*
The writer of the *Letter to the Hebrews* concentrates in this reading on the uniqueness of Christ's sacrifice. It is a single event, unlike the sacrifices of the high priests, which one older commentary likens to the endless additions of zero to zero with nought as the end result. Christ waits at God's right hand until the Second Coming when his foes will be overwhelmed. The one unique offering has achieved perfection.

Gospel: *Mark 13.24-32*
Whether the violent disturbances in the form of physical phenomena are symbolic or literal is for each to decide. The language comes from the *Old Testament* Prophets (e.g. *Joel 2.28 -32*), who used such language to describe events of their time such as the fall of Babylon, *(Isaiah 13.10)*. The fig tree, so common a sight, provides the second parable (*Mark 11.13*). The last sentence is a good antidote to the nonsense of those who hawk prophecy from door to door.

---

[1] See Notes Third Sunday in Ordinary Time, Year B.

Last Sunday in Ordinary Time
OUR LORD JESUS CHRIST, UNIVERSAL KING
YEAR B

First Reading: *Daniel 7.13-14*
The first six Chapters of *Daniel* [1] are narrative; at Chapter 7 the
section on visions begins and it is in this chapter that the First
Reading is found. Chapter 7 commences with the visions of the
four beasts; the present reading then follows. In the language of
visions, supernatural beings are represented by men. The Church
has seen Christ as the fulfilment of this section of the book,
Christ whose Kingdom embraces all nations and all time.

Responsorial Psalm: *Psalm 92.1-2,5*
This psalm is one of the Enthronement Psalms that celebrate
the Kingship of God, though where they fitted into the ancient
Jewish liturgy is disputed; possibly they were associated with the
New Year festival. The thought in this short, but magnificent
poem is expressed with great simplicity; like an earthly king
gloriously apparelled, God is robed in power; he rules from
eternity for ever. The selected verses end on the note of God's
holiness.

Second Reading: *Apocalypse 1.5-8*
The Apocalypse is addressed to the Seven Churches of Asia, but
the mystic number suggests that in reality there are no
geographical boundaries to its reception. The reading begins
with an elaborate salutation which covers Our Lord's redemptive
work and ends with a kind of "Thus said the Lord", expressed
symbolically through the first and last letters of the Greek
alphabet. The salutation gathers up the Church's teaching
throughout the year about Christ. In "coming on the clouds"
there is an echo from the First Reading.

Gospel: *John 18.33-37*
Alone now with Pilate in the Governor's residence, Jesus is master
of the situation; Pilate almost seems to be the prisoner. But it is
not the trial that concerns us in this Mass, but the Kingship of
Our Lord. John allows Jesus to declare here more fully than in
the Synoptic Gospels, the nature of his Kingship, that he came
to bear witness of the truth. John's account also records that his
Kingdom does not belong to this world.

---

[1] See Notes, First Reading previous Sunday.

SUNDAY MASSES
Year C

FIRST SUNDAY OF ADVENT
YEAR C

First Reading: *Jeremiah 33.14-16*

Israel represents the northern kingdom of the Jews, Judah the southern. At the time when Jeremiah was exercising his ministry, Israel was in Assyrian hands and the situation for Judah was perilous. Deportations of Jews to Babylon had begun; the puppet king Zedekiah was on the throne in Jerusalem. Yet Jeremiah could see beyond these national disasters to a time when God, true to the Covenant, would raise up one of David's line and the city would be renamed. The Church has declared Christ to be the Son of David. The reading is part of what is known as the *Book of Consolation*.

Responsorial Psalm: *Psalm 24.4-5,8-9,10,14*

A note of deep humility runs through the psalm which reflects in the omitted verses the mind of one whose piety admits to sin and seeks forgiveness. God's mercy includes instruction of those who stray. The last stanza shows what God offers to those who seek him.

Second Reading: *I Thessalonians 3.12-4.2*

Probably the first part of the New Testament to be written, *I Thessalonians* is very much a personal letter to loved friends of whom Timothy had brought a glowing report to Paul. In the first paragraph we have Paul's prayer for the growth of his friends' character. The words "When Christ comes" are built around a noun meaning the "official visit of a king". In the second paragraph the advice to go on developing in Christ is continued.

Gospel: *Luke 21.25-28,34-36*

Jesus speaks of the end of the age and the Coming of the Son of Man. The turbulence which heralds an entirely new order is depicted in cataclysmic language found in the *Old Testament,* as in *Joel 2.20-11,31-32.* The account given in the reading of the Second Coming draws on the "traditional stock of apocalyptic ideas". Our limited minds cannot grasp the form these events will take; but this we can do: keep our spiritual sensibilities sharp and unsullied.

First Reading: *Baruch 5.1-9*
Baruch [1] was traditionally a disciple of Jeremiah and wrote for the exiles in Babylon. His message is one of hope for a people to whom everything seemed lost. There is a vital message for us, for we have in large part made ourselves exiles from God. The reading is addressed to Jerusalem: she is to put on the robes of royalty to fulfil her new status with the nations. The latter part recalls *Isaiah* 40.3-5 which is quoted in the Gospel for the Mass.

Responsorial Psalm: *Psalm 125*
This is one of the fifteen Songs of Ascent sung by pilgrims on their way up to Jerusalem for the great festivals. The first two stanzas reflects the anticipated joy of return from Babylon to Jerusalem; even the pagan nations marvelled, but like a dream, there was unreality in it. This is apparent in the last two stanzas which refer to the many difficulties which faced them on their return, but hope breaks through the last barrier.

Second Reading: *Philippians 1.3-6,8-11*
The Church at Philippi [2] had a special place in Paul's affections. Its growth in Christ and its generosity to Paul, now in prison, prompted this letter of joy in which he commends the Philippians for their part in spreading the Gospel. He is sure their spiritual development will continue. His advice on preparing to meet the Day of Christ reaches down through the ages to us.

Gospel: *Luke 3.1-6*
After an opening which elaborately fixes the date in terms the ancient world understood, Luke quotes a well known passage from *Isaiah* 40 in which God's coming to his people is likened to the progress of an oriental king before whom heralds paved the way; roads were made; valleys were filled in and hills were levelled. In the Gospel John is the herald; The King is on his way.

---

[1] See Notes Sixth Reading Easter Vigil.

[2] See Notes Twenty-fifth Sunday in Ordinary Time, Year A.

THIRD SUNDAY OF ADVENT
YEAR C

First Reading: *Zephaniah 3.14-18*

Zephaniah [1], roughly a century later than the author of *Isaiah 1-39*, had spoken severely to Jerusalem. Now he looks beyond the days of God's anger against the city and speaks comforting words to the faithful remnant. The reading is a psalm of pure joy; enemies have been repulsed; God as a victorious warrior is in the city's midst. The passage rings with the hope of Advent. This is a wonderful introduction to *gaudete* Sunday (*Gaudete in domino semper*: Rejoice in the Lord always).

Responsorial Psalm: *Isaiah 12.2-6*

The reading has been described as two small psalms sung by those who have been redeemed. It is considerably later than the part of *Isaiah* in which it has become embedded. It should be read in conjunction with the end of the preceding chapter which speaks of times of deliverance. While not being specifically Messianic, it has a Messianic quality. The reading overflows with the joy of God's salvation which is like the inexhaustible springs of water from a well.

Second Reading: *Philippians 4.4-7*

There is an unmistakable note of joy and peace in the passage before us. Paul had a very real expectation of the Lord's return, yet it was not a time for anxiety. In expressing the thought "pray..... with prayer.." the writer uses two different words, one expressing the whole aspect of prayer, the other denoting petition for needs. The reading concludes with a reference to God's peace which will guard us, will in fact be a garrison, for that is what the Greek means.

Gospel: *Luke 3.10-18*

Only Luke records the passage to be read. Many of those who came to John for baptism sensed that there was something wrong in their lives. John gave no general answer, but prescribed a different treatment for each group. Each was touched differently, where it hurt most, yet in each part of his advice there was a common factor. The reading concludes with an ancient picture of winnowing by throwing grain and chaff into the wind with a winnowing fan shaped like a shovel. John's last word is to remind his listeners that the Messiah is standing with his winnowing fan in his hand.

---

[1] See Notes, Fourth Sunday in Ordinary Time, Year A.

FOURTH SUNDAY OF ADVENT
YEAR C

First Reading: *Micah 5.1-4*
Micah belonged to the same period as the Isaiah of Chapters 1-39 and faced the same scene, but like Amos was a man of the soil with more concern than Isaiah for the poor farmer. From his more famous contemporary he drew many of his ideas. One hears *Isaiah 7.14* in this present reading which presents a prophecy of the birth of a child who will usher in a new era for the Jews. The Church has applied the prophecy to Christ.

Responsorial Psalm: *Psalm 79.2-3,15-16,18-19*
The psalm is a national lament in which God is seen as the all-powerful Shepherd and Israel as a wilting vine that has been brought from Egypt. The purpose of the psalm is a plea to God to restore the northern kingdom of Israel, now broken and dispersed. The "man you have chosen" refers to Israel. Restoration and the "man you have given your strength" point symbolically to Advent.

Second Reading: *Hebrews 10.5-10*
The theme of this letter is that the new Covenant with God through Christ is superior to the old as given by Moses. The sacrificial code of the *Old Testament* is replaced by the perfect sacrifice of Christ. The quotation is from *Psalm 40.6-8*, which differs considerably from what is found in the *Jerusalem Bible,* because the writer of *Hebrews* has used the Greek translation of the *Old Testament* which does not always accord with translations made from the Hebrew. The psalmist is saying that he will offer no more animal sacrifices, but instead will devote himself to God. The writer of *Hebrews* has applied this to Christ.

Gospel: *Luke 1.39-44*
Following the Annunciation of her Holy Motherhood, Mary heeds the angel's bidding and sets out to see Elizabeth. The passage to be read deals with the meeting of Mary and Elizabeth and in it Luke displays two of his most obvious characteristics, concern for women and the work of the Spirit. The movement of the child most beautifully tells of the nearness of Advent. The *Ave Maria*, so dear to Catholics, is scriptural with additions authorised in the twelfth and sixteenth centuries.

CHRISTMAS DAY: VIGIL MASS
See above p. 16

CHRISTMAS DAY: MIDNIGHT MASS
See above p. 17

CHRISTMAS DAY: DAWN MASS
See above p. 18

CHRISTMAS DAY: DAY MASS
See above p. 19

First Reading: *Samuel 1.20-22,24-28*

This beautiful story of a mother's dedication of her son to God sets the scene for the Mass. Weaning, which took place when the child was between two and three years old, was usually celebrated as an important occasion. In this case there was a generous sacrifice. In the Hebrew there is a play on the words "ask" and "make over", both forms of the same word. We note that the surrender of little Samuel was complete. Any mother will appreciate the depth of Hannah's devotion.

Responsorial Psalm: *Psalm 83.2-3,5-6,9-10*

The psalm is a pilgrim psalm belonging to autumn when work in the fields was over and thanks were due to God for the year's activity. The first stanza reflects the longing of those who have not had the opportunity to enjoy the Temple of God. In the second stanza the psalmist declares the blessedness of those who can share in this worship. Finally, by "your anointed" the writer means the king whose prosperity is the prosperity of his people.

Second Reading: *I John 3.1-2,21-24*

There is a sense in which we can all be part of the Holy Family by becoming children of God. We are warned that it is no easy way that lies ahead. In the second part of the reading we are told how to enjoy God's very presence. Belief in Our Lord and loving one another are conditions for God's dwelling in us through the Spirit.

Gospel: *Luke 2.41-52*

The Lord's devoted parents make the long journey to the Passover at Jerusalem. Jesus at twelve was now a man and every Jew aimed to make the journey at least once. The magnificent Temple and the huge colourful crowds would make the occasion memorable. Various attempts have been made to explain his parents' apparent lack of supervision. The most convincing is that men and women travelled in separate caravans and that the women who travelled more slowly set out ahead of the men. When they camped for the night each parent thought Jesus was with the other. The reply which Our Lord gave when he was found seems rather pert. Said with winsome gentleness it loses its precocity.

164   1 January: Octave of Christmas
       SOLEMNITY OF MARY, MOTHER OF GOD
See above p. 21

                    6 January or
       Sunday between 2 January and 8 January
             THE EPIPHANY OF THE LORD
See above p. 23

                  Sunday after 6 January
                 BAPTISM OF THE LORD
              (First Sunday in Ordinary Time)
                        YEAR C

First Reading: *Isaiah 40.1-5,9-11*
The prophet Deutero- or Second Isaiah sees an end to the
Babylonian captivity of the Jews. The reading falls into three
parts: first, it is made clear that enough is enough; the sins that
brought the people to Babylon have been atoned for. Then a
voice rings out. It is God who will bring his people back to
Jerusalem and he shall be as an eastern potentate for whose
progress hills will be levelled and valleys filled in. Finally a
messenger is bidden to go up to the vantage point of a high
place and tell of God's coming in power, yet with the tenderness
of a shepherd.

Responsorial Psalm: *Psalm 103.1-2,3-4,24-25,27-30*
In a long psalm consisting of thirty-five stanzas the writer, in beautiful Hebrew poetry, glorifies God for his work of creation. There are three other such poems in the Psalter. This one includes thoughts gathered from the creation myths of other lands. Jewish thought had no place for natural causes; God was the cause and source of everything. The only living sea known to the Jews was the Mediterranean. The last stanza recalls the divine cycle of life and death with the renewal of the earth as one of its phases.

Second Reading: *Titus 2.11-14,3.4-7*
Paul, having given Titus some advice on various matters, offers in the passage before us the doctrinal basis of his teaching, namely what God did for us in sending his Son into the world and what obligations it imposes on us. Two points may be made: the words "giving up everything that does not lead to God" look like a definite renunciation such as was made at Baptism in the early Church, and is made now at Confirmation; the "cleansing water" is another reference to the sacrament of Baptism. The mention of water and the Spirit prepare the reader for the Gospel of the Mass.

Gospel: *Luke 3.15-16,21-22*
The three Synoptic Gospels agree in likening the Spirit at Our Lord's baptism to a descending dove. A symbol of reconciliation and peace (*Genesis 8.11*), the dove frequently forms a type of the Holy Spirit. Much has been written to explain "with the Holy Spirit and fire". Two and a half centuries ago a German scholar writing in Latin said: "The Holy Spirit with which Christ baptises has a force like fire". Or is the reference to the events of Pentecost? Our Lord did not need to be baptised, but submitted to its regenerative power as the representative of sinful humanity. The heavens opened and he was given a vision of the glory beyond, a world that was his and one to which he would return.

ASH WEDNESDAY

See above p. 25

FIRST SUNDAY OF LENT
YEAR C

First Reading: *Deuteronomy 26.4-10*
The long list of laws to regulate the lives of the Israelites in the Promised Land is drawing to a close. The reading records instructions in the matter of first fruits and their presentation to God as an annual obligation of gratitude, a remembrance of rescue from Egypt and of the gift of the Promised Land. So we on this Sunday are reminded of our redemption and of our Promised Land.

Responsorial Psalm: *Psalm 90.1-2,10-15*
The Jews had a profound belief in demons and evil spirits. This psalm which has been called a "Song for Evil Encounters" was used to avert the assaults of evil spirits. First God is invoked under four different names. Then in the full version there is reference to these evil spirits in their various manifestations. Opinions vary to what extent we should recognise the existence of evil spirits. On the other hand few can deny the need for protection against evil. This is the psalm which Satan used to tempt Our Lord in the wilderness.

Second Reading: *Romans 10.8-13*
This reading is part of a statement Paul made regarding the Jews and their rejection of Christ. Having set forth the idea of divine sovereignty, he then presents the concept of human responsibility. In the exercise of this the Jews failed to realise that the period of the Law was closed and that the way of salvation for Jews and Greeks alike was through faith in Christ and his Resurrection.

Gospel: *Luke 4.1-13*

There are frequent references in the *Old Testament* to "forty", the period of the flood, giving of the law, time in the wilderness and now to Our Lord's temptation or testing. All his replies to Satan are quotations from *Deuteronomy*. The reason for this is apparent in the first temptation, for *Deuteronomy 9.9* records how Moses stayed forty days and nights on the mountain without food. The first temptation was an endeavor to persuade Our Lord to be diverted from the role of Suffering Servant and to win followers by supplying their physical needs, to be, as some one has said, a "bread king". In the second temptation a political messiahship is offered. The third temptation was designed to put God to the test. Perfect trust calls for absolute obedience. The Tempter's aim was to break the intimate bond between Father and Son.

First Reading: *Genesis 15.5-12,15-18*

Abraham's misgivings about God's promise of descendants who would number more than the stars are finally overcome. For Abraham it became an act of faith and as a result God counted him as righteous. But Abraham was not satisfied; he wanted God's promise in the form of a covenant, the making of which is described in the reading. God passed through the halves of a divided carcase, his presence indicated by the mingling of smoke and fire while Abraham was deep in supernatural sleep. The ancient ritual of making (literally cutting) a covenant bound the parties in a death compact.

Responsorial Psalm: *Psalm 26.1,7-9,13-14*

The psalm is in reality two psalms, each very different from the other. The extent of this difference is best seen in the full version. In the first part we have a picture of faith that cannot be shaken, for the psalmist has been through great trial. In the second part the writer is in deep despair with dangers all about. But withal, he does not waver. There is radiance in stanza one; a cloud passes in the next two stanzas and then in the last the light returns.

Second Reading: *Philippians 3.17-4.1*

Here is a glimpse of mysteries beyond this world of ours, with the changing of the outward form of our lowly bodies to share the form of Our Lord's glorious body. It is idle to speculate beyond what Paul tells us, but two thoughts will help: Paul clearly does not think that the eternal state involves a separation of body and soul; again, when Our Lord appeared to Thomas after the Resurrection, it was not a disembodied spirit that the disciples saw (*John 20.24-29*). The phrase "into copies of his glorious body" could also be translated "to share the essentials of his glorious body". In a way beyond our comprehension, we will be transfigured, clad in the splendour of another world, no longer a body of decay and death.

Gospel: *Luke 9.28-36*

The Transfiguration, with its glimpse of the world from which Our Lord had come and to which he was going to return, marks the beginning of the Passion. Earlier he had told of his coming death. The Transfiguration confirmed him in his intention as it also confirmed the doubting disciples (*Matthew 16.21*). The unique experience of the Transfiguration would also predispose his disciples to listen to his less palatable utterances. The presence of Moses and Elijah showed that Jesus was the embodiment, purpose and fulfilment of the Law and the Prophets. Only Luke refers to his "passing", his "exodos". His death was to be an even greater exodus for all who believed, an exodus from bondage.

First Reading: *Exodus 3.1-8,13-15*
The story of Moses and the burning bush is one of several in the *Bible* that tell of God breaking into history, in this instance, to rescue from oppression the people he had chosen to be his revelation to the world. God calls himself "I am who I am". This unusual phrase implies that God cannot be explained by anything other than himself. The Lenten message of deliverance comes through clearly.

Responsorial Psalm: *Psalm 102.1-4,6-8,11*
This long psalm is frequently used in the Missal in different [1] forms; it is of unsurpassed beauty and represents a personal outpouring in song. The blessings of God are many; he forgives, heals and redeems. He cares for the oppressed; he is rich in compassion and love. The psalm deserves to be read and reread.

Second Reading: *1 Corinthians 10.1-6,10-12*
This is a very difficult passage. Paul has in mind the disorders and irregularities in the Corinthian church regarding the Eucharist. Turning to the *Old Testament* he refers to the crossing of the Red Sea, the manna and the water that gushed at Horeb, thus reading spiritual meaning into the wilderness experience. The omitted verses tell of those who died and why. Paul's point is that the good and the evil alike shared in God's desert mercies. The warning is there for the people of Corinth lest they be guilty of the Body and Blood of Christ.

Gospel: *Luke 13.1-9*
In this passage, found only in *Luke*, Our Lord dispels the idea that great disasters are a punishment for great evil. This *Old Testament* idea dies hard. Only repentance, a change of mind and intent, will ensure that man escapes death, that is the death of the soul. To impress the need for urgency in repentance, the story of the fig tree is told. How often we have done the same thing in our own garden! Why should we expect otherwise?

---

[1] See Index of Passages.

First Reading: *Joshua 5.9-12*
The Israelites had passed from the desert into the Promised Land. From being nomads they were now set to become an agricultural people, and for the first time the Passover was celebrated with the produce of the soil. The gift of manna was now withdrawn. We note that whether in wandering or in settled life the Passover, the festival of deliverance, had to go on.

Responsorial Psalm: *Psalm 33.2-7*
As so often happens, a personal deliverance seems to be the motive which prompted the psalm. The writer's joy in God and his gratitude for rescue from whatever it was that beset him, spills over into a desire that others should share in his joyful experience. The psalm is an acrostic [1] in its structure.

Second Reading: *I I Corinthians 5.17-21*
There had been a severe crisis in Paul's relationship with the church in Corinth. The breach had, however, been healed and in this portion of a very difficult letter which is possibly bits and pieces of three letters put together, the writer's thoughts draw from recent experience and expand into the wider field of reconciliation, that of man to God.

Gospel: *Luke 15.1-3,11-32*
Luke's compassion for the lost is most evident in Chapter 15 with its stories of the lost coin, the lost sheep and the lost son. The coin was lost through no fault of its own, the sheep because it knew no better, and the son by deliberate intention. The first two were found by the efforts of others, the third by his own choice through repentance. Of the two sons, it has been said: "One stayed; the other strayed". Who do you think stood more in need of his father's compassion?

---

[1] See Notes, Fourteenth Sunday in Ordinary Time, Year A.

First Reading: *Isaiah 43.16-21*
Deutero-Isaiah is speaking to the exiles in Babylon; his theme is a great deliverance in the past and another that is yet to come. The first stanza reviews Israel's escape from Egypt. Then comes a promise of a highway through the terrible desert from Babylon, a way of return from exile. The desolate wilderness will flow with water; even wild animals will pay their homage to God.

Responsorial Psalm: *Psalm 125*
This is one of the fifteen Songs of Ascent sung by pilgrims on their way to Jerusalem for the great festivals. The first two stanzas reflect the anticipated joy of return from Babylon to Jerusalem. Even the pagans marvelled, but like a dream, there was unreality in it and this is apparent in the last two stanzas which refer to the many difficulties that faced them on their return, but hope breaks through this second barrier.

Second Reading: *Philippians 3.8-14*
Paul had listed all the privileges conferred on him by being a Pharisee. These he now rejects as a worthless means of gaining Christ. Faith alone will bring him to that goal, a righteousness by faith. As we draw near to Easter, listen to references to the Resurrection and how Paul applies it to himself. He is fond of metaphors from games, with the striving and the prize of victory. Athletic contests were a common feature of the Greek world in which he moved.

Gospel: *John 8.1-11*
The passage fairly bristles with difficulties; it is generally agreed that John did not write it, though it could well be an "authentic piece of early tradition". The early Fathers seem to have been unaware of its existence. The incident was an attempt to trap Jesus, for the woman if guilty faced the death penalty (See *Leviticus 20.10* and *Deuteronomy 17.5*). Much has been written about what Our Lord wrote on the ground. Two different verbs are used, one of which could mean "to draw". The thrust of the passage is against those who would condemn in others the faults they see in themselves.

PASSION SUNDAY (PALM SUNDAY)
See above pp. 31-34

HOLY THURSDAY: CHRISM MASS
See above p. 35

THE EASTER TRIDUUM

HOLY THURSDAY (Mass of the Lord's Supper)
See above p. 36

GOOD FRIDAY (Celebration of the Lord's Passion)
See above p. 37

EASTER VIGIL
See above pp. 38-43

THE SEASON OF EASTER
EASTER SUNDAY

See above p. 43

SECOND SUNDAY OF EASTER
YEAR C

First Reading: *Acts 5.12-16*

Luke is at pains to show us the early beginnings of the Church and the way in which it was growing in popular esteem. In so doing he puts special emphasis on the work of the apostles. The signs and wonders done by them are given special prominence. The word used of Peter's shadow is found elsewhere, but only to describe some form of divine presence.

Responsorial Psalm: *Psalm 117.2-4,22-27*

This long psalm has been used in the Missal several times in different forms. [1] Thanksgiving for deliverance is at the heart of it. It appears to have been used at the Feast of Tabernacles and sung antiphonally. The first stanza is a general call to give thanks to God. Then follows the familiar reference to the massive block of stone sunk in the ground to hold two meeting walls. Israel is the stone, seen by the psalmist as rejected and later to be restored to a position of honour among the nations. The psalm ends on the note of God's salvation. In the period after Easter we apply the reference to the rejected stone to Our risen Lord.

Second Reading: *Apocalypse 1.9-13,17-19*

It is uncertain who wrote the *Apocalypse*, but this is sure: like other writing of its kind e.g. *Daniel*, it is the product of trial and crisis. Written in times of persecution, the message of encouragement to those suffering for their faith is necessarily obscure and often beyond our understanding. John who for his faith had, according to tradition, slaved in the marble quarries of Patmos, repeats the Lord's uplifting words: "Do not go on being afraid". He urges his readers to put aside their fears and hold to the risen Christ.

Gospel: *John 20.19-31*

In a passage teeming with power there are glimpses of the post-Resurrection form of Our Lord; the voice, so beloved of the disciples, speaks to allay their fears. Anxieties at rest, the Lord gives his commission. The doubting Thomas whose image fits so many of us, bursts forth in the ecstasy of "My Lord and my God". The risen Lord breathed on his disciples as his Father breathed on the world at its creation. The passage contains the only reference in the Gospels to the nails of the Cross.

---

[1] See Index of passages.

First Reading: *Acts 5.27-32,40-41*
The passage to be read presents an extraordinary reversal of what is found in the Passion narrative. Peter and the other apostles are no longer fearful and uncertain of themselves. They are in complete control of the situation, in contrast to the authorities who are now on the defensive. From the very beginning, the power of the Holy Spirit is being acknowledged. The first signs of martyrdom are beginning to appear.

Responsorial Psalm: *Psalm 29.2,4-6,11-13*
The psalm is a personal thanksgiving for recovery after illness during which the writer nearly died. Listen for the words: "Lord you have raised my soul from the dead". Not to be taken literally, the words mean that God rescued him as he was going down to Sheol, the Underworld. He calls on others who love God to join him in his overflowing joy. A true chord of life is struck in the words: "All night there are tears, but joy comes with dawn".

Second Reading: *Apocalypse 5.11-14*
In the greatest chorus ever of man and nature, the praise of the Lamb is sung. The strains of this music come from in the air and on the ground, from under the ground and in the sea, all to the praise, not of some powerful beast, but of the Lamb of God who was slain to redeem the world.

Gospel: *John 21.1-19*
Peter's work in laying the foundation of the Church dominates the first part of *Acts*, not the Peter who lost his nerve in Holy Week, but a daring and revitalised Peter who knew no fear. We shall hear again how his threefold denial of the Lord is offset by a threefold declaration of his love and loyalty. Warned that he will suffer for his faith, he goes to obey his Lord's commission: "Feed my sheep".

First Reading: *Acts 13.14,43-52*

Our reading is part of the narrative that tells how the Gospel began to be carried to the ends of the earth, for the Jews had consistently rejected the Gospel. The events recorded in this reading took place in southern Asia Minor, the modern Turkey. Listen for the words: "We must turn to the pagans". The quotation is from *Isaiah 49.6* [1]. With these words the Gospel burst its Jewish bonds and became a world-wide crusade. Of that great event we are heirs.

Responsorial Psalm: *Psalm 99.1-3,5*

This is the psalm widely known as "Old Hundredth" [2]. It was sung in procession to the Temple when the thank offering was to be made. A call to sing with gladness to the Lord is followed by the people's acknowledgement of their allegiance to God. The psalm ends on the note of God's eternal goodness. It rings with the joy of worship, which in turn springs from the sense of the divine presence.

Second Reading: *Apocalypse 7.9,14-17*

Christians down the ages have drawn comfort from this portion of Scripture. There would scarcely be an older member of any congregation who has not at some time and in some crisis found consolation in its message. We miss the primary purpose of the *Apocalypse* if we forget that it was written for those undergoing intense persecution for their faith. Known periods of persecution were in the 60's A.D. under the Roman Emperor Nero and in the 90's A.D. in the time of Domitian. The latter is probably the occasion to which the *Apocalypse* refers.

Gospel: *John 10.27-30*

In a tense situation in which the Jews were ready to stone Jesus, he speaks to them of the union that exists between his followers, mentioned under the guise of sheep, and himself. Because his works and words are the works and words of God, the disciples who are united to him are united to God also. No one can tear us from the Father.

---

[1] See Reading and Notes Second Sunday in Ordinary Time, Year A.

[2] Psalm 100 in most translations, including the *Jerusalem Bible*

First Reading: *Acts 14.21-27*

On the surface the passage may seem uninteresting; the many strange names do not help to grip our attention. There is to it, however, more than meets the eye. Paul went back to Lystra, Iconium and Antioch where he and Barnabas had been stoned, worshipped and expelled. This they did with personal disregard, to strengthen the small groups of converts there. With courage the Church was being built up. Some may wish to follow Paul on a biblical map. Here are the basics: Lystra, Iconium and Antioch are in central Asia Minor; from there they moved due south to Pisidia, Pamphylia and Perga and then to Attalia. The second Antioch is a different place, in northern Syria.

Responsorial Psalm: *Psalm 144.8-13*

The spiritual quality of this psalm is attested by its frequent use in the Missal. The last of the alphabetical or acrostic psalms, it could have been composed only by one who had had a profound experience of God. The first stanza reads like a personal testimony. Next comes the note of universalism that runs through the full version. Then all the glory of God's reign is brought to mind. Finally the eternal nature of his rule is praised.

Second Reading: *Apocalypse 21.1-5*

Since Easter we have been reading from the *Apocalypse*, but between this Mass and the last there is a gap of fourteen chapters. In it are trumpets, dragons and beasts, Armageddon, Babylon and the end. This symbolism had meaning for those suffering persecution in the 90's A.D. For us the key is lost and so the chapters find no place in our Missals. House to house pedlars of "literature" which interprets these chapters in terms of current world events should not be taken seriously. In the passage to be read, John sees beyond the turmoil of his day to a time when a new society is formed with God as its centre.

Gospel: *John 13.31-35*

The writers of the *New Testament* often had to coin new words or give old ones a new meaning. The Christian doctrine of love could not be expressed with words tarnished by debased ideas and practices. So two words, a verb and a noun that had been little used were brought into service to express "not an emotional experience, but a principle of the mind". Hear now how John records Our Lord's discourse on love.

First Reading: *Acts 15.1-2,22-29*
As the Church grew, a dilemma arose: should the new Israel be required to conform to the requirements of the old, in particular to the rite of circumcision? The apostles and elders met in Jerusalem and made an historic decision that freed the new Israel: the use of certain foods, murder and immorality were forbidden. No other restrictions were imposed; the tie with Judaism was cut for ever.

Responsorial Psalm: *Psalm 66.2-3,5-6,8*
The full version reveals the psalm as a harvest thanksgiving and then the thought extends into the harvest of the world, an idea present in each stanza. The limits of God's grace are the very ends of the earth; all peoples and nations are under his beneficent rule; the last stanza has a strong missionary note, "till the ends of the earth revere him".

Second Reading: *Apocalypse 20.10-14,22-23*
John's description of the new Jerusalem is continued. The city conforms with the best architecture of the day, high walls and gates with massive foundations linked by inscription to early beginnings of Jewish society. The ancient world had no answer to the problem of lighting, but this city had no such difficulty. God and the Lamb were its perfect Light.

Gospel: *John 14.23-29*
There are three aspects of this portion of John's Gospel: the discourse on love is continued, simple, yet profound; there is a reminder that Pentecost is drawing near and that the Spirit will continue the teaching ministry of Jesus. Finally Our Lord speaks of that peace which he gives, not the absence of strife which is the world's negative definition, but a positive quality of life.

First Reading: *Acts 1.1-11*
The reading begins with a reference to "my earlier work" which is Luke's Gospel, and to "Theophilus" who is anybody's guess. The writer then mentions in general terms Our Lord's Resurrection appearances. The promise of the gift of the Holy Spirit—*Acts* has been called the *Book of the Holy Spirit*—is repeated; questions about the political future of Jerusalem are not answered and with that, the earthly ministry of Our Lord ends in his Ascension.

Responsorial Psalm: *Psalm 46.2-3,6-7,8-9*
This is one of the Enthronement Psalms used to celebrate the Kingship of God, possibly in association with the festival of the New Year. While there may be a reference to some great deliverance, more probably the writer in this psalm looks towards God's future universal rule. It has a traditional association with Ascension Day. After discussing possible divisions into stanzas, one commentator prefers to see it as "one trumpet blast with many ringing, melodious notes".

Second Reading: *Ephesians 1.17-23*
Paul's *Letter to the Ephesians*, written from prison, was a circular letter to the churches of Asia Minor; it represents his spiritual genius in full flower. The theme is the Church as the Body of Christ, embracing Jews and pagans without distinction. The reading deals with Christ's supremacy and sets out what he who has triumphed over angelic and demonic hosts will confer on believers. The terms "Sovereignty, Authority, Power or Dominion" refer to levels in the hierarchy in the spirit world. The terms can not now be identified and refer in any case to ideas which are no longer tenable.

Optional Second Reading: *Hebrews 9.24-28,10.19-23*
Unlike the high priest on earth with his many sacrifices and many entries over the years into the Holy of Holies, Christ's perfect sacrifice of himself has given him permanent place in the heavenly Sanctuary, even God's presence. In the second paragraph we are reminded that whereas Jews had no access into the sanctuary, the blood of Christ provided an access into God's presence. The constantly recurring reference to baptism is noted. The reading provides an awe inspiring vision of the ascended Christ.

Gospel: *Luke 24.46-53*

There are ten post-resurrection appearances of Our Lord of which Luke records only three. In these last precious moments with him, it emerges that repentance is to be the basis of all preaching; that the evangelisation of the world would begin in Jerusalem and that the disciples were to wait in that city for the promised gift of the Holy Spirit. It is an ancient custom of the Church to extinguish the Pascal Candle after this Gospel and thus to indicate the removal of the Lord's visible presence for all time.

First Reading: *Acts 7.55-60*
The reading records the death of Stephen, who was one of that group of seven elected to lighten the apostles' load. Having been brought before the *Sanhedrin* for alleged impiety, he so vigorously defended himself that the infuriated Council vented their wrath by illegally stoning him to death. (See *Leviticus 24. 14-16* and compare *John 18.31*). So Stephen, dying a death which like his Lord's seemed outwardly to be of no avail, became the Church's first martyr. We remember his sacrifice on December 26th.

Responsorial Psalm: *Psalm 96.1-2,6-7,9*
This is another of the Enthronement Psalms that celebrate the Kingship of God. The first stanza proclaims the fact of God's rule and that its basis is moral. Then comes a declaration that all the world is aware of this. The short selection of verses concludes with the recognition that God is above all creation, creatures and the spirit beings who are conceived as part of the heavenly company.

Second Reading: *Apocalypse 22.12-14,16-17,20*
These are the last words in the *Bible*. The New Jerusalem with its materials, the finest known to man, has been described. The reading is part of what is generally called the *Epilogue* in which ideas flow quickly and in some disarray, so that some scholars see a dislocated text. Jesus speaks, declaring his Coming to be near, that he represents a completeness such as alpha and omega, the first and last letters of the Greek alphabet. Those entitled to enter the New Jerusalem are bidden to come in. Finally the Spirit and the Bride (Church) make an appeal to come and drink of the water of life.

Gospel: *John 17.20-26*
On the Seventh Sunday of Easter a portion of *John* Chapter 17 is always used. Described as "One of the most sacred passages in the *New Testament*", Chapter 17 is a long prayer uttered just before the arrest of Jesus. He prays for the unity of all believers present and future. He wants them to be so knit to him that through them his glory will be seen by the world. The reading closes on the note of the Lord's love.

PENTECOST SUNDAY
VIGIL MASS

See above p. 52

MASS DURING THE DAY
YEAR C

First Reading: *Acts 2.1-11*
Pentecost was originally a festival of the crops. This reading tells
how it became one of the greatest occasions in history when God
the Holy Spirit burst into human affairs. In all great religious
experiences words become inadequate. In spite of his mastery of
language, Luke can only say that the coming of the Holy Spirit
was like a powerful wind and like tongues of fire. There is
mention of people from many places. These were Jews, citizens
of the countries into which over the years they had been
scattered, but always Jews, who returned to Jerusalem for the
festival of Pentecost and found themselves caught up in the
outpouring of the Spirit.

Responsorial Psalm: *Psalm 103.1,24,29-31,34*
Gathering thoughts from various accounts of creation that
circulated in other lands, the psalmist has put together a
magnificent hymn of praise to God the Maker of all things. In
the reading which is a small part of the full version, God's majesty
in creation is praised. Man and nature draw their life from God.
Finally the psalmist declares God to be the centre of his joy.

Second Reading: *Romans 8.8-17*
Paul's theme in this well known passage is the new life in the
Spirit, a word used nearly thirty times in this chapter. As a
result of our being declared righteous, there is a transformation
brought about by the Holy Spirit. This indwelling Spirit raises
us from our former life just as God raised Jesus from the dead.
Life in the Spirit is life indeed and provides the status of sonship,
and that in turn makes us heirs with Christ to share his suffering
and his glory.

Gospel: *John 14.15-16,23-26*
As the shadow of the Cross begins to fall upon Our Lord, he
speaks of the love [1] that exists between God and the believer. As
the Lord's departure is near he speaks of the Advocate, the Spirit
who will take his place. It is a word almost impossible to
translate, with the basic meaning of "One called to be beside".
However translated, the word refers to the Holy Spirit who will
guide believers in the way of truth.

---

[1] See Notes, Fifth Sunday of Easter, Year C.

First Reading: *Proverbs 8.22-31*
The reading deals with Wisdom, but it will very soon be realised that Wisdom is not an idea or an abstract concept, but a person who was with God before creation [1]. Here is the beginning of the idea of the Trinity whose festival is celebrated in this Mass.

Responsorial Psalm: *Psalm 8.4-9*
This psalm has been called *"Genesis 1* Set to Music". It was probably associated with the treading of the grapes in autumn. It honours God who made the world and set man within what he had fashioned, giving him honour and power. It is God the Creator and Father who emerges from this psalm.

Second Reading: *Romans 5.1-5*
Through the work of the Lord Jesus Christ who came to earth as God's Son we see the redemptive work of God. The gift of grace is not earned, but is free to all who believe. Having stated this tremendous fact, Paul then sets out the process of human development within the sphere of grace. So, in addition to the work of God the Father there is added in this passage a clear reference to God the Son.

Gospel: *John 16.12-15*
These and other well known verses from *John* Ch.16 explain the operation of the Holy Spirit whose influence was so soon to be felt by the disciples. Jesus declares that his teaching will be continued after his departure by the Holy Spirit. In the first reading the notion of the Trinity was foreshadowed and then followed references from Scripture to God the Father, God the Son and God the Holy Spirit.

---

[1] See Notes, Twentieth Sunday in Ordinary Time, Year B.

184   **Thursday or Sunday after Trinity Sunday**
THE BODY AND BLOOD OF CHRIST
YEAR C

First Reading: *Genesis 14.18-20*
Melchizedek is one of the most mysterious figures in the *Old Testament.* The writer of the *Letter to the Hebrews* says it all: "he has no father, mother or ancestry and his life has no beginning or ending; he is like the Son of God, a priest for ever" (Ch.7.3). His gift to Abraham of bread and wine represents royal hospitality and these gifts are symbolic of the Eucharist.

Responsorial Psalm: *Psalm 109.1-4*
This psalm, most frequently quoted of any in the *New Testament,* is addressed to a king, possibly on the occasion of his enthronement. The noble language of the psalm also suggests that it is prophetic of the Messiah. The king in question and the Messiah to whom he points have the priestly qualities of Melchizedek, and this for all time.

Second Reading: *I Corinthians 11.23-26*
There are four accounts of the Last Supper. Matthew, Mark and Luke each record their version. The passage to be read was written by Paul at least a decade earlier and was composed in the first place to show his authority for rebuking disorders in the Corinthian church in connexion with the Eucharist. In Paul's letters one observes how little there is of the life and teaching of Our Lord, yet here there is great detail and the reason is clear: he received it from the Lord. It emphasises also the importance of the Eucharist in God's plan.

Gospel: *Luke 9.11-17*
The Feeding of the Five Thousand is the only miracle recorded in all four Gospels. Our Lord who in his temptation refused to turn stones into bread was acutely aware of the needs of other people. In this provision for them there is a glimpse of the Messiah's banquet in heaven and a foretaste of the Eucharist that feeds the souls of God's people on earth.

THE SACRED HEART OF JESUS
YEAR C

First Reading: *Ezekiel 34.11-16*
This section of *Ezekiel* (Chs.33-39) contains prophecies that deal with the redemption of God's people in exile in Babylon, awaiting the rebuilding of their national hopes. In the reading the prophet thinks of rulers who have misused their kingly power and so have contributed to the state of the nation. Henceforth God himself will be the Shepherd of his people. The reading clearly introduces Jesus Christ as Shepherd Saviour.

Responsorial Psalm: *Psalm 22*
The Shepherd psalm is unique in the Psalter and probably the best known; this is its fifth use in the Missal. Into his image of the good shepherd the writer, traditionally said to be David, projects all the qualities of the keeper of sheep on the hill side. What more could he do for his charges than is set out in the first two stanzas? Then the picture changes to a banquet where God is the host. The psalm ends with a feeling of security prompted by the divine Shepherd. All we like sheep have gone astray, and we find in this psalm the Great Shepherd who gently leads the lost back to the fold.

Second Reading: *Romans 5.5-11*
Continuing the theme of righteousness through faith, Paul deals with the efficacy of Christ's sacrifice which was made not for godly men, but for sinners. Thus reconciled to God, we are assured of salvation in the consummation of all things to which we look forward now, not in fear, but in "joyful hope".

Gospel: *Luke 15.3-7*
The reading is part of what has been called "a Gospel within a Gospel" and in its application we see the compassion of Our Lord. We note that the shepherd's concern for the one that is lost outweighs consideration for the rest of the flock, that when found, the sheep is not driven home, but carried, and that the shepherd, so far from being in any way put out by the wandering animal, rejoices that he has found it. So in every way is it with him whose compassion we celebrate today.

First Sunday in Ordinary Time
THE BAPTISM OF THE LORD
YEAR C

See above page 164

First Reading: *Isaiah 62.1-5*

As noted previously, *Isaiah* is the work of two different hands [1].
The reading belongs to *Deutero-Isaiah* and is set in the years
after the Babylonian captivity when the Jews had returned, not
to a Utopia, but to hardship and difficulty from which they
scarcely at times seemed to be emerging. Yet the prophet can see
a new Jerusalem with future glory, the religious centre of the
world, no longer forsaken as an unmarried girl, but married and
loved by God as a bridegroom adores his bride. Her new names
are Hephzibah (My delight is in her) and Beulah (Married).

Responsorial Psalm: *Psalm 95.1-3,7-10*

This is one of a group of psalms that celebrate the Kingship of
God and are known as Enthronement Psalms. First comes a call
to all nations to praise God and to declare his concern for the
affairs of men. In the third and fourth stanzas the call is renewed
to worship God. The Temple is to be open to all, Jews and pagans
alike.

Second Reading: *I Corinthians 12.4-11*

This is the first of seven readings from *I Corinthians* [2]. The
Corinthian church, in which spiritual gifts were clearly evident in
many forms, seems to have assessed some manifestations of the
Spirit more highly than others. Paul stresses that all are the work
"of one and the same spirit". Though not every congregation may
be familiar with these gifts, the practical principles Paul lays
down speak to us all: no one is more important than another
before God in the exercise of his gift in service. To clean the
brass in an empty church and to be an acolyte before a packed
congregation are gifts of equal service.

---

[1] See Notes, Nativity of the Lord, Vigil Mass, Year A.

[2] See Notes Second Sunday in Ordinary Time, Year A.

Gospel: *John 2.1-11*
The story of the wedding at Cana is told with great simplicity.
Two points call for comment: First the words: "Woman, why
turn to me?". This and similar translations have puzzled
Christians. "Woman" in Greek is not harsh as in English, quite
the opposite in fact. "Why turn to me?" is a translation which,
along with other crude attempts, overlooks what is a Semitic
idiom and an idiom can not be translated literally. So "Mother,
let me do it my way" gives the meaning without offence. Second,
the whole occasion shows how elevated is any function at which
Our Lord is present, turning into best quality wine water meant
only for washing hands and feet.

THIRD SUNDAY IN ORDINARY TIME
YEAR C

First Reading: *Nehemiah 8.2-6,8-10*
When Cyrus King of Persia captured Babylon in 538 B.C. the
Jews were permitted to return to Jerusalem and the long task of
reconstruction began. Not only had buildings to be remade, but
codes of spiritual and moral behaviour had to be refashioned. In
this process Ezra the priest played a prominent part. There was an
extensive reading from the Book of the Law which was probably
the *Pentateuch* or part of it. If the reference to translating is a
correct rendering — and many doubt it — it implies that the Jews
during the exile had forgotten the Hebrew in which the Law was
written.

Responsorial Psalm: *Psalm 18.8-10,15*
This psalm consists of two separate parts, the first showing how
God is seen in nature, the second, which is the portion in the
Missal, revealing God in his Law which is variously called rule,
precepts, command, fear and decrees. The Law of God directs
the psalmist's life; God is his rock which provides security. It is
generally agreed that this psalm is the composition of two
different writers.

Second Reading: *I Corinthians 12.12-30*
This reading follows on from the Second Reading of last Sunday.
Paul is speaking to the divided church in Corinth (See Ch.1.10-
17). As a pastor trying to heal wounds of division he tells the
Corinthians that they are the Body of Christ. No member of the
body has a separate existence; on the contrary, each functions in
harmony with the others. For its proper function each needs the
well-being of all the others.

Gospel: *Luke 1.1-4,4.14-21*
The Gospel is a composite passage, beginning with the formal
opening with which Luke launches his Gospel. The opening in the
Missal is unrelated to what follows, but it has been inserted
because *Luke* is the Gospel in Year C, and the Third Sunday in
Ordinary Time marks the beginning of consecutive use of this
Gospel. The rest of the reading deals with the commencement of
the Galilean ministry. Worshipping in his home town on the
Sabbath, Jesus read from *Isaiah Ch.61* [1]. Luke, as is his custom,
quotes from the Greek version of the *Old Testament*, not from
the Hebrew. The prophet saw Israel renewed and glorious,
nurturing the world in a new era of spirituality. Our Lord, in his
first public statement reshaped all this and applied the words of
the prophet to himself. This is therefore the first promulgation
of what was to be a progressive revelation of the New Law. Only
Luke records what Our Lord said in the synagogue and in the
reference to the underprivileged he gives his readers a first glimpse
of one of the outstanding characteristics of his Gospel,
compassion for the poor and the oppressed.

---

[1] See Notes, Third Sunday of Advent, Year B.

First Reading: *Jeremiah 1.4-5,17-19*
The whole purpose of this Mass will be clouded over unless there
is a clear understanding of the function of a prophet. He was
first and foremost a preacher, attacking some political, social
or moral weakness of the day. Often prophets tried to forecast
future events arising from unchecked evils. Their task was not to
issue a blue print for the future, most certainly not for the times
in which we live. Their task was to forth-tell, not to foretell. The
call of Jeremiah, as in the case of others, is represented as a
personal dialogue with God. Though destined to be the most
tragic and loneliest of prophets, Jeremiah could never escape
from the powerful forces that kept him on his prophetic way.

Responsorial Psalm: *Psalm 70.1-6,15,17*
The psalm is an old man's acknowledgement of God as his life-
long hope and trust; it is also the same man's plea not to be
abandoned, for presumably in sickness, he has suffered the taunts
of cruel men. The voice of this aged saint, still confident of his
God, deserves to be heard by pilgrims only just setting out on the
same journey.

Second Reading: *I Corinthians 12.31-13.13*
Commentators vie with one another to find adequate praise for
this "Hymn of Love" which is probably Paul's noblest utterance.
Translations vary; most have something to offer if only in a single
phrase. If you have access to other translations — and none is
perfect — read them, but above all read the passage and read it
over and over, for this is the best commentary on it. The Christian
concept of love was something new to the pagan world and was
expressed by a word virtually unused hitherto[1]. Paul would have us
remember that without love all the prophecy of the Church is in
vain.

---

[1] See Notes, Fifth Sunday of Easter, Year C.

Gospel: *Luke 4.21-30*
Jesus leaves no doubt that he is the fulfilment of the hopes and
expectations of the *Old Testament*. The new age is not near; it
has arrived. Later in his ministry Our Lord said: "Happy are those
who have not seen and yet believe" (*John 20.29*). There is a hint
of this attitude here in his refusal to repeat what he had done at
Capernaum. Already the element of faith in Jesus rather than in
his works was emerging. Only Luke records the references to
Elijah and Elisha (*I Kings 17.9-16; II Kings 5.1-14*) and this is
highly significant: the miracles done by these two prophets
were for the benefit of pagans. The universalism of Luke's Gospel
is widely recognised as one of its main characteristics, for the
writer was not a Jew. Recognising that Jesus was preaching
salvation for all men, the Jews were shocked and enraged and
sought to kill him by throwing him over a cliff.

FIFTH SUNDAY IN ORDINARY TIME
YEAR C

First Reading: *Isaiah 6.1-8*
When God called Isaiah there was conflict within Isaiah himself
and this may have been partly connected with the death of King
Uzziah. This splendid ruler, dying of leprosy, must have revealed
the tenuous nature of life and helped Isaiah to fasten his thoughts
on the power and majesty of God. Realising the absolute holiness
of God, Isaiah saw himself for what he was. It is at this stage
that God can act. Cleansed, in the magnificent words of our
passage, by the live coal, he was ready to hear the voice of God
and able to respond. In so few words we are given the essential
details of a profound religious experience.

Responsorial Psalm: *Psalm 137.1-5,7-8*
This Psalm is an expression of great gratitude to God, though
there is little to indicate the circumstances. The tone of the psalm
suggests some great deliverance. The writer's trust in God is
unshakable. Whatever it is that God has done for him, he feels
that the kings of the earth will learn of it, to the further praise
of God.

192

Second Reading: *I Corinthians 15.1-11*

In the main part of the passage, Paul seems to be covering some very obvious ground. We must remember that as yet, none of the Gospels had been written, but chiefly, that there were some in Corinth who in true Greek fashion denied the possibility of resurrection. A reference to the apostles (the "sent-out ones") leads into a digression on his own status. To glorify the saving grace of God he recounts his own unworthiness to be called an apostle, even using of himself the insulting term "miscarriage" which no doubt some one had hurled at him. Central to our belief and to the very nature of our apostleship is the Resurrection. As Paul was to say later, we are buried with Christ through baptism into his death that we may live a new kind of life.

Gospel: *Luke 5.1-11*

We shall never know what Our Lord taught from the vantage point of Peter's boat, but it does remind us how little we have of his teaching. Two aspects of Peter's conversion arrest our attention: first, a man tired after a night's heavy and futile work does not usually take a silly order seriously - fish are not netted in the middle of the day - but in this case the order came from one who had been observed healing the sick. Though the command ran counter to all his experience as a fisherman, he agreed, with dramatic change to his whole life. Second, one would not normally compare the Galilean fisherman with the greatest of the *Old Testament* prophets, yet there is a strong common element; both recoiled with a sudden awareness of their sinfulness and their inadequacy. This recognition is the basis on which in both cases God could build a spiritual edifice beyond human imagining. To those who are afraid in their apostleship there is a voice that says: "Launch out into deep water and stop being afraid".

First Reading: *Jeremiah 17.5-8*

The *Book of Jeremiah* has been called "a rather bewildering collection of sayings, and historical and biographical stories". In the study of any prophet it is imperative to have the background of his utterances. In the present instance it is impossible to be more specific than to say that Jeremiah prophesied (preached) in the decadent period before the Babylonian captivity. The two stanzas in the Missal present a striking contrast between the man of worldly interests and the man of spiritual discernment. In the one, a stunted shrub barely ekes out an existence, its roots sodden in salty water, while the other, its roots in fresh water, thrives in all seasons.

Responsorial Psalm: *Psalm 1.1-4*

This psalm bears striking resemblance to the First Reading, but a real difference emerges at the end. Though the psalmist does not say outright that divine retribution will overtake the evil, a principle which the psalmists in the main apply, he comes very near to such a declaration. Jeremiah and other prophets see sin as a self-destructive force. God leaves the sinner to his sin and in the end it destroys him. The main thrust of the psalm is in the call to a godly life.

Second Reading: *I Corinthians 15.12,16-20*

When Paul addressed the Athenians on the Areopagus he held his audience until he spoke of the Resurrection. At this they began to sneer. Even among his Corinthian converts there were some who could not accept this idea. Paul then shows them what happens to their faith if resurrection is denied. The Resurrection is central to our faith; without it we have no hope; there is no expectation of reunion with our beloved dead. At this point with joyful outburst Paul uses his own emphatic two word phrase of contrast: "But now Christ is risen ..." (not "has been raised", but "was raised and is now in a risen state")... "the first fruits". Christ rose from the dead at the time when the first sheaf of barley was being offered in the Temple. As the first fruit was followed by the full harvest, so also will Christ's Resurrection be followed by the full harvest of those who are his.

Gospel: *Luke 6.17,20-26*
Luke's presentation of the Beatitudes is different from Matthew's
(Matthew 5.3-12) and is probably nearer to the original. Observe
how the fourfold use of "Happy" is balanced by a fourfold
"alas". A famous scholar has said of the Beatitudes: "They are
flashes of lightning followed by a thunder of surprise", for in
them ordinary values are reversed. However when poverty,
hunger, weeping, social rejection occur, they have Our Lord's
blessing only when these situations are for his sake. Similarly
riches etc. merit his censure only when these conditions have
become an end in themselves. In short, he will bless the poverty
of the religious, but pious platitudes spoken to a starving widow
and her family are pure humbug. Our Lord spoke not to the
crowd, but to his disciples who were already being moulded by
his teaching. The Beatitudes are not designed to reform society
at large, but to guide us who have already, by the grace of God,
developed some spirituality.

First Reading: *I Samuel 26.2,7-9,12-13,22-23*
Relations between Saul and David had never been smooth and
even. Although he was Saul's son-in-law, David was at the time of
this incident, a fugitive from Saul in west Judaea. The reading tells
how David had Saul at his mercy and with a generous spirit
spared him because he was the Lord's anointed. David had
displayed the same magnanimity on a previous occasion (Ch.24).

Responsorial Psalm: *Psalm 102.1-4,8,10,12-13*
This beautiful psalm, used seven times [1] in various forms in the
Missal, was written by one who had communed long with his
God and from the needs of his own soul found the many
responses of the Divine, forgiveness, healing, redemption, long
life and mercy. Scholars date the psalm, but in another sense it is
timeless, Everyman's theology of God.

Second Reading: *I Corinthians 15.45-49*
Paul's discussion of Resurrection is carried a further step and in
this reading he grapples with the nature of the Resurrection body.
The first Adam possessed a soul that had life, as we all have;
Christ, the last Adam, was animated by the life of the Spirit of
God. Paul then contrasts the first Adam with the last; the first
comes from the dust (*Genesis 2.7*), the last from heaven. After
the resurrection we shall share Christ's life and we shall wear his
likeness as a garment.

Gospel: *Luke 6.27-38*
Our Lord, in laying down the basis on which the new society will
function and in setting forth the Law of love, turns upside down
the accepted moral values and attitudes of the world. Greek has
two verbs meaning "to love", one based on the emotions, the
other on the will. This latter word, with its noun that was
unknown outside Biblical usage, was used in the *New Testament*
to convey the action and idea of love that seeks another's good.
Listen now to the application and demands of the new law of
love.

---

[1] See Index of Passages.

First Reading: *Ecclesiasticus 27.4-7*

Written approximately two centuries before the Christian era, *Ecclesiasticus* provides our second meeting in this series with Wisdom Literature which includes *Proverbs, Job, Ecclesiastes* and the *Wisdom of Solomon.* Wisdom is an emanation (flowing forth) from God, almost a person; she is the inspiration of those qualities that make for right living. Out of Wisdom and other ideas grew John's concept of the Word (*John 1.1*). In *Ecclesiasticus* the author, Ben Sira, devotes much space to the nature of Wisdom and in our reading, set in a contrast between wise and foolish men, shows how what we say reveals what we are.

Responsorial Psalm: *Psalm 91.2-3,13-16*

In the full version the psalmist grasps the nettle of goodness and evil in relation to prosperity and suffering and thinks he has disposed of it! Before us is only the picture of the prosperity of the godly man; omitted verses give the fate of the wicked. The Palmist uses the morning and evening services to thank God for his own position. He likens himself to the fruitful date palm and the lovely cedar tree which is the symbol of strength and long life.

Second Reading: *I Corinthians 15.54-58*

The discourse on immortality continues. Paul visualises a dramatic transformation in which, under the familiar image of putting on garments, the perishable in us is replaced by the imperishable. Then, taking liberties with quotations from *Isaiah* and *Hosea*, Paul shows how fear has gone out of death. Inability to keep the Law creates sin and sin contributes to death. Finally on a practical note, he urges the Corinthians to keep up their Christian work.

Gospel: *Luke 6.39-45*

The message is straightforward: unless the disciples learn the truth they will not be able to teach others, any more than the blind can lead the blind. Soundness, be it of tree or people, is right through and not on the surface only. In the Parable of the Plank and the Splinter there is one of the best examples of Semitic exaggeration to enforce a point. The word "hypocrite" comes from the Greek word for an actor. He could reach twenty thousand people in an open air theatre, assisted by his mask with its megaphonic effect. From the basic meaning of answering from under a mask comes the secondary sense of "hypocrite".

First Reading: *1 Kings 8.41-43*

About 970 B.C. Solomon came to the throne of Israel and four years later began the famous Temple associated with his name. The reading contains part of Solomon's prayer at the dedication of the Temple. In the prayer Solomon specifies the various occasions when prayers would be offered in the Temple and in the verses before us he indicates that foreigners may use it.

Responsorial Psalm: *Psalm 116*

This is the shortest of the psalms and for this reason some have thought that it may be only a fragment. It is a call to all peoples to praise God for his love and faithfulness to Israel. Paul quotes the psalm in *Romans* 15.11 to prove that the Gospel is for all nations.

Second Reading: *Galatians 1.1-2,6-10*

This is the first of six readings from *Galatians*. The Galatians were located somewhere in Asia Minor; they had been converted by Paul on his second missionary journey, from possibly some form of astrology. Then came troublemakers who tried to persuade them that the Mosaic Law was essential for their faith and it is to refute this version of salvation that Paul wrote the letter. The phrase "he is to be condemned" is hardly strong enough. "Let him be anathema". The word meant an ornament, then an offering in a temple and finally something offered to God for destruction.

Gospel: *Luke 7.1-10*

The centurion, a non-commissioned officer in the service probably of Herod Antipas, was not a Jew, but one who found the Jewish religion attractive. He emerges from the story as a humble man. His knowledge of what it meant to obey and to be obeyed was the basis of an unquestioning faith. Our Lord, in noting that the soldier's faith was greater than that of his own people, was pointing to the wide acceptance of the Church's message.

First Reading: *I Kings 17.17-24*
Few characters in the *Old Testament* stand out more clearly than
Elijah. He wrote nothing, yet he is seen as the greatest of the
early prophets. The first mention of him enlivens the narrative
of the *Book of Kings*. Chapter 17 tells how Elijah restored to life
the dead son of a widow in whose house he was staying. Taking
the child to the upper room which was a flimsy structure on the
flat roof, Elijah lay upon him in the belief that thus his own
health would be transferred to the child. Similar incidents are
recorded in *II Kings 4.34* and *Acts 20.10.*

Responsorial Psalm: [1] *Psalm 29.2,4-6,11-13*
The psalmist had been near to death, to the joy of his enemies,
but God restored him. He invites his friends to join him in praise
of God. The intensely personal nature of the psalm, the writer's
uncomplicated faith and his desire to share with his friends make
the psalm a joy to read.

Second Reading: *Galatians 1.11-19*
To cut the ground from under his opponents' feet and to draw his
foolish Galatians back into a correct understanding of their faith,
Paul sets out to show that he received his Gospel, not from men,
not even from the apostles, but from God through a revelation of
Jesus Christ. He gives an account of his early life and then of his
conversion.

Gospel: *Luke 7.11-17*
The only son of a widow had died. Gone also were her hopes of
support and the continuance of her husband's name. The mention
of Nain as the scene of the miracle gives a touch of reality. So
also in a different way does "sat up", a rare word which is part of
Luke's medical vocabulary. Some commentators doubt the story,
bandying such words as "trance", "coma", "popular tale". Our
Lord later burst the bonds of death; why could he not do it now?

---

[1] See Notes, Third Sunday of Easter, Year C.

First Reading: *I I Samuel 12.7-10,13*
As king, David inherited Saul's house and his wives, yet he sought Bathsheba and to gain his end, he sent her husband to his death. This is the sin Nathan exposes in the passage to be read. When David confessed his sin he received absolution from the prophet.

Responsorial Psalm: *Psalm 31.1-2,5,7,11*
One of the seven great penitential psalms, Number 31 has been ascribed by some to David as a confession of the sin described in the First Reading. This psalm was a great comfort to Augustine in his last hours. It expresses the mind of one who, convinced of God's forgiveness, finds great peace.

Second Reading: *Galatians 2.16,19-21*
Galatians began to feature in Second Readings two Sundays ago[1] and will continue for another three. So we must see why Paul wrote to the Galatians. To this people of uncertain location somewhere in the interior of Asia Minor, Paul came on his second missionary tour (*Acts 16.6*). Others came after him, trying to impose on the Galatians a form of Christianity with a heavy overlay of Jewish legalism. This is clear in the reading in which Paul emphasises that by faith alone in Jesus Christ is a person saved and made righteous.

Gospel: *Luke 7.36-8.3*
The passage has been described as an "artistic triumph" and along with others shows Luke's great understanding of women, a recognised feature of his Gospel. People were horrified to learn that Jesus could accept the homage and the gift of a woman with a bad name. She must have heard Jesus preach and in some way beyond our knowing found forgiveness. If read carefully, the passage becomes a cycle of love which begins with the Lord's love for the sinner and ends with the penitent's love for the Lord.

---

[1] These Sundays are often omitted and hence the repetition of previous material.

First Reading: *Zechariah 12.10-11,13.1*
This reading is difficult and obscure. The reference is to the time after the exile when the Jews were striving to remake their city. Divine gifts are to be poured out on the people. Suddenly the prophet's mood changes: the nation is to be plunged into mourning for some martyr (unknown to us) whom they have killed. In *John* this piercing is applied to Jesus.

Responsorial Psalm: *Psalm 62.2-6,8-9* [1]
The psalm may express David's longing for God in the wilderness, or the feelings of an exile separated from the familiar things of worship. Be that as it may, a deep yearning for God and a sense of the value of communion with him, reflect a hunger greater than any physical need.

Second Reading: *Galatians 3.26-29*
Society has always created divisions in the community. Paul speaks of Jew and Greek, slave and free etc. We have artificial lines drawn between rich and poor, black and white etc. But if we put on Christ — an expression which Paul often used – then we grow like what we wear and all divisions lose their meaning for we are all God's children.

Gospel: *Luke 9.18-24*
With his ministry well advanced, Our Lord must have wondered to what extent his disciples appreciated who he really was. The question he asked — and it is given in the passage to be read – showed that Peter at least knew. And then came the bombshell: the way was through suffering for himself, and an act of renunciation for his disciples and a following of him that had no end. Greek can often express shades of meaning that are impossible in English. The self-denial and the taking up of the cross are single acts; the following is an ongoing action.

---

[1] See also Notes, Twenty Second Sunday in Ordinary Time, Year A.

First Reading: *I Kings 19.16,19-21*
Our reading deals with the prophet Elijah, a figure of great
importance in the *Old Testament*. We shall hear now he passed
close to Elisha and threw his cloak over him. This cloak was a
symbol of Elijah's prophetic gift; what he did was, in fact, to
transfer that gift to Elisha, in effect to call him to prophetic
service.

Responsorial Psalm: *Psalm 15.1-2,5,7-11*
This is a psalm in which the key note is total devotion to God.
For the writer, God is his refuge and portion; from him also come
counsel and fulness of joy. Here is one who so communes with his
God that his course of life is sure. The second half of the third
stanza is not a plea for immortality, nor is it a prophecy of the
Resurrection. It is only a prayer for a life of normal length.

Second Reading: *Galatians 5.1,13-18*
There are references to law, liberty and slavery. To understand
this reading, these terms must be grasped. Paul's work in Galatia
was being undone by those who wanted the people to accept a
Jewish form of Christianity with devotion to a complicated
ceremonial law which was only slavery. From this Paul would free
the Galatians with the Law of Christ. This Law of love through
the Holy Spirit would save them from slavery to pettiness and
indulgence.

Gospel: *Luke 9.51-62*
This passage deals mainly with candidates for discipleship. When
Our Lord says: "Follow me", the word is in a form which means
"follow and keep on following continuously", as was pointed out
in the notes last Sunday. He will allow no shadow of uncertainty
in their minds. By vigorously enforcing his challenge he makes
very clear the expected quality of discipleship.

First Reading: *Isaiah 66.10-14*
When the Jews returned from exile, difficulties abounded. Here
the prophet looks beyond the troubles that beset his people, to
the full glory of the Messianic Age. As a mother comforts her
child at her breast, so Jerusalem will give her peace and comfort
to those who rejoice for her.

Responsorial Psalm: *Psalm 65.1-7,16,20*
The portion of the psalm before us falls into two sections: first
there is a hymn of praise for God's mighty works, especially the
parting of the Red Sea when the Israelites fled from Egypt, and
the crossing of the Jordan to enter the Promised Land; the psalm
ends with an invitation to hear the writer's personal testimony of
answered prayer.

Second Reading: *Galatians 6.14-18*
In a final thrust at his opponents, Paul decries the value of Jewish
rites. To be a new creation in Christ is all that matters. Slaves and
devotees of pagan religions bore marks that gave protection and
showed to whom they belonged. Paul has a last word for his
enemies: he wants no more trouble; he bears the stigmata of
Jesus. But what were these stigmata? Reproduction of the
wounds of Christ's Passion as in the case of St. Francis of Assisi
and others? In Paul's case, the explanation probably lies in the
experiences set out in *II Corinthians 11.24.*

Gospel: *Luke 10.1-12,17-20*
In a passage of great content, space allows only four remarks: the
reading is part of what has been called the "Travel Narrative" (9.
51-18.14), the very core of Luke's Gospel with much material
found nowhere else; the figure 72 represents the 72 nations of
earth as in *Genesis 10*; missionaries throughout the ages have
accepted the spirit of Our Lord's instruction to limit provision for
their needs and to rely on God; finally, it has been said that "the
unheeded peace comes back and blesses the heart that wished it".

First Reading: *Deuteronomy 30.10-14*
The Covenant had been given to Israel (Chapters 12-28) and now, Moses, near the end of his life, makes a series of exhortations for its keeping. Our reading is the conclusion of these exhortations: God's Law is not in heaven where only holy men may find it or overseas in foreign custody, but on people's lips that they may speak of it, and in their hearts that they may keep it.

Responsorial Psalm: *Psalm 68.14,17,30-31,33-34,36-37*[1]
The psalmist is in great trouble; poor and ill, he waits on God with fervent hope. He uses his distress to assure others like himself that God will revive their hearts and refurbish their land. The psalm is much quoted in the *New Testament*.

Alternative Responsorial Psalm: *Psalm 18.8-11*
This psalm which is almost certainly two psalms blended together, begins with a wondering look at the nightly sky and ends with the psalmist's delight in observing the Law, that is the Mosaic Law, before the Pharisees converted it, with their burdens, into a yoke. It is the latter portion of the psalm that will be read. We turn from the grandeur of the heavens that make us feel insignificant, to the moral law which lifts man to his highest dignity.

Second Reading: *Colossians 1.15-20*
This is the first of four readings from *Colossians*. Colossae was a city in the heart of Asia Minor. Though Paul did not found the church here, he was concerned for its faith, for heresy was rife. Their worship was an incredible hotch-potch including bits of astrology, asceticism, worship of demons and angels, and some Jewish rites (Chapter 2.16-18). Perhaps worst of all was their belief that Christ was only one of the ways of approaching God. Paul writing from prison, here sets out the absolute supremacy of Christ, Lord of the universe, reconciling God and man through the Church which is his Body.

---

[1] A different selection of verses appears on the Twelfth Sunday in Ordinary Time, Year A. See Notes there.

Gospel: *Luke 10.25-37*

The story of the Good Samaritan is one of the best known and best loved of *Bible* stories. To get most out of the parable, one needs to know something about the Samaritans. The Jews despised them because of their mixed origin - poor Israelites and heathen immigrants - their refusal to use all the *Old Testament* and their failure to worship at Jerusalem. All Our Lord's references to the Samaritans are compassionate.

First Reading: *Genesis 18.1-10*
This is the story of Abraham's reward for entertaining three
mysterious wayfarers: Sarah would conceive in her old age and
thus the promise to Abraham of descendants more numerous
than the stars would be fulfilled. The Bedouin sheik of today
receives travellers in just the same way. Who were these three?
Were they angels? Could it be that we have here a primitive
concept of the Trinity, God in three Persons?

Responsorial Psalm: *Psalm 14.2-5*
The first line of the psalm (omitted in the Missal) "God, who has
the right to enter your tent?", explains all. Pilgrims asked this
question and a priest gave them this psalm for an answer. There is
emphasised throughout, a strong link between religion and ethics
(moral conduct). In the last stanza we are reminded that Jews
were forbidden to lend to each other at interest (*Leviticus 25.
36*); it amounted to profiting from another's distress.

Second Reading: *Colossians 1.24-28*
Paul has spoken of reconciliation and now turns to the purpose of
his own ministry. The passage begins with a difficult statement
which seems to mean that Paul is part of all that suffering which
the Church must endure until victory over evil is won. Let us
remember that we are Paul's heirs. Then there is a reference to "a
mystery hidden for generations". The word "mystery" does not
mean something that baffles, but a secret long hidden and at last
revealed, in this case God's redemptive purpose in Christ. It was
part of Paul's ministry to reveal this mystery.

Gospel: *Luke 10.38-42*
Only Luke records this conversation with Martha and Mary. But
what did Our Lord mean when he said to Martha: "You worry
and fret about so many things and yet few are needed, indeed
only one"? Matters are not helped by the poor state of the Greek
text at this point. Our Lord was on his way to Jerusalem and
needed fellowship, not material things; he probably said in effect
to Martha: "You are preparing a lavish spread; just a snack will
do!"

First Reading: *Genesis 18.20-32*
Abraham is with the same company he had entertained in his
tent. Before Sodom, he is given a view of the way divine justice
works as he bargains with God in deep concern for God's justice
and his power to destroy. Abraham's pleading also shows his own
faith in the justice of God. For today's Mass the special point in
all this is the fact of Abraham's approach to God.

Responsorial Psalm: *Psalm 137.1-3,6-8*
The psalm falls into two parts. In the first the writer refers to
some great personal deliverance. Some imagine he was among
compatriots in exile. Then in the latter part the psalmist speaks
generally of present and future. God has regard for the lowly and
will afford protection in days to come. In the last line "work of
your hands" is best taken as a reference to the psalmist himself.

Second Reading: *Colossians 2.12-14*
Just before our passage, Paul tells the Colossians in general terms,
the errors in their faith. Then with the words we will hear he
speaks of the Christian's dying with Christ, of his baptism with
him and of his rising to new life with him. The record of the debt
which the Law would have demanded is cancelled, or in Paul's
vivid language, the I.O.U. with the debtor's personal signature has
been wiped clean (as with a sponge).

Gospel: *Luke 11.1-13*
At the beginning of this passage you will be struck by a form of
the Lord's Prayer that is different from the one we know so well
from *Matthew*. In writing their Gospels the Evangelists used much
common material, but also had sources of their own. Matthew
and Luke, in recording the Lord's Prayer drew on sources
apparently unknown to each other. With all their differences —
and they are many — each preserves the spirit of the other. The
Parable of the Persistent Friend stresses that we wrestle for our
blessing in the belief that God will give what is best.

First Reading: *Ecclesiastes 1.2,2.21-23*
The *Book of Ecclesiastes* is a kind of essay, presented through one who calls himself the "Preacher". Written about 300 B.C. when Jewish thought had exhausted its spiritual wealth, the book is pessimistic. Though the Preacher believes in the supremacy of God, God yet remains beyond man's knowing. From the emptiness of life, from the vanity of vanities in which all is vanity, the writer would lead men to pursue a more moral existence. The passage to be read, with its example of life's futilities, prepares us for the riches that are in Christ.

Responsorial Psalm: *Psalm 89.3-6,12-14,17*
The psalm falls into two clearly defined parts: the fleeting nature of man's life is set against the eternity and timelessness of God. In the third stanza the psalmist begins a steady ascent, through a plea to know God's Wisdom, to exultation and rejoicing in the favour of God.

Second Reading: *Colossians 3.1-5,9-11*
Having condemned the false elements in the worship of the Colossians (Chapter 2.16-18), Paul directs his readers to the new life in Christ. There are things that must go from their lives; this is expressed in one of his favourite figures of taking off old garments and putting on new. In this process all racial distinctions will disappear. In this letter as in others, doctrine is presented first and then conduct is related to it.

Gospel: *Luke 12.13-21*
Though there are no quotations from the *Book of Ecclesiastes* in the *New Testament*, there is a ring of the First Reading in the parable we are about to hear. Through the ages men have fought over property. In this dispute between brothers, Our Lord refuses to do what the rabbis often did, and arbitrate. On the contrary, in this parable which appears only in *Luke*, he shows that love of possessions does not contribute to the things of the Spirit.

First Reading: *Wisdom 18.6-9*
The *Book of Wisdom* was written in Greek about a century before
Our Lord's birth and was one of the last parts of the *Old
Testament* to be composed. Our reading is an extract from a
survey of the circumstances of Israel's deliverance from the
Egyptians. Their wickedness against Israel resulted in their
punishment and the rescue of Israel from bondage. The reference
to the "sacrifice in secret" is to the Passover. It is possible that
what we are to hear was recited by Greek-speaking Jews at
Passover celebrations.

Responsorial Psalm: *Psalm 32.1,12,18-20,22*
Praise in a ringing cry of joy is to be offered by those with most
to give, the just and the loyal. God is not absent from their
affairs; in fact he has rescued them from peril and famine. The
past illumines the future; the psalm ends on a note of expectancy
and hope. The psalm features several times in the Missal in
different forms. See the Index of Passages.

Second Reading: *Hebrews 11.1-2,8-19*
This is the first of four readings from *Hebrews*, the author of
which has never been identified [1]. Its basic message is the
superiority of Christ to all that made up the old Covenant, angels,
priests and the sacrificial system. As an exhortation to greater
faith the writer sets out a catalogue of heroes of the faith. This is
where our reading begins.

Gospel: *Luke 12.32-48*
The Gospel falls into three parts: first, there is instruction what
to do with our possessions; a spiritual use of them for the good of
others is the essence of Our Lord's command. Then follows the
parable with is message of watchfulness, for the Master will return
without warning. The crux of the final part is that we are
expected to give as freely as we have received.

---

[1] See Notes, Twenty-seventh Sunday in Ordinary Time, Year B.

First Reading: *Jeremiah 38.4-6,8-10*
Not by nature a prophet of woe, perhaps more likely the noblest character in the *Old Testament*, Jeremiah stands supreme as a suffering servant in a personal relationship with God. When the might of Assyria was waning, the Jews courted Egypt against the power of Babylon. Jeremiah prophesied the destruction of Jerusalem and the Temple, and counselled submission to Babylon. For his unpopular stance he was imprisoned. The details of this experience will now be read.

Responsorial Psalm: *Psalm 39.2-4,18*
Near to death in serious illness, the psalmist tells how he waited for God to deliver him from the pit of the Underworld. The vivid language, especially the reference to the "miry clay" reminds us of the First Reading. The third stanza suggests that what the psalmist has endured will strengthen the faith of others. As they stand, the last four lines are a plea for speedy deliverance in the future.

Second Reading: *Hebrews 12.1-4*
The reading is an exhortation to emulate the heroes of faith, the catalogue of whose names has just been recorded. The writer imagines the scene of an athletics contest at which the heroes of faith are the dense crowd of onlookers, while on the course are the runners of the day. Like good athletes they have discarded all encumbrances; they press on steadily for the race is long; in their minds is the athlete of all time, Jesus who overcame all the obstacles in his way.

Gospel: *Luke 12.49-53*
The passage is short and difficult. First there is, "I come to bring fire". Is it the fire of strife? Or the fire that separates gold from dross (*Malachi 3.3*), or the fire that is spiritual baptism (*Matthew 3.11*) or the fire of holiness that creates divisions such as the reading goes on to describe? Many a person has taken Holy Orders in the face of violent parental opposition. An old commentary quotes two sayings of Jesus recorded outside Scripture, "He who is near me is near the fire" and "Near me, near the sword".

First Reading: *Isaiah 66.18-21*
Isaiah looks beyond the broken dreams of Judah's return from
exile to the glorious future when nations will stream into
Jerusalem to see the holy Mountain of the Lord. Numerous
peoples are mentioned in the reading; they lived in the western,
eastern and southern parts of the Mediterranean, the world as
the Jews knew it. The spirit of the passage is part of our Christian
heritage and certainly part of our hope.

Responsorial Psalm: *Psalm 116*
The shortest of all the psalms takes up the call to all nations to
worship God, and clearly states the reason; his love and his
faithfulness are sure. Paul quotes this psalm in his *Letter to the
Romans* (Chapter 15.11) to prove his claim that the Gospel is for
all nations.

Second Reading: *Hebrews 12.5-7,11-13*
The central theme of *Hebrews* is the eternal High Priest "who has
offered one single sacrifice for sins and then taken his place for
ever at the right hand of God" (*Hebrews 10.12*). Through Christ
we can enter the same Sanctuary with the status of sons, but as
sons of God we must submit to the correction that human fathers
apply. The reading deals with this chastisement and the results it
produces.

Gospel: *Luke 13.22-30*
When some one, clearly referring to the Jews, asked if only a few
would be saved, Our Lord applied the answer to those present.
They were on their way up to Jerusalem and there was an
increasing urgency about issues involved. Luke attributes to Our
Lord a Greek figure of speech from the athletics track: "Continue
to strain every nerve to enter by the narrow door". They will
come from all directions, as Isaiah saw, and when the door is
finally closed, no more will be admitted.

First Reading: *Ecclesiasticus* [1] *3.17-20,28-29*
One of the late books of the *Old Testament* and not to be confused with *Ecclesiastes*, the Preacher, *Ecclesiasticus* is part of what is called Wisdom Literature. Wisdom is not an idea, but almost a person who existed before creation. *Proverbs 8.22-31* helps us to understand. The First Reading deals with humility as part of the practical observance of Wisdom.

Responsorial Psalm: *Psalm 67.4-7,10-11*
The psalm is a medley, difficult to interpret and without an obvious thread to link the various parts. Equally unclear is the purpose for which it was composed. In the small portion before us there is an exuberant call to rejoice in God; the outcasts of society are his special concern. Finally God's breaking of a drought is called to mind.

Second Reading: *Hebrews 12.18-19,22-24*
Much has been made in the *Letter to the Hebrews* of God's two Covenants with man, and in this, the last reading from *Hebrews,* we shall hear of the terrifying natural phenomena that accompanied the giving of the Law at Sinai; by contrast, those who belong to the New Covenant draw near to the heavenly Jerusalem with its divine company and its communion of saints.

Gospel: *Luke 14.1,7-14*
We have come full circle and are back to the thought of the First Reading, but with this difference, that there, humility was stressed for daily living, whereas here it is a prerequisite for life in the Kingdom. The parable, which is not in the usual narrative form, is directed against the Pharisees who considered that they were entitled to the best places in the Kingdom. The reading concludes with an injunction against doing things with the calculated motive of getting a return, again as the Pharisees did.

---

[1] See Notes, Eighth Sunday in Ordinary Time, Year C.

First Reading: *Wisdom* [1] *9.13-18*

We meet again the *Old Testament* concept of Wisdom as a "breath of the power of God, a pure flowing forth of the glory of the Almighty" (*Wisdom 7.25*). In the passage to be read the writer declares that man cannot by himself fathom the mind of God, but Wisdom provides the enlightenment necessary for this purpose.

Responsorial Psalm: *Psalm 89.3-6,12-14,17*

The psalm falls into two clearly defined parts: the fleeting nature of man's life is set against the eternity and timelessness of God. In the third stanza the psalmist begins a steady ascent, through a plea to know God's Wisdom, to exultation and rejoicing in the favour of God.

Second Reading: *Philemon 9-10,12-17*

Onesimus, a runaway slave belonging to Philemon had found his way to Paul in prison, probably in Rome. Paul wrote to Philemon and begged him to take Onesimus back, not as a slave, but as a brother. Fugitive slaves were subject to the cruellest of punishment, but the conversion of Onesimus to Christianity and the fact that Philemon was a Christian eased the way for Paul's request. We note that Paul did not ask for Onesimus to be freed, for Paul was not concerned with social problems; they would all be solved when the Lord returned. There is no massive theology in this letter, only tender concern for one who was on the lowest rung of the social ladder.

Gospel: *Luke 14.25-33*

With the shadow of the Cross beginning to fall across the company as they journeyed to Jerusalem, Our Lord speaks of the cost and perils of discipleship. The remark that we must hate our kin is a good example of Semitic exaggeration to enforce a point: the claims of Christ come before those of the family. The examples of the builder of the tower and the king at war emphasise the need to count the cost of discipleship.

---

[1] See Notes, Thirty-second Sunday in Ordinary Time, Year A.

TWENTY-FOURTH SUNDAY IN ORDINARY TIME 213
YEAR C

First Reading: *Exodus 32.7-11,13-14*
The Israelites grew anxious as Moses tarried with God on Sinai,
and needing a tangible object to worship, made a golden calf from
their jewellery, the calf being a symbol of strength and fertility
and a memory of what they had seen in Egypt. This is the scene
that greeted Moses when he returned. The rest of the reading
deals with Moses and his pleading with God for mercy on his
errant people.

Responsorial Psalm: *Psalm 50* [1] *3-4,12-13,17,19*
This is the greatest of all the penitential psalms and is often
wrongly applied to David's treatment of Uriah (*II Samuel 11*).
Through the centuries the psalm has echoed the desire for
forgiveness of those who have a burden to cast on God. First,
there is the frankest plea for forgiveness, then a desire for inner
renewal; finally, the penitent promises to declare God's goodness,
and with that he returns to his own contrition.

Second Reading: *I Timothy 1.12-17*
This is the first of seven readings from Paul's two *Letters to
Timothy*. Whether these and *Titus* were written by Paul as they
stand, or are fragments of Pauline correspondence or even the
work of another hand, need not concern us. Timothy is Paul's
representative in Ephesus faced with false teachers, and Paul
writes to encourage him by referring to his own early career and
how Christ's salvation came to him.

Gospel: *Luke 15.1-32* [2]
The reading deals with the joy that comes when the lost is found.
The passage tells of the **Lost Sheep**, the **Lost Coin** and the well
known story of the **Prodigal Son**, the last two being recorded
only in *Luke*. The sheep was lost because it knew no better, the
coin because of another's carelessness and the son by deliberate
intention. The first two were found by the efforts of others, the
third through his own choice in repentance. Of the two sons it
has been said: "one stayed; the other strayed". Who do you think
stood more in need of his father's compassion?

---

[1] See Index of Passages.

[2] See Notes, Sacred Heart, Year C.

First Reading: *Amos 8.4-7*
Amos [1] was the first of the canonical prophets (those whose
teaching was written down). A herdsman called by God to
prophesy to Israel, he knew that the country's wealth was built
on social injustice and that the people had no real regard for their
religion. In the reading, he attacks the use of false measures and
the practice of selling sweepings of wheat for wheat itself,
actions directed against the poor.

Responsorial Psalm: *Psalm 112.1-2,4-8*
Psalms 112-117 are psalms of praise and were used at the great
religious festivals of the Jews. The theme of this psalm is simple,
but profound: God who is Lord of the universe is concerned
with the lot of the poor.

Second Reading: *1 Timothy 2.1-8*
Much of this letter is devoted to advice how to behave in God's
house, advice Timothy was to put into practice in his duties at
Ephesus. In the reading, prayers for all men are enjoined,
especially those in high places of authority, and for the pagans
around them. We note that following the Lord's example (*Mark
12.17*), Christians had no wish to turn the world upside down
politically.

Gospel: *Luke 16.1-13*
The Parable of the Unjust Steward is one of the most difficult
passages in Scriptures. In spite of an enormous literature on the
subject, there is no one explanation which is wholly satisfactory.
It helps to remember that in a parable there is only one teaching
point; the mass of detail is only colouring matter. There are two
interpretations that have an appeal: lowered standards are always
passed on, and just as the steward with all his faults used
circumstances to serve his own ends, so we should use material
advantages to provide for the future needs of the kingdom.

---

[1] See Notes, Fifteenth Sunday in Ordinary Time, Year B.

TWENTY-SIXTH SUNDAY IN ORDINARY TIME 215
YEAR C

First Reading: *Amos 6.1,4-7*
Amos continues his trenchant attack on the debased social life
of Israel. Their furniture and food are the choicest in the land.
Their music, drinking habits and use of cosmetics receive the
prophet's lash as sins of luxury. The prophecy that they would be
exiled was fulfilled when Assyria overran the kingdom of Israel
in 721 B.C.

Responsorial Psalm: *Psalm 145.6-10*[1]
Five psalms at the end of the Psalter are known as "Alleluia
Psalms" because they begin and end with the word "alleluia".
They were used each morning in the services of the Synagogue. In
this psalm God is praised for his concern for the socially
oppressed and the handicapped. They are all his care. The psalm
ends on a note of triumph: the Lord will reign for ever.

Second Reading: *I Timothy 6.11-16*
The letter has ranged over many issues such as worship, church
officials, false teachers and the position in the Church of various
sections of the community. Paul now turns to Timothy with
some advice and encouragement: Timothy must maintain the
highest standards in his own life. To the words "Fight the good
fight" one could add "and do not give up", to express more fully
the force of the Greek. The phrase takes us back again to the
sports arena. The passage concludes with a doxology.

Gospel: *Luke 16.19-31*
Only Luke records the Parable of Dives and Lazarus, the last in
a series dealing with the misuse of wealth. Dives who had refused
to listen to Moses and the Prophets in his lifetime regarding the
treatment of the poor, suffers misery in the hereafter, while
Lazarus has his reward in the bosom of Abraham at the banquet
of the blessed. It is not the having of wealth that Our Lord
condemns, but the misuse of it.

---

[1] See Notes, Twenty-third and Thirty-second Sundays in
Ordinary Time, Year B.

First Reading: *Habakkuk 1.2-3,2.2-4*

A little later than Jeremiah, Habakkuk lived in the period when Assyrian power had waned and Egypt, after a brief ascendency, declined before the might of Babylon. Habakkuk wrote just before Babylon overwhelmed Jerusalem. The reading contains, first, the prophet's complaint to God that he does nothing about the evil ways of his people. Then God tells Habakkuk to write down the prophetic message he is about to receive: their enemies are puffed up with pride, but the righteous man will live by his faithfulness. This last sentence, with a slight alteration, became the key stone of Paul's *Letter to the Romans* (1.17). The second last line of the reading refers to the enemies of the Jews.

Responsorial Psalm: *Psalm 94.1-2,6-9*

This psalm was sung on the way to the Temple. St Benedict in the sixth century required the monks of his order to say it daily on waking. In the psalm God is approached with a joyful noise in characteristic Oriental manner. In the second stanza one feels the hush of awe. References to the rock, Meribah and Massah show how the desert experience stands as a perpetual warning to God's people.

Second Reading: *II Timothy 1.6-8,13-14*

In this *Second Letter to Timothy*, Paul continues to encourage his protege in the face of the difficulties that beset him. In the passage to be read, Paul would have Timothy stir into white heat the smouldering embers of what he received at ordination. The word "pattern" in the latter part means a preliminary sketch. Paul says in effect: you have the rough outline of what I have taught; fill it out so that it becomes your own.

Gospel: *Luke 17.5-10*

The reading is in two parts, the first dealing with the power of faith and the second with the insufficiency of works, the latter being found only in *Luke*. In the first part we note that the mustard seed was considered the smallest of all seeds and yet the source of a large tree. We note, too, the typical Semitic exaggeration in "be planted in the sea". The second part is a strong corrective to any feeling of superiority that might be occasioned by works of faith. We are servants, unpaid as of old; our service is our bounden duty.

First Reading: *II Kings 5.14-17*
Naaman the Syrian suffered from one of those skin ailments which the Jews classified as leprosy. Through his Israelite slave girl, he heard of Elisha who instructed him to do what is described in the reading. Naaman, cleansed from his disease, in his gratitude, wanted to be always near to Elisha's God; so he took home some of the soil on which the God of these people resided, for the ancients believed a god was god only of his own territory.

Responsorial Psalm: *Psalm 97.1-4*[1]
The psalmist calls on the people to sing a new song, "new" suggesting a special occasion, possibly deliverance from Babylon, or maybe, because his psalm is another in the Enthronement series. God has shown his justice by the rescue (salvation) of his people. All the world has seen and is called to rejoice. The psalmist thus sees the God of the Jews as the God of all nations.

Second Reading: *II Timothy 2.8-13*
Paul continues to encourage Timothy to face hardship, using the soldier, the athlete and the farmer as examples. In the first sentence of the reading, Paul refers to his own plight as a criminal in prison for the sake of the Gospel. He accepts all this in the belief that the Cross comes before the Crown. Then follows a fragment of a hymn — there are several incorporated into the *New Testament* — and from what Paul quotes, it would appear to have been part of a martyr's hymn.

Gospel: *Luke 17.11-19*
The Jews despised the Samaritans for their mixed origin, their refusal to worship at Jerusalem and their reliance on part only of the *Old Testament*. On this occasion, ten lepers, one a Samaritan, were bonded in a common suffering and exclusion from society. Our Lord answered a cry for pity by sending them, in accordance with the Mosaic Law (*Leviticus 14*), to the priests. On the way they were healed, not by the Lord's touch, but by their own faith. Only the Samaritan returned to express his gratitude, a reproach to the elect of all ages.

---

[1] See Notes, Nativity of the Lord, Mass during the Day.

First Reading: *Exodus 17.8-13*
On their way to the Promised Land the Israelites were attacked
by the Amalekites, descendants of Esau and destined for
centuries to be their implacable foes. On this occasion, Israel
gained victory by the intercession of Moses. In the reading there
is a reference to Moses' arms uplifted in supplication. This was a
common posture of prayer (*Psalm 134.2*).

Responsorial Psalm: *Psalm 120*
This is the second of the Gradual Psalms sung by pilgrims,
probably in some response form, as they ascended Zion's hill. As
they approached their destination, uplifted eyes saw the
mountains round about Jerusalem. The psalm is a beautiful
expression of trust in God who is the Helper of his people and
who is ever on guard for their good and watchful in every
circumstance of danger. Every Jew recited the last sentence as he
entered or left his home.

Second Reading: *I I Timothy 3.14-4.2*
Paul's advice to Timothy continues. As a counter to the current
false teaching, he must look to Paul's example (4.10) and to the
Scriptures in which he was brought up. The Scriptures are not the
New Testament, for the only part as yet in existence was Paul's
correspondence, but the *Old Testament* and most probably the
Greek version of it, for Timothy's mother and grandmother were
Greeks. Paul asserts that these Scriptures provide a wisdom that
leads to salvation. Who the false teachers were is a complex
problem; put simply, their teaching was a mixture of Jewish
thought and ascetic practice.

Gospel: *Luke 18,1-8*
This parable is found only in *Luke*; it is an encouragement to
pray unceasingly that no matter what problems beset the Church,
Our Lord will return. The vehicle of his teaching is the widow,
who was too poor to bribe and had no protector. Her persistence
eventually induced the judge to act, for the judge said: "She will
worry me to death". Was that what the judge really said? The
Greek verb means "to give someone a black eye".

First Reading: *Ecclesiasticus 35.12-14,16-19*
Once again we meet the *Book of Ecclesiasticus* which has been described as "the gem of the *Apocrypha*" (books of the *Old Testament* not considered genuine by the Jews). It was a late composition, best known in a Greek translation and regarded as a kind of handbook covering a wide range of life's situations. These are dealt with in relation to Wisdom[1]. Our reading shows God's concern for the oppressed.

Responsorial Psalm: *Psalm 33.2-3,17-19,23*
The writer is full of thanksgiving, for God has rescued him from some serious trouble. He must tell God's praises, but with the dubious assurance that the wicked will be punished. In the last stanza the psalmist is surely speaking from his own experience. The psalm is an acrostic in its structure [2].

Second Reading: *I I Timothy 4.6-8,16-18*
This is the last of the readings from Paul's letters to Timothy and in it we hear some of the writer's final words. There is a quiet and confident expectation of the end. He finishes with three vivid metaphors: he is already being poured out in the way the pagans and the Jews made drink offerings to their gods; it is time to strike camp—Paul was a tent maker by trade—and looking back over his life, he lets his thoughts turn to Olympic and other games and to the athletes' track in particular. Victory is assured, no crown of laurel wreath which must wither and die, but the Crown of righteousness which never fades.

Gospel: *Luke 18.9-14*
On paper the Pharisee had a most impressive list of virtues, some in excess of what the Law required; the tax collector had only a debit column. The parable illustrates the incorrect use of prayer and shows that God reads these balance sheets of human virtues in a manner very different from the way the world does. The Pharisee sought to give himself status with God; the tax collector, admitting that he had none, was given status by God.

---

[1] See Notes, Sixteenth Sunday, in Ordinary Time, Year A.

[2] See Notes, Fourteenth Sunday in Ordinary Time, Year A.

First Reading: *Wisdom 11.22-12.2*

The *Book of Wisdom* is in three parts: the first section deals with the destinies of the good and the evil; in the second, Wisdom herself speaks in the form of a meditation; finally Israel's early history is reviewed. It is here that our reading belongs. The writer uses the ideas in this passage to show the operation of God's forbearance.

Responsorial Psalm: *Psalm 144.1-2,8-11,13-14*

The spiritual quality of this psalm is attested by the frequent use of it in the Missal [1]. The psalm is a hymn of praise, described as "one of the most inspiring in the Psalter"; it could have been composed only by one who had had a profound experience of God. It is the last of the alphabetical or acrostic psalms in which each verse begins with the succeeding letter of the Hebrew alphabet. First the greatness of God, then his compassion are praised. In the third stanza the psalmist strikes a universal note and concludes with the praise of God's faithfulness and love.

Second Reading: *II Thessalonians 1.11-2.2*

It is very appropriate as the year draws to a close and Advent approaches, that we should be directed to this early letter of the great apostle with its fervent expectation of the Lord's Return. It was at Thessalonika, overlooking the northern waters of the Aegean Sea, that Paul established his second European church. In the passage to be read there is a prayer that the Thessalonians will be worthy of their calling, and then with a relevance that applies to all times, he warns against preoccupation with the Lord's Return, because some of his friends in Thessalonika were so sure of the immediacy of the event that they had ceased to work. Furthermore, what appeared to be a letter forged in Paul's name had fired rumours that the great event had taken place.

Gospel: *Luke 19.1-10*

We are indebted to *Luke* alone for the story of Zacchaeus. On their way to Jerusalem, the little band reached Jericho, an important centre in the tax collecting industry of the Roman empire. As a prominent figure — Luke rarely uses names — Zacchaeus was despised by the local population. In the story of his dramatic conversion, it is noted that Zacchaeus did not abandon his calling, but continued to pursue it, a new man in Christ.

---

[1] See Index of Passages.

THIRTY-SECOND SUNDAY IN ORDINARY TIME 221
YEAR C

First Reading: *I I Maccabees 7.1-2,9-14*
Alexander the Great having conquered the world, ruled for two
years and died in 323 B.C. His vast empire was split into three
parts, Syria and adjacent areas falling to Seleucus who founded a
dynasty. Its fifth member, the eccentric Antiochus 1V is the king
mentioned in the reading. He stirred up violent opposition by
imposing Greek culture on the Jews in an attempt to stamp out
their religion. The reading describes one such act of oppression.
The date is about 165 B.C.

Responsorial Psalm: *Psalm 16.1,5-6,8,15*
It is obvious from the complete form of the psalm that the writer
is in great danger, though who his enemies were we cannot tell.
With a clear conscience, he begs God to help him and goes on to
tell God why he should! "Shadow of your wings" could suggest a
mother bird's protective care, an idea found elsewhere in the
Psalms. The psalmist has a very pronounced sense of his own
righteousness.

Second Reading: *I I Thessalonians 2.16-3.5*
Paul has dealt with mistaken ideas about the Lord's Return and
then prays for the Thessalonians that they may be strengthened,
for their position in a hostile world is not easy. A request that
they pray for him changes to a prayer for the missionary work of
the Church, and that he and they may be protected from their
enemies, who were most likely Jews or Jewish Christians with
an emphasis on Judaism. They were active in Thessalonika and
Corinth where Paul was writing.

Gospel: *Luke 20.27-38*
Three points will help our understanding of this passage: first, the
Sadducees were a priestly aristocracy who refused to accept what
was outside the Mosaic Law. They rejected later views in the *Old
Testament* regarding bodily resurrection and angels (*Acts 23.8*);
second, the Mosaic Law required a man to marry his deceased
brother's wife to preserve the family name (*Deuteronomy
25.5-6*); finally, Our Lord refutes the Sadducees by referring to
Moses at the scene of the Burning Bush (*Exodus 3.1-6*): if God is
God of Abraham, Isaac and Jacob, then these three are alive. Our
Lord is saying that the bonds and relationships that exist on earth
do not apply in heaven.

First Reading: *Malachi 3.19-20*
Malachi, the last of the books in the *Old Testament*, is not the last in time. We know almost nothing about the writer, perhaps not even his name, for Malachi means "my messenger". The Jews had returned from exile; the Temple had been rebuilt, but all was not well: they were beset by poor seasons; neighbours were hostile; there was no heart in their religion and moral standards had fallen. Malachi sees the Day of the Lord as a fierce oven into which the wicked will be cast as fuel, but for the righteous this same event will be as the dawn.

Responsorial Psalm: *Psalm 97.5-9*
This is one of the Enthronement [1] Psalms which were used to celebrate God's enthronement over creation, at a festival marking the beginning of the Jewish year. In this psalm all are invited to salute their king with voice and musical instruments; then nature is invoked to join the acclamation. In the last stanza, it has been pointed out that the thought is echoed in "Thy Kingdom come".

Second Reading: *I I Thessalonians 3.7-12*
Still on the subject of the Lord's Return, Paul directs his attention to those who are so preoccupied with the immediacy of the event that they refuse to work and are living off their Christian brothers. Quoting his own example of industry in their midst, he urges that loafers should not be fed. The letter speaks pertinently to all those who get the Second Coming out of perspective.

Gospel: *Luke 21.5-19*
Writers, ancient and modern, run out of words trying to describe the magnificence of Herod's Temple. It symbolised the very existence of the Jewish nation. Our Lord prophesied its destruction. The description of the last times continues: everything will be shattered, international relationships, the order of nature and basic human ties. Faced with all this, the elect will win through with endurance, defined by one scholar as "the spirit to bear with blazing hope".

---

[1] See Notes, Nativity of the Lord, Mass during the Day.

OUR LORD JESUS CHRIST, UNIVERSAL KING
YEAR C

First Reading: *I I Samuel 5.1-3*
Saul was dead and the choice of a new king fell on David whom they anointed. This ceremony was common to many ancient religions. Probably Egyptian in origin, its use in the *Old Testament* implied a special endowment of God's Spirit. From the Hebrew verb "anoint" comes "Messiah", (the anointed one), and this translated into Greek becomes "Christos".

Responsorial Psalm: *Psalm 121.1-5*
In this gradual psalm there is an expression of a pilgrim's joy when he joins others who have invited him to go to Jerusalem. Travel in groups was a necessary precaution against brigands. Then comes the sheer delight of being in the city of cities. The second stanza may refer to the dense array of buildings in the city or to its solid unity and the joy of its people going up to the festivals. The final thought is of this ancient seat from which the civil power of kings was administered. Portion of this psalm is used on the first Sunday of Advent in Year A. We have come full circle.

Second Reading: *Colossians 1.12-20*
Paul had heard that the Colossian church was riddled with heresy that centred chiefly on the belief that there were many ways by which God could be approached. Here Paul sets out the absolute supremacy and uniqueness of Christ. The passage has attracted an enormous literature, but by reading slowly and often, its message comes through.

Gospel: *Luke 23.35-43*
The Church's year has run its cycle and we are standing at the foot of the Cross. We hear the soldiers' cruel jibe "If you are King of the Jews, save yourself" and the plea of the penitent thief "Remember me when you come into your Kingdom". To the former Our Lord made no response; to the latter he gave a kingly reply, "Today you will be with me in Paradise". "Paradise" is a Persian word; it is used of the Garden of Eden in the Greek version of the *Old Testament* and in Greek literature it describes the royal parks of Persian kings and nobles. Luke, who alone gives us this word from the Cross, uses "Paradise" to describe the Intermediate State of the dead.

HOLY DAYS
FEASTS OF THE LORD
SOLEMNITIES

GENERAL CALENDAR

PRESENTATION OF THE LORD
Second Form: Solemn Entrance

First Reading: *Malachi 3.1-4*

Malachi [1] is concerned to answer the question whether God really cared to distinguish between good and evil (2.17). He declares dramatically that the Lord will suddenly appear in his Temple; spiritual longings will be satisfied; the priesthood will be purified. The First Reading is a beautiful preparation for the Presentation of the Lord in the Temple, the Candlemas of the early Church.

Responsorial Psalm: *Psalm 23.7-10*

The psalm was used at one of the great festivals which celebrate the Ruler of the universe as he enters his chosen dwelling. A priest asks who may climb Zion's hill and is answered by another declaring that it is he whose hands are clean and whose heart is pure. In the portion before us two thoughts alternate: the ancient gates are bidden to open for the King's entry; and the question is asked who the King is. The answer gives his qualities. In the words "grow higher" it is suggested that the ancient doors guarding the city are barely high enough to receive the lofty King of Glory.

Second Reading: *Hebrews 2.14-18*

Having declared the superiority of Jesus, the unknown writer of this letter sets out in detail his humanity, an idea most appropriate for this Mass. The main thought of the passage lies in the words "It was not angels that he took to himself". Jesus was not an angel, but a man. The benefits to mankind that flowed from his humanity are declared in the reading.

Gospel: *Luke 2.22-40*

The presentation of the Child Jesus in the Temple shows both the poverty (*Leviticus 12.6,8*) and the piety of Mary and Joseph. Revealed too is the fact that Jesus was under the Law. The story of Simeon indicates the acute spiritual perception of holy men which in this case gave the Church the little gem we call *Nunc Dimittis*. The first shadow falls across a mother's joy as she catches a fleeting glimpse of her future role of *mater dolorosa*. Finally, over the scene comes Anna's gentle voice, Anna the type of many an elderly nun, rich in years and wisdom.

---

[1] See Notes Thirty-first Sunday in Ordinary Time, Year A.

19 March
ST. JOSEPH
HUSBAND OF THE BLESSED VIRGIN MARY

First Reading: *I I Samuel 7.4-5,12-14,16* [1]
David, his warfare accomplished, was troubled in his conscience because he was better housed than the ark of God. Nathan, the prophet, made it clear that another would build for him and establish a dynasty. Joseph who was of David's lineage fulfilled this promise as husband of the Blessed Virgin Mary.

Responsorial Psalm: *Psalm 88.2-5,27,29*
The full version of this psalm is composite; the verses before us reflect the facts of the First Reading; In the first stanza, the writer declares his intentions of ever proclaiming God's love which is as sure as the heavens. In the next stanza the permanence of the Davidic covenant is affirmed. Finally the psalmist echoes the conclusion of the First Reading in the words: "You are my father".

Second Reading: *Romans 4.13,16-18,22* [2]
The First Reading told of God's promise to David. Now we read how God's promise to Abraham, against impossible odds, extended much farther back in time. In David's case no great demands were made of him; Abraham was required to exercise faith in the extreme. Joseph's righteousness (which is rather obscured in the *Jerusalem Bible*)—*Matthew 1.19*—puts him in Abraham's lineage.

Gospel: *Matthew 1.16,18-21,24*
Only Matthew gives us these precious details of Joseph's reaction to Mary's holy pregnancy, details that required a faith comparable to Abraham's. This lovely incident gains greater meaning when it is recalled that betrothal created a bond so close that if the man died the girl became a widow. In Mary's condition Joseph could not simply walk away from her. The scandal of a divorce or a writ and the payment of a fine were the options. Joseph, intending to take the latter course, was stopped by an angel.

---

[1] See Notes, Fourth Sunday in Advent, Year B.
[2] See Notes, Tenth Sunday in Ordinary Time, Year A.

Alternate Gospel: *Luke 2.41-51*

The Lord's devoted parents make the long journey to the Passover at Jerusalem. Jesus at the age of twelve was now a man and every Jew aimed to make the journey at least once. The magnificent Temple and the huge colourful crowds would make the occasion memorable. Various attempts have been made to explain his parents' apparent lack of supervision. The most convincing is that men and women travelled in separate caravans and that the women who travelled more slowly set out ahead of the men. When they camped for the night each parent thought that Jesus was with the other. The reply which Jesus gave when he was found seems rather pert. Said with winsome gentleness it loses its precocity.

24 June
BIRTH OF ST JOHN THE BAPTIST
VIGIL MASS

First Reading: *Jeremiah 1.4-10* [1]
Jeremiah, alone and often apparently forsaken, and John, austere
and unyielding, have much in common. Three points emerge in
the dialogue between God and Jeremiah: first, God's purposes are
not haphazard decisions; Jeremiah's destiny was determined
before he was born. Scripture holds many examples of men
shrinking from the purposes of God [2]. See *Isaiah 6.5.* Finally,
Jeremiah is commissioned for his work; the lips that were to
speak for God were touched by God.

Responsorial Psalm: *Psalm 70.1-6,15,17*
The psalm is an old man's acknowledgement of God as his life-
long hope and trust; it is also the same man's plea not to be
abandoned, for, presumably in sickness, he has suffered the
taunts of cruel men. The voice of this aged saint, still confident of
his God, deserves to be heard by pilgrims only just setting out on
the same journey.

Second Reading: *I Peter 1.8-12*
The first paragraph establishes how precious salvation is and in
the second, the writer declares, in a passage of great difficulty,
that the prophets were looking for this salvation and satisfied
themselves that they had found it in the Law and the Prophets of
the *Old Testament.* Suffering features prominently in *I Peter*;
there is a reference to it in the reading. St John the Baptist met a
cruel death.

Gospel:*Luke 1.5-17*
Here is the central theme of the mass. Actually after a brief and
very formal opening, Luke inserts this passage to give his readers
the details of the one who was to be the forerunner of Christ.
Three points stand out: Zacharias' vision was given to him at the
holiest moment of his service; references to angels are a marked
feature of Luke's Gospel; John was to be a Nazarite (*See
Numbers 6.3ff.*).

---

[1] See Notes, Fourth Sunday in Ordinary Time, Year C.
[2] Francis Thompson's poem *The Hound of Heaven* centres on
this theme.

First Reading: *Isaiah 49.1-6*
In *Second* [1] *Isaiah* there are four Songs of the Suffering Servant
and the second of these is in the First Reading. Speaking in exile,
the Servant sees the restoration of his country as a God-given
task. He is the means by which salvation comes not only to those
near by, but also to those far away. The Servant declares that he
was divinely appointed to this purpose even before birth.

Responsorial Psalm: *Psalm 138.1-3,13-15*
The psalm reflects a profound trust in God. The writer
acknowledges that his whole life is as an open book before the
Lord and that even before he was born, God was with him. The
psalm has been called "the greatest gem in the Psalter". There is
a lovely metaphor at the end of stanza one: just as grain is
separated from chaff by winnowing, so God assesses the value of
this man's actions. "You mark when I walk or lie down" does
not adequately express this.

Second Reading: *Acts 13.22-26*
Paul was making his first missionary journey in Asia Minor and at
Antioch — there were other cities so named — in the Roman
province of Galatia, he preached in the Synagogue. Before us is
part of his thumb-nail sketch of Jewish history in which he
presents Jesus as part of David's line and, more to the point for
this Mass, John as his forerunner.

Gospel: *Luke 1.57-60,80*
Apparently only Blessed Mary knew of Elizabeth's pregnancy for
she had gone into retirement (*Luke 1.24*). Of the reasons offered,
the most attractive is that she was not really in retirement, but
rather in retreat, for the child she was carrying was of God and
for God. As he grew up John also went into retreat in the
"deserts", a phrase suggesting that in these preparatory years, he
moved about freely in his self-imposed seclusion. The beautiful
Benedictus, Zacharias' song of praise, has been omitted from the
reading.

---

[1] See Notes, Second Sunday in Ordinary Time, Year A.

Sunday on or after 29 June
SS PETER AND PAUL, APOSTLES
VIGIL MASS

First Reading: *Acts 3.1-10*
It was mid-afternoon and people were gathering for prayers in the
magnificent and partly built Temple which Herod had started. In
stark contrast was the pitiful beggar, crippled and in the rags of
poverty. This was to be the first healing recorded in *Acts*. In
response to the man's plight Peter showed that he had more to
offer than money. The very power of God flowed through
Peter to meet the needs of this distressed man.

Responsorial Psalm: *Psalm 18.2-5*
Just as Peter and Paul were to take the gospel to the ends of the
earth, so since time began, God's wonders of creation have been
proclaimed for all to see. The silent preaching of the nightly sky
is an unending homily of which we never weary.

Second Reading: *Galatians 1.11-20*
Paul had made many converts among the Galatians, a people of
uncertain location in Asia Minor. Others came and preached false
doctrine so that Paul had to write a corrective letter. In the
passage before us he states that Christ himself revealed the truth
of the Gospel to him and that God chose him for his missionary
work before he was born. Chosen by the Father and taught by
the Son, could his message fail to be true?

Gospel: *John 21.15-19*
In a passage full of pitfalls for the translator, two basic facts stand
out. Peter who three times denied his Lord is required to make a
threefold assertion of his love; he is taken back to the point of his
failure and given the chance to claim victory there. As a pointer
to the great things ahead, he was given a threefold commission:
"Feed my lambs", "Look after my sheep", "Feed my sheep".
The words "take you where you would not go" are seen as a
reference to his martyrdom, crucifixion upside down.

First Reading: *Acts 12.1-11*
In times similar to those in which his Lord was crucified, Peter
was imprisoned by the implacable Herod. It was a crisis of
diametrically opposing forces, Herod, cruel friend of the Jews,
with soldiers to execute his whim and the Church in unremitting
prayer. We wait for the thrill of this immortal story and note that
as he passed from his prison with angelic escort, Peter, the first
home missionary of the Church, joined the prayer group that had
rescued him.

Responsorial Psalm: *Psalm 33.2-9*
The psalmist had been in great trouble, but the Lord answered his
needs and set him free and angels watched over him. Throughout
the psalm the friends of the writer are invited to join with him in
praising God. Try to recall as many incidents as you can in the
life of Peter and Paul and see how apt the psalm is for today.

Second Reading: *II Timothy 4.6-8,17-18*
As Paul, the first foreign missionary of the Church, brings his last
letter to a close, his writing becomes vivid and arresting. He is
already being poured out in the way the pagans and the Jews
made drink-offering to their gods. It is time to strike camp—
Paul was a tent maker—and looking back over his life, he lets his
thoughts turn to Olympic and other games and to the athletes'
track in particular. Victory is assured, no crown of laurel leaves
which must wither and die, but the crown of righteousness which
never fades.

Gospel: *Matthew 16.13-19*
Peter's realisation who Jesus really was, led Our Lord to declare:
"On this rock—'petra' means a rock—I will build my Church". In
Matthew alone of the Gospels is there reference to the Church
and then only three times. The word has a remarkable history.
When the ancient Greeks were experimenting with democracy,
'ecclesia' denoted those who were eligible to vote and to legislate.
Later, when a Greek translation of the *Old Testament* was made
for Jews scattered far and wide, the same word bore the meaning
of 'the sacred assembly of Israel'. Finally, 'ecclesia' with its basic
meaning of a 'called-out body' answered a Christian need for a
word to denote the Church. On Peter Our Lord declared his
intention to build his 'ecclesia'.

6 August [1]
THE TRANSFIGURATION OF THE LORD

First Reading: *Daniel 7.9-10,13-14*
The last six chapters of *Daniel* [2] are devoted to a series of visions
and in this part of the book the First Reading is set. These
visions along with similar parts of the *Apocalypse* belong to what
is known as Apocalyptic literature, which is the successor of
prophecy and concentrates on the great consummation of all
things. In the First Reading there is a vision of the "Ancient of
Days" and "One like a son of man". This is no place to go into
interpretation; suffice it to say that as an introduction to the
Transfiguration it is without an equal.

Responsorial Psalm: *Psalm 96.1-2,5-6,9*
This is another of the Enthronement Psalms that celebrate the
Kingship of God. The first stanza proclaims the fact of God's
rule. With a touch of the mysterious, the writer declares that this
rule has a moral basis. The power, justice and glory of God come
through in the second stanza. The short selection of verses
concludes with the recognition that God is above all creation and
the spirit world.

Second Reading: *I I Peter 1.16-19*
Apparently countering criticism, the writer declares that the
teaching of the apostles is not an excursion into mythology, but
is based on the experience of eye-witnesses at the Transfiguration.
The word "coming" in the first sentence is an important word;
outside the *New Testament* it is used of the official visit of a
king; adopted into the *New Testament* it became the regular
word to describe the Lord's Return. The last paragraph means
that the whole of the *Old Testament* and not just the Prophets,
foreshadow Christ's Coming.

---

[1] The Transfiguration is celebrated also in the Masses of the
Second Sunday of Lent each year.

[2] See the Thirty-third Sunday in Ordinary Time, Year B.

Gospel: *Matthew 17.1-9*

When Paul wrote to the Philippians (2.6) and referred to Christ as "being in the form of God", he used a word which is part of the Greek verb "to be transfigured". Our Lord was changed into a form that revealed the Godhead. The presence of Moses and Elijah on the Mount of Transfiguration symbolised the Law and the Prophets, the old order summed up in two persons. Peter the impetuous wanted to hold the moment for all time, not realising that as the voice at the Lord's baptism set the seal on his ministry, so now it confirmed the way to the Cross.

YEAR B

Gospel: *Mark 9.2-10*

As Peter, James and John were the only witnesses of the Transfiguration and as Mark is the source of Matthew and Luke's Gospels, Peter is the obvious source of this material in the Gospels. From the days of the early Fathers the belief has been strong that Mark was Peter's interpreter. Three brief observations are offered: Our Lord's changed form revealed his Godhead; Peter the impetuous had to say something, so he suggested the three tents! The voice from heaven that had set the seal on Our Lord's ministry now confirmed the way to the Cross.

YEAR C

Gospel: *Luke 9.28-36*

The Transfiguration, with its glimpse of the world from which Our Lord had come and to which he was going to return, marks the beginning of the Passion. Earlier he had told of his coming death. The Transfiguration confirmed him in his intention as it also confirmed the doubting disciples (*Matthew 16.21*). The unique experience of the Transfiguration would also predispose the disciples to listen to his less palatable utterances. The presence of Moses and Elijah showed that Jesus was the embodiment, purpose and fulfilment of the Law and the Prophets. Only Luke refers to his "passing", his "exodos". His death was to be an even greater exodus for all who believed, an exodus from bondage.

234 15 August
THE ASSUMPTION OF THE BLESSED VIRGIN MARY
VIGIL MASS

First Reading: *I Chronicles 15.3-4,15-16;16.1-2*

We find the original record of the way David brought the ark into Jerusalem, in *II Samuel 6.11ff.* Before us now is a much later account, updated to accord with practices and ideas of the time. We note that the Levites, supposedly all of one tribe, included the "Sons of Aaron" and were the traditional ministers of the sanctuary; that the Chronicler represents David as the organiser of Temple music and that the overall picture is one of national rejoicing, with sacrifices presided over by David in honour of the ark's permanent resting place.

Responsorial Psalm: *Psalm 131.6-7,9-10,13-14*

This psalm for soloists and choir is one of the Songs of Ascent or Gradual Psalms [1] and again takes up the theme of David and the ark. In the first stanza, a choir ("we"), representing David and his men, tells of the finding of the ark and then going to worship the Lord. The two places mentioned are in Bethlehem. In the second stanza the psalmist turns from what appears to be the setting of the ark in its new place to a declaration in the last stanza that this home is the home of the ark for ever. The early Fathers saw in the ark that contained the Law, a symbol of Mary who bore within herself God's new Law.

Second Reading: *I Corinthians 15.54-57*

We pass from the theme of the ark to part of Paul's famous discourse on immortality, in which he visualises a dramatic transformation; under the familiar image of putting on garments, the perishable in us is replaced by the imperishable. Then taking liberties with quotations from *Isaiah* and *Hosea*, Paul shows how fear has gone out of death. His concept of passing from mortality to immortality finds expression in The Assumption of the Blessed Virgin Mary.

Gospel: *Luke 11.27-28*

This precious fragment is preserved only in *Luke* and typifies the writer's concern for women. It has been suggested that the unknown woman's remark came from a heart yearning over an errant son. Her admiration for the Lord bursts forth into praise of his Mother and this is the theme of the Mass. Our Lord's reply to the woman in the crowd lifts the thought of sustenance from the body to that of the soul.

---

[1] See Notes First Sunday in Advent, Year A.

First Reading: *Apocalypse 11.19;12.1-6,10*

In a passage of great difficulty amid a labyrinth of different interpretations, this much clearly emerges, that we wrestle not against flesh and blood, but that our warfare is in the heavens (*Ephesians 6.12*). The ark was captured when Jerusalem was taken. The Jews believed that Jeremiah rescued it (*II Maccabees 2.1-8*) and that it would be restored to Israel. In the reading this idea is spiritualised; God's intervention in the struggle between the woman and the dragon declares the triumph over evil. The Church sees in the woman, crowned and powerful, a symbol of the Blessed Virgin Mary.

Responsorial Psalm: *Psalm 44.10-12,16*

In this song for a royal marriage, it is recognised that Christ is prefigured with his bride, the Church. Thoughts turn also to the queenly grace of the Blessed Mother. In the first stanza, the bride, probably non-Jewish, is urged to give total devotion to her husband. In the second stanza the couple are escorted into their palace with the blessings of their people.

Second Reading: *I Corinthians 15.20-26*

It is in Chapter 15 that Paul comes to grip with the question of resurrection. There was nothing in Greek thought to help the Corinthians in this matter. Their kinsmen in Athens poured scorn on the idea *(Acts 17.32)*. So Paul states resurrection as a fact and using a favourite contrast between Adam and Christ, declares that the faithful departed will be brought to life in Christ who was the first of the harvest, to be followed by the full ingathering.

Gospel: *Luke 1.39-56*

Following the annunciation of her Holy Motherhood, Mary heeds the angel's bidding and sets out to see Elizabeth. The passage to be read deals with the meeting of the two women and in it Luke displays two of his most obvious characteristics, concern for women and the work of the Spirit. The *Ave Maria*, so dear to Catholics, is scriptural with additions authorised in the twelfth and sixteenth centuries. The Gospel concludes with Our Lady's hymn, the *Magnificat*, so named from the first word of the Latin translation. Put together with phrases from the psalms, and resembling, but surpassing Hannah's song, the *Magnificat* is Mary's reaction to Elizabeth's congratulations. Whether it is her own or a hymn she had learnt as a girl, she has made it her own for all time.

First Reading: *Numbers 21.4-9*
Much of the *Book of Numbers* is devoted to the wanderings of
the Israelites in the wilderness. In fact, the Hebrew Title is "In
the Wilderness". The complaint about "this unsatisfying food"
refers to the manna which God had provided. The bite of the
serpents produced a burning irritation. The strange story of the
bronze serpent which belongs to one of the oldest strands in the
Pentateuch may be an example of explaining back in the past a
later form of worship, in this instance Canaanite in origin
(II Kings 18.4).

Responsorial Psalm: *Psalm 77.1-2,34-38*
This long historical psalm reviews the nation's early history; it
extols Judah at the expense of Israel, the northern kingdom. The
writer invokes the lessons of history, points out the sham of
past acts of repentance and concludes with a declaration of
God's compassion despite the back sliding of his people.

Second Reading: *Philippians 2.6-11*
Paul, writing to the Philippians from prison, is speaking about the
Christian life and in Chapter 2, in response to a local situation,
makes a plea for unity. Into this setting he places what is
generally agreed was a Christian hymn and it is this that
constitutes the reading. This is not the only hymn that has
found its way into the *New Testament*. Their identification is not
easy as there was no literary code regarding quotations. The
hymn to Christ falls into two parts, his Humiliation and his
subsequent Glorification. The volume of literature on this
hymn is second only to that dealing with the Lord's Prayer.

Gospel: *John 3.13-17*
Nicodemus, unknown outside the Fourth Gospel, represents the
quiet seeker, the best of the Jewish race. Our Lord tells him he
must be born again (or from above) and illustrates his meaning
from *Numbers (21.7)* with the story of the fiery serpents as told
in the First Reading. So the Son of Man, a title with origins in the
Book of Daniel, is used by the Lord of himself, as the Messiah
will, when lifted up on the Cross, be the remedy for the
poisonous sins of the world.

ALL SAINTS

First Reading: *Apocalypse 7.2-4,9-14*
Apocalyptic writings [1] have a background of crisis and persecution and this is certainly true of the last book of the *Bible.* The reading declares the final triumph of God's saints on whom the seal of security is set in the midst of persecution. A paean of praise to God follows and then comes the assurance of triumph. The word "saint" does not imply of necessity a special endowment of moral or spiritual worth, but denotes a state of being set apart for God and his Christ.

Responsorial Psalm: *Psalm 23.1-6*
The psalm was used at one of the great festivals. The first stanza affirms the divine creation and the Lord's possession of his own. Then a priest in the pilgrims' midst asks who may climb Zion's hill; the question is answered by another priest and in stanza three the rewards of those fit to ascend are set out. The second half of this psalm may be seen in the Mass of the Presentation of the Lord.

Second Reading: *I John 3.1-3*
God's love has been lavished on us, his children; all our future is not clear, but this is, that we shall eventually see him in all his glory. Set in this spiritual gem is a centre of darker hue: the world did not recognise Our Lord; it may well do the same to us.

Gospel: *Matthew 5.1-12*
The Beatitudes, ten in number and forming a new Decalogue, reverse all the world's values regarding what constitutes happiness. These were delivered on a mountain, as was the original Decalogue. Mountains play a big part in Matthew's Gospel as places of importance in the life of Jesus. The phrase "poor in spirit" (Luke omits "in spirit") means having an awareness of spiritual need, absence of intellectual pride. The Beatitudes depict the quality of life which God's saints set as their goal.

---

[1] See First Reading, Transfiguration of the Lord.

2 November
THE COMMEMORATION OF ALL THE FAITHFUL DEPARTED

First Reading: *Isaiah 25.6-9*
These words are addressed to the exiles in Babylon and follow the invitation to the Messiah's banquet [1]. Here are words of earnest pleading, for many have grown cold and even sought heathen gods. But God is forgiving; his thoughts soar above the limits reached by man. There is comfort in these words for us as we think of our beloved dead.

Responsorial Psalm: *Psalm 26.1,4,7-9,13-14*
The portion in the Missal suggests a man whose joy in the Lord comes from a life without a care. The full version, which is in fact two psalms joined together, shows him battered and bruised by the calumnies of men, a fact which makes his joy all the more attractive. The second stanza expresses a beautiful thought, the peace that comes from being in the house of the Lord. He knew the presence that is so real in holy places. In the last stanza the psalmist's confidence soars and he urges others to be like-minded.

Second Reading: *Romans 5.5-11*
The use of the word "hope" in the Pauline writings, both as a noun and a verb, is more frequent than in all the other parts of the *New Testament*. Hope is a very important element of this Mass. Paul reminds us that hope is not an illusion, because God has made contact with us by the outpouring of his love like water in a parched land. This hope is for all because Christ's sacrifice was not made for godly men, but for sinners. Thus reconciled to God, we are assured of salvation in the consummation of all things to which we look forward, not in fear, but in "joyful hope".

---

[1] See Notes, Twenty-eighth Sunday in Ordinary Time, Year A.

Gospel: *Matthew 11.25-30*
Following the pronouncement of doom on the unrepentant cities,
comes this passage with its two distinct sections, first, what has
been called "Matthew's pearl of great price", and then the
"ecstasy of Jesus", which is almost Johannine in character, as
Our Lord gives a self revelation that indicates a oneness with the
Father. Then like Isaiah with his call to come to the waters and
drink, Our Lord issues a gracious invitation that has been
accepted through the centuries by those who have sought relief
from the burdens of life. The yoke to which Our Lord refers is
primarily the burden of the Pharisaic Law. His yoke, like those
he made in his workshop, fits lightly and does not chafe.

YEAR B

Gospel: *Mark 15.33-39;16.1-6*
Greek verbs can be made very intensive by compounding with
prepositions. The verb "deserted" is a double compound,
"utterly abandoned". From the deepest depths of despair the
narrative soars to the sublime heights of the Resurrection. How
better can hope be lifted up on this the day of the dead?

YEAR C

Gospel: *Luke 7.11-17*
The only son of a widow had died. Gone also were her hopes of
support and the continuance of her husband's name. The mention
of Nain as the scene of the miracle gives a touch of reality. So
also in a different way does "sat up", a rare word which is part of
Luke's medical vocabulary. Some writers doubt the story,
bandying such words as "trance", "coma", "popular tale". Our
Lord later burst the bonds of death; why could he not do it now?

9 November
DEDICATION OF THE LATERAN BASILICA

First Reading: *Ezekiel 47.1-2,8-9,12*

The prophet is looking beyond the tragedy of the present, the exile of his people, to a Messianic future. From Chapter 40 onwards is the vision of the Temple and the people of the future. In the reading, the stream is described that flows from under the Temple giving fertility to the desert and sweetening the Dead Sea with life. So also is the invisible stream that flows from the Great Basilica that is mother and head of all the churches of the world.

Responsorial Psalm: *Psalm 45.2-3,5-6,8-9*

The purpose for which this psalm was written has created much diversity of opinion: celebration of a great deliverance, the occasion of a national festival, an expression of apocalyptic hope, are views expressed by scholars. In the first stanza the writer expresses his unshakable trust in God. The second stanza introduces the idea of a river refreshing all that it touches and suggesting God as the Fountain of living water (*Jeremiah 17.13*). The stanza closes with a return to the theme of the first four lines. The same thought is repeated in the last stanza, in all an ideal psalm for the Mass.

Second Reading: *I Corinthians 3.9-11,16-17*

Dealing with the clash of personalities and the ensuing partisanship, Paul declares that he laid the foundation for the Corinthian Church and that foundation is Jesus Christ, but others may build on it. He likens the structure to a temple, and with the thought that the Corinthians are the real Temple, he warns them of the sanctity of the Temple. The references to foundation and building are particularly apt, given the history of the Lateran Basilica, destroyed by earthquake and later by two separate fires and built under the direction of several popes.

Gospel: *John 2.13-22* [1]

The commercial traffic in the Temple arose from the sale of sacrificial animals and from the changing of money into acceptable coinage. Both forms of activity were legal, but full of abuse and it was to these that Our Lord objected. Two points are made: it is a distinct feature of John's style that he has a passion for synonyms, different words with the same meaning. The word for "money-changers" occurs twice, the first word in no other known writer, the second, the regular word; God constantly cleanses his Church; the Lateran Basilica, home of Popes until the early fourteenth century witnessed the excesses of the early Papacy.

_____

[1] See Notes, Third Sunday of Lent, Year B.

THE IMMACULATE CONCEPTION OF
BLESSED VIRGIN MARY

First Reading: *Genesis 3.9-15,20*

The reading seeks to explain through one of the earliest strands in *Genesis* how man, created in the first instance by God for his fellowship, fell from that state of bliss. We observe how the blame was first placed on the woman and then how she attributed her plight to the serpent and finally how the serpent, identified in later thought with Satan (*Wisdom 2.24*) was cursed for his part in the Fall. *Genesis 3.15* is taken to support the doctrine of the Immaculate Conception of the Blessed Mary.

Responsorial Psalm: *Psalm 97.1-4*

The psalm had its origin in some great deliverance and the writer turns the occasion into an opportunity for God to show the nations his concern for his people. The use of "new" denotes another psalm in the Enthronement series, or because it is a special occasion, deliverance from Babylon. All the earth is invited to rejoice in what God has done for his people, to rejoice in his saving and rescuing power.

Second Reading: *Ephesians 1.3-6,11-12*

Ephesians was a circular letter written to the churches of Asia Minor and is considered by some to be Paul's greatest composition. Its purpose, unlike some of his other epistles is not corrective, but is the flowering of Paul's spiritual genius to be shared with his Christian converts. Its theme is the Church as the Body of Christ. The reading describes God's intention for man, holiness and adoption to the status of sonship, all predetermined "by him who guides all things".

Gospel: *Luke 1.26-38*

One of the most loved and most precious stories in the Bible, the Annunciation is recorded only in *Luke*, who is certainly using a documentary source. Three points are offered: The link with David's line is through Joseph; when Luke wrote "The power of the Most High will cover you with its shadow", he used a rare word which appears again in all accounts of the Transfiguration; finally it is noted that Mary, unlike Zacharias in a lesser annunciation, offered no protest, gave no thought to her social position as pregnant and unmarried, but rendered total submission to the will of God.

17 March
ST PATRICK BISHOP

First Reading: *Jeremiah 1.4-9* [1]
Jeremiah, alone and often forsaken, is one of the most tragic figures in the *Bible*. In the account of his call he tells how he shrank from the driving purpose of God, only to find that he could not fight against what had been ordained from the beginning. Scripture records and personal experiences attest that God gives his servants what to say in his service. The prophecy can be dated precisely, the year 626 B.C.

Responsorial Psalm: *Psalm 116*
This is the shortest of the psalms and for this reason some have thought that it may be only a fragment. It is a call to all peoples to praise God for his love and faithfulness to Israel. Paul quotes the psalm in *Romans 15.11* to prove that the Gospel is for all nations. Like the First Reading, the psalm is ideal for this Mass.

Second Reading: *Acts 13.46-49*
Preaching in Asia Minor at Antioch, Paul and Barnabas met fierce opposition which created a turning point in history, a decision to take the Gospel to the pagan world. The quotation is from *Isaiah 49.6*. The words were originally addressed to the Servant[2] and are here made to refer to the Apostles.

Gospel: *Luke 10.1-12,17-20*
In a passage of great content, space allows only four comments: the reading is part of what has been called the "Travel Narrative" (9.51-18.14), the very core of Luke's Gospel with much material found nowhere else; the figure 72 represents the 72 nations of the earth as in *Genesis 10;* missionaries throughout the ages have accepted the spirit of Our Lord's instruction to limit provision for their needs and to rely on God; finally it has been said that "the unheeded peace comes back and blesses the heart that wished it".

---

[1] See Notes, Fourth Sunday in Ordinary Time, Year C.
[2] See Notes, Second Sunday in Ordinary Time, Year A.

First Reading: *Ecclesiasticus 4.11-18* [1]
As often observed in these notes, Wisdom is not an abstract idea in the *Old Testament*, but a person, a flowing forth from the Almighty. The reading sets out the rewards for those who seek Wisdom. The passage, so simple and so beautiful, enshrines the central thoughts of the Mass.

Responsorial Psalm: *Psalm 112.1-8*
Psalms112-117 are psalms of praise and were used at the great religious festivals of the Jews. The theme of this psalm is simple, but profound: God who is Lord of the universe is concerned with the lot of the poor and lowly whom he sets amid the company of the exalted.

Second Reading: *I Corinthians 1.18-25* [2]
Having dealt with the problem of partisanship, Paul now speaks to those at Corinth who, on intellectual grounds, cannot accept the Cross or find salvation in the paradox of a crucified Christ. Man's acquired knowledge could not bring him salvation; only the folly of the Cross could do that. The passage requires careful working out along these lines.

Gospel: *John 19.25-27*
Matthew (27.55) mentions women looking on from a distance. The company to whom John refers were closer, for Our Lord spoke to them. His concern for his Mother is central to the passage before us. He wanted to be sure that she would be cared for and so committed her to the beloved disciple. As noted elsewhere "Woman" is not harsh in Greek, but rather like "Lady". As she was in his concern to the end, so she ever holds us in hers.

---

[1] See Notes, Holy Family, Year A.

[2] See Notes, Second and Third Sundays in Ordinary Time, Year A.

First Reading: *Proverbs 31.10-13,19-20,30-31*
Proverbs is part of the Wisdom literature of the *Old Testament*.
The book consists of several collections of sayings, with dates of
composition spread over some centuries. *Proverbs* is a book of
searching for practical Wisdom and man's chances of success in
this endeavour are good. Chapter 31.10-31 which should be read
in full, describes the perfect wife: she is virtuous, possessed of
many skills and a shrewd business-woman. Yet she had hardly
any rights at law; her virtues were her own reward.

Responsorial Psalm: *Judith 13. 18-20*
The *Book of Judith* is unhistorical, was written in the second
century B.C. and is known only in a Greek translation. It tells
how Judith, a beautiful young woman, outwitted and slew
Holofernes, Nebuchadnezzar's general who was threatening the
Jews. Before us is the Jewish King's song of praise in her hour
of victory. The language of Elizabeth's greeting to Mary is
reminiscent in the Greek of the King's opening words to Judith.

Second Reading: *James 3.13-18*
It has been argued by some that this letter [1] is the earliest part of
the *New Testament* and by others that it is quite late! Though
not stated in the First Reading in so many words, clearly the
perfect wife is drawing on Wisdom as understood in the *Old
Testament*. In the Second Reading James compares the right use
of Wisdom "that comes down from above" and knowledge, with
man's distorted concept of these qualities. False and true Wisdom
are then described.

Gospel: *Luke 1.39-56*
Following the annunciation of her Holy Motherhood, Mary heeds
the angel's bidding and sets out to see Elizabeth. The passage to
be read deals with the meeting of the two women and in it Luke
displays two of his most obvious characteristics, concern for
women and the work of the Spirit. The *Ave Maria*, so dear to
Catholics, is scriptural, with additions authorised in the twelfth
and sixteenth centuries. The *Gospel* concludes with Our Lady's
hymn, the *Magnificat*, so named from the first word of the Latin
translation. Put together with phrases from the psalms and
resembling, but surpassing Hannah's song, the *Magnificat* is
Mary's reaction to Elizabeth's congratulations. Whether it is her
own, or a hymn she learnt as a girl, she has made it her own
for all time.

---

[1] See Notes, Twenty-second and Twenty-fifth Sundays in
Ordinary Time, Year B

First Reading: *Genesis 3.9-15,20*
The reading seeks to explain through one of the earliest strands in *Genesis*, how man, created in the first instance by God for his fellowship, fell from that state of bliss. We observe how the blame was first placed on the woman and then how she attributed her plight to the serpent and finally how the serpent, identified in later thought with Satan (*Wisdom 2.24*) was cursed for his part in the Fall. *Genesis 3.15* is taken to support the doctrine of the Immaculate Conception of the Blessed Mary.

Responsorial Psalm: *Psalm 102.1-4,8-9,11-12*
This is the sixth time that this psalm has been used in the Missal, but always in a different form [1]. One senses a long communion with God in which the writer has found from the needs of his own soul the responses of the Divine, forgiveness, healing, redemption, mercy and love. In a sense we have a complete theology of God.

Second Reading: *Ephesians 3.14-19* [2]
Paul is praying for the deepening of his readers' spiritual life, for Christ to dwell in their hearts so that they may comprehend the love of Christ in all its dimensions. The phrase "planted in love" is rather flat. A more vigorous and more accurate rendering would be "firmly fixed by the roots"; "with love as a foundation" brings out the metaphor which "built on" obscures.

Gospel: *Luke 8.19-21*
All three Synoptic Gospels record this saying of Our Lord. In *Matthew* and *Mark* it is in a fuller form and placed differently in the narrative. When Our Lord stated who his true relations were he was transcending all ties of family and blood. In *Luke* alone these three verses which are like a flash of light that illumines the whole sky follow closely on the parable of the Sower. To accept this concept of a universal family is to be part of the seed that fell on good ground.

---

[1] See Index of Passages and relevant notes.

[2] See Notes, Sacred Heart, Year B

Owing to the demand of space it is possible to give only the first and last verse of a reference especially as so many are composite, e.g. *Genesis 2.7-9,14-15,20-21* will be given as *Genesis 2.7-21*. By turning to the passage in the Missal, the reader will find the exact reference. Where a passage is used more than once and the substance of the notes is the same, the subsequent references may not be given.

*The Missal follows the numeration and the versification of the *Grail Psalms*, but gives the versification of the Hebrew as well. To avoid making confusion worse confounded, only Grail numbers are given in the Index. "For most of the psalms the Greek numeration is one behind that of the Hebrew", *Psalms Singing Version* p.15 where full reconcilliation of the two systems is given.

248

252